Robert Douglas

The Story Of China

Robert Douglas

The Story Of China

ISBN/EAN: 9783741103476

Manufactured in Europe, USA, Canada, Australia, Japa

Cover: Foto ©Lupo / pixelio.de

Manufactured and distributed by brebook publishing software
(www.brebook.com)

Robert Douglas

The Story Of China

IDOL AT THE RACE-COURSE, AMOY.

BY

PROFESSOR ROBERT K. DOUGLAS

London

T. FISHER UNWIN

PATERNOSTER SQUARE

NEW YORK: G. P. PUTNAM'S SONS

MDCCCXCIX

PREFACE

THE antiquity of China is so great, and the history of the Empire covers so vast a period that it was plainly impossible to compress the whole subject within the limits of a single volume of this series. It was determined, therefore, to limit the record, in the present instance, to the annals of the Empire from the time of Marco Polo to the present day, leaving the earlier history of the country to appear later.

As is well known, the Chinese possess histories of their various dynasties, and they attempt to insure that these should be truthful records by ruling that the events of each dynasty should not be described by contemporary historians but by authors under the succeeding *régime*. It might be supposed that this system would entail the compilation of biased and *ex parte* chronicles. But happily Chinese historians, like the rest of their countrymen, are so entirely devoid of patriotism that they have no inducement to pervert facts, or to trim their sails to the necessities of party feeling.

Generally truthful as these historians are, however, their works yet labour under the defect common to all Oriental histories of being records of the Court and camp rather than of the life of the people; and it is only by reference to miscellaneous works that it is possible to obtain the side-lights necessary to illustrate the true progress of the nation.

Among the authorities I have consulted are the following:—The native dynastic histories; the *Shêng Wu Ki*, or the wars of the present dynasty, by Wei Yuen; various native biographical works; the *Peking Gazette*; the Parliamentary Blue Books; the Histories of Wells Williams, Boulger, and Macgowan; "The Jesuits in China," by R. Jenkins; "A Narrative of Events in China," by Lord Loch; "The Ever Victorious Army," by Andrew Wilson, &c.

ROBERT K. DOUGLAS.

January, 1899.

CONTENTS

___

I.

VII.

VIII.

IX.

X.

XIV.

LIST OF ILLUSTRATIONS

I

THE EARLY HISTORY OF THE EMPIRE

OF all the great Empires of antiquity, China alone has preserved its existence in defiance of the disintegrating effects of time and the assaults of her enemies. While the ancient Empires of Egypt, Babylonia, and Assyria have waxed and waned, she has maintained her position in the Eastern world, and has enlarged rather than diminished her boundaries.

The earliest existing records of the people describe them as a small body of settlers dwelling in the fertile regions of North-eastern China, in the neighbourhood of the Yellow River. By degrees as they consolidated their Empire and established a definite form of government, they forced back the native tribes which had originally hemmed them in, and extended their rule over the regions lying to the west and south of their original location. As centuries went by they threw out colonies into the outer regions, and after the manner which may still be observed in their dealings with the Manchurians and Mongolians, made these colonies first centres for the spread of Chinese

2

influence, and then bases on which to work the
lever of empire. Pushing on in this way they
crossed the Yang-tsze-kiang southwards in the
third century B.C., and thenceforth adding province
to province they established the Empire as it now
exists. Throughout their whole history they have
shown a marked capacity for acquiring territory, and
this rather by the peaceful method of settling on the
neighbouring lands than by invasion and conquest.
They have none of the characteristics of a warlike
race, and their triumphs over less cultivated peoples
have been gained rather by peaceful advance than by
force of arms. In almost every respect we are taught
by their records that they differed essentially from
the tribes by whom they first found themselves surrounded, and hence the question naturally arises who
they were, and whence they came?

Many suggestions have been made as to the earlier
habitat of this people. It has been surmised that
they may have migrated from the plains of Sennaar ;
that they were a colony from Egypt ; and that they
possessed a Scythic origin. No proofs in support of
these guesses at history have been, however, forth-
coming, and it was reserved for the late Professor
Terrien de Lacouperie to establish with many incon-
testable proofs the theory that they had migrated
eastward from a region on the south of the Caspian
Sea in about the twenty-third century B.C. In
support of his proposition Professor Terrien de
Lacouperie was able to show a marked connection
between many of the primitive written characters
of the languages of Akkadia and China ; as well as

a marked affinity between the religious, social, and scientific institutions and beliefs of the two peoples. In the twelve Pastors, among whom the Emperor Yao (2085–2004 B.C.) apportioned the Empire, he saw a reflection of the twelve Pastor Princes of Susiana. In the worship of Shang-Ti and the six Honoured Ones he recognised the supreme god and the six subordinate deities of the Susians. In the knowledge possessed by the Chinese of astronomy and medicine he recognised an identity with the condition of those sciences in Mesopotamia ; and he also drew attention to the fact which recent excavations in Babylonia have brought to our knowledge, that the canals and artificial water-ways of China suggest a striking likeness to the canals with which the whole of Babylonia must have been intersected, and which cannot but have been as characteristic a feature of that country as similar works are of China at the present day.

Vast migrations have been by no means uncommon in Asiatic history, and even as late as the end of last century we know that a body of Kalmucks, numbering six hundred thousand, journeyed from the frontiers of Russia to the confines of China. This migration, which De Quincey has made immortal, is but an example of the movements which have constantly taken place in the populations of Asia. Plague, famine, political disturbances have all had their influences in the constant distribution of the tribes and nations of the East, and there is, therefore, nothing improbable in the supposed movement of the Chinese tribes from Mesopotamia to the banks of the Yellow

River. It is unnecessary here to discuss at any further length the early habitat of the Chinese people. In this work we are mainly interested in them after their arrival in China, and for the purpose of this preliminary sketch we are not called upon to go beyond the traditional records of the nation.

In the native histories the records of the race are traced back to a period which dwarfs into insignificance the antiquity of Egypt or Chaldea, and though their earlier pages rest on no better foundation than traditional fables, there is yet preserved a substratum of fact on which it is safe to rest. Like the first founders of every Imperial race the Chinese leaders of antiquity are represented as possessing the wisdom, and almost the power of the gods. One of their first leaders, Fuhsi by name, has earned eternal fame as having designed the six classes of written characters ; invented the system of horary and cyclical notation ; and established the laws of marriage, as well as having devised the celebrated eight Diagrams which are popularly supposed to be the basis of the renowned " Book of Changes." His successor, Shennung, is supposed to have instructed the people in agriculture ; to have established public markets ; and to have discovered the medicinal properties lying dormant in the herbs of the field. In the portraits common to official biographies, this ancient sage is depicted chewing a long stalk of some herb, which from the expression of his face is plainly unpleasant to the taste, however efficacious it may be as a medicine. Hwangti, the next sovereign, came to the throne, such as it was, in 2332 B.C. Like those of his predecessors his reign was long, and is said to have extended over a full century. He taught his people to manufacture utensils of wood, pottery, and metal, and invented a medium of currency. Professor Terrien de Lacouperie finds a resemblance between his second name, Nai Hwangti, and the Nakhunte of Elamite history, and is of opinion that he never ruled in China. But however that may be, native historians dwell on his wisdom and virtue with untiring unction.

With the advent to power of the Emperor Yao (2085–2004 B.C.), the purely fabulous chapters of Chinese history may be said to come to a close, and at this point Confucius takes up the pen. According to that sage Yao was " all informed, intelligent, accomplished, and thoughtful." With a godlike instinct he ruled the "black-haired" race, and by the influence of his example, as Confucius insists, he led all men to him. Under his benign administration the frontiers of the Empire were extended from 23° to 40° N., and from 6° west of Peking to 10° east of that city. On his becoming a " Guest on high," Shun was chosen to succeed him, and it was during the reign of this monarch that a great flood, which was considered by the early Jesuit missionaries to have been the flood of Noah, devastated large districts of the Chinese states. *Pace* the missionaries, this catastrophe was probably nothing more than one of those outbreaks of the Yellow River which periodically lay waste the country lying on its banks. In this case Yü, a certain official, was appointed to lead the waters back to their original channel. His labours, we are told, extended

over nine years, and we are asked to believe that so
absorbed was he in his work that he thrice passed the
door of his house without once stopping to enter.   As
a reward for this signal service he was raised to the
throne on the death of Shun, and became the first
sovereign of the Hsia dynasty (1954–1687 B.C.).
Among the other exploits of this sovereign was a
redivision of the Empire into nine instead of eleven
Provinces, a description of which rearrangement was
engraved, for the benefit of posterity, on nine brazen
vessels ; and as a crowning testimony to his worth,
an inscription on a stone monument, raised for the
purpose on Mount Hêng, recorded the benefits which
he is believed to have conferred on his subjects.

Sixteen sovereigns ruled in succession to Yü, and
as has been constantly the case, not only in China
but in other Oriental countries, there was a woful
falling off in his successors on the throne from the
higher standard which the founder of the dynasty had
set them.   The earnestness and single-mindedness
which belonged to Yü, and on which the native
historians delight to linger, no longer animated his
unworthy followers on the throne.   Self-indulgence
and cruelty became more and more accentuated as
ruler after ruler accepted the sceptre of empire, until
all the worst passions of his predecessors found expression in the conduct of Chieh Kwei, who reigned
from 1739 to 1687 B.C.   According to the traditional
belief of the ancient Chinese, a belief which was
strongly insisted upon by the philosopher Mencius,
it becomes the bounden duty of a people to raise the
standard of rebellion when the ruler persistently

acts in opposition to the laws of heaven. Such a crisis had now arrived. By public oppression of the people, and private outrages on their properties and persons, Chieh Kwei placed himself beyond the pale. With one consent his subjects rose against him under the leadership of a man named T'ang, " the Complete," who justified this epithet by dethroning the Emperor and proclaiming himself sovereign by the grace of God.

The story of the Shang or Yin Dynasty, as it is variously called, is but a repetition of that of Hsia. The virtuous impetus which placed the sceptre in T'ang's hand was gradually dissipated in the twenty-eight reigns which followed in succession to his. Historians make a distinction in favour of one or two of his descendants, but the general tendency was downwards, and like another Chieh Kwei, Chow Sin brought the dynasty to an end by his crimes and iniquities. "Wild extravagance, unbridled lust, and the most ferocious cruelty, are enumerated among his vices. To please his infamous concubine, T'aki, he constructed vast palaces and pleasure grounds where every form of wild debauchery was continually practised." As was said by a famous statesman of the time, "the house of Yin can no longer exercise rule over the four quarters of the Empire. The great deeds of our founder have enjoyed and still enjoy a wide renown, but we by being lost and maddened with wine have destroyed the effects of his virtue in these latter days. The people of Yin, both small and great, are given to highway robberies, villainies, and treachery. The nobles and officers imitate one

another in violating the laws.   Evil-doers receive no
punishment, and the people rise up and commit
violent outrages on one another.   The dynasty of
Yin is now sinking to its ruin.   Its condition is like
one crossing a river who can find neither ford nor
bank."

To the remonstrances of his ministers Chow Sin
turned a deaf ear, and, in a conversation reported by Confucius,
comforted himself with the reflection that as Emperor he was under
the protection of high Heaven.
"Your crimes," replied the officer,
"which are many, are chronicled
above, and how can you speak of
your fate as though it were in the
charge of Heaven.   Yin will shortly
perish.   As to your deeds they can
but bring ruin on the country."
This prophecy was soon to be fulfilled.   A leader of rebellion was
found in the "Warlike Prince," who
drove the Emperor from his throne
and urged him to suicide.   This
action, which has all the appearance
of being revolutionary, was nevertheless strictly in
accordance with Chinese morality and met with the
entire approval of the philosopher, Mencius.   "He
who outrages benevolence," said that sage, "is called
a ruffian : he who outrages righteousness is called a
villain.   The ruffian and the villain we call a mere
fellow.   I have heard of the cutting off of the fellow

T'A KI, CHOW SIN'S
EMPRESS.

Chow, but I have not heard of the putting of a ruler to death."

Following the usual precedent of successful rebel leaders the "Warlike Prince" seized the Imperial sceptre with the full approval of the nation. Historians of every class, from Confucius downwards, have poured unceasing praise on the administration of the ursurper, who, if these authorities are to be believed, was graced with every virtue that befits a monarch. By his magnanimous conduct he fulfilled the criterion of an exemplary ruler laid down by Confucius, by drawing all men to him. During his reign Embassies arrived from the Kings of Korea, Cochin China, and other distant regions. In his warlike expeditions he was uniformly successful, and he left to his successor a frontier which was respected by his enemies, and an Empire which was the envy of his allies. Happily for the State the succeeding two or three sovereigns worthily maintained the standard set them by their great predecessor. They consolidated the Empire and secured the loyalty and service of the feudal states. History does not concern itself much with the majority of the later rulers of the house of Chow, as the new dynasty was styled, but draws attention with some emphasis to Mu Wang (B.C. 1001–946), and finds food for reflection in his conduct. To his charge is laid the crime of having introduced the system of redeeming offences by the payment of fines, and of having thus set the example of bribery and corruption which has since wrought such havoc in the morals of the people and their rulers. On the other side of the shield

there is told of him that he prosecuted successful
wars against the tribes on the western frontier, a fact
which has given rise to a legendary account of a
journey which he is supposed to have made to the
borders of the Lake of Gems, where he is said to
have been hospitably entertained, with all the
delights of a Mussulman's Paradise, by the "Royal
Mother of the West."

Rightly to understand the condition of the country
at this period, it is necessary to remember that the
kingdom was formed of a congerie of states, each of
which was ruled over by its own sovereign, and each
of which owed the limp and uncertain fealty common
to subordinate Oriental princedoms to the elected
sovereign of the predominant kingdom of Chow. No
common patriotism bound these feudatories to their
liege lord, and it was only by the strength of his
right arm that he preserved his lordship over them.
Any sign of the weakening of his authority was
naturally the signal for a rising on the part of the
more restless princekins against his power. As time
went on and the Chow state fluctuated in wealth and
influence, the uprisings of the more ambitious feudatories became more threatening and frequent. The
country became distracted by obscure quarrels, and
open disorder, until as the philosopher Mencius
graphically writes: " A host marches and stores of
provisions are consumed, the hungry are deprived of
their food, and there is no rest for those who are
called on to toil. Maledictions are uttered from one
to another with eyes askance, and the people proceed
to the commission of wickedness. Then the royal

ordinances are violated, the people are oppressed, and: the supplies of food· and drink flow away like water. The rulers yield themselves to the current, or they urge their way against it. They are wild, they are lost. The crime of him who connives at it and aids the wickedness of his ruler is small, but the crime of him who anticipates and excites that wickedness is great. The great officers of the present day are all guilty of this latter crime, and I say that they are sinners against the princes. Sage kings do not arise, and the princes of the states give reins to their lusts. In their stalls there are fat beasts, and in their stables there are fat horses ; but their people have the look of hunger, and in their fields there are those who have died of famine. This is leading on beasts to devour men."

It was while the country was in a condition similar to that described above that Confucius was born. We might leave the legendary accounts of his miraculous birth and early days to the recounters of fables, and it is only necessary for us here briefly to consider his influence on politics. To students of Chinese history that influence appears to be out of all proportion to the weight of his words, and the convincing force of his doctrines. He found the Empire tempest-tossed with faction and disloyalty, and he believed it to be his mission to lead back the sovereign and his people to the orthodox condition of affairs which existed when Yao meted out the heavens and the "Warlike Prince" exercised his patriarchal sway. His constant theme was the virtue of the ancient sages, and his panacea for all political ills was a return to the traditional virtue of those great men. During his lifetime he was scouted by not a few rulers and princekins, and achieved success only when his influence was regarded as necessary for the support of some ruler or cause. It was only after his death that people turned to him as to a great leader of mankind, and for the last three and twenty centuries his teachings have been the guiding star of the nation through all its many changes and

CONFUCIUS WITH HIS DISCIPLES.

chances. Loudly he deplored the anarchy of the time, and as an illustration in point it is told of him that on one occasion as he journeyed from his native state to that of Ch'i he saw a woman weeping by a tomb at the roadside, to whom, having compassion upon her, he sent a disciple to ask the cause of her grief. "You weep," said the messenger, "as if you had experienced sorrow upon sorrow." "I have," said the woman. "My father-in-law was killed here by a tiger, and my husband also ; and now my son has met the same fate." "Why then do you not move from this place?" asked Confucius. "Because

GRAVE OF CONFUCIUS.

here there is no oppressive government," answered the woman. Turning to his disciples Confucius remarked, "My children, remember this, oppressive government is fiercer than a tiger."

In spite, however, of the warnings of Confucius and the more philosophical teachings of Lao Tsze, the founder of Taoism, disorders increased on every side, and there were not wanting ominous signs which were regarded by native authorities as foretelling the downfall of the Chow Dynasty. The brazen vessels which had been set up by the great Yü were seen to shake and totter as though presaging a political catastrophe; famine and pestilence stalked through the land; and on all sides men's hearts failed them for fear. It is at such times as these that an ambitious leader can find his opportunity, and in this case the ruler of the Ch'in Dynasty, seizing his advantage, made war against the Imperial state, which was already tottering to its fall. After a series of victories he claimed the throne by right of conquest, and established himself as the first sovereign of the short-lived Ch'in Dynasty. Neither this man nor his two successors on the throne were men of mark, and if it had not been for the sovereign who followed them the Imperial line would have sunk into oblivion "unwept, unhonoured, and unsung." They initiated little and accomplished little, but this at least cannot be said of their successor.

The evils of the feudal system had long been patent, but no one had hitherto arisen who was bold enough so to fly in the face of precedent and history as to attempt a reform in the constitution. Ascribing all the evils under which his country had so long suffered to the system which for so many years had guided its destiny, Shih Hwangti determined once and for all to put an end to the petty jealousies among the States by establishing an Empire, and proclaiming himself the first Universal Sovereign.

To this reform the literary classes offered a determined opposition. All the national love for antiquity accentuated by the sayings and writings of Confucius and his followers was outraged by this draconic measure. They pointed back to the halcyon days when the "Warlike Prince" and his immediate followers ruled over the United States in peace and harmony, and quoted the works edited by Confucius as evidence of the prosperous condition which existed under those favoured circumstances. So serious was the opposition thus presented that the Emperor, who knew nothing of half measures, determined to wrest from his critics the evidences which they were so fond of producing. With this intention he issued an edict commanding that all the existing literature in the country, with the exception of works on divination and medicine, should be destroyed. From the nature of this decree it was plainly impossible that it could be carried out in its entirety. But so far as possible it was given effect to, notwithstanding the determined resistance of the *Literati*, many of whom perished at the block rather than commit their cherished volumes to the flames. To a certain extent the immediate effect of the measure was successful, and the prosperity which the new policy secured for the nation at large gained for its author very general support. With genuine zeal he also set himself to improve the material condition of the country, and recognising the importance, both political and commercial, of

providing means of communication between the
several States, he constructed roads in all directions,
spanned the river with bridges, and encouraged by
every method in his power the means of locomotion.
At this time the Tartars were constantly threatening
the northern frontier, and realising that it was as
necessary to protect his subjects from foreign foes as
to promote their internal prosperity, he constructed
the Great Wall which, stretching from the sea at the
120th degree of longitude, and fringing the northern
frontier of the Empire to the 100th degree, still
stands as a monument of the energetic administration of this great Sovereign.   Unhappily, no
hereditary instincts guided his successor into his
paths, and during the short reign—three years—of
this last Emperor of the Ch'in Dynasty, the country,
instead of advancing toward consolidation, became
the prey of constant civil war, and of every form of
brigandage.

With dramatic propriety a leader arose at this
troublous period who showed himself to be a man
standing head and shoulders above his compeers.
The historian of the Han Dynasty tells us that, like
another Macbeth, when first taking the field this man
encountered a soothsayer who foretold his future greatness. With commendable rapidity this prophecy was
fulfilled, and the object of it was universally hailed
as the first Emperor of a new dynasty, to which he
gave the title of Han from the name of his native
state. Time had at length accustomed the people of
all classes to the abolition of the feudal States, and
the new Emperor, Kaoti, felt that there was no

longer any need to cut the nation adrift from the sheet anchor of its native literature. The *Literati* also were still hankering after their literary gods. Their influence was also plainly an appreciable quantity, and Kaoti determined to secure it on his behalf by resuscitating such works as it was possible to recover. Under his protecting influence the *Literati* undertook the congenial task of searching for any stray copies of the classics and other works which may have escaped the holocaust of the books. Phœnix-like the old literature rose from its ashes. From the sides of caves, from the roofs of houses, and the banks of rivers, volumes were produced by those who had risked their lives for their preservation, and history states that from the lips of old men were taken down ancient texts which had everywhere perished except in the retentive memories of veteran scholars. While reversing this part of the work of the first great Emperor, Kaoti followed his example in still further improving the means of communication in the Empire, and to engineers employed by him belongs the credit, among other enterprises, of having constructed the first suspension bridges known to exist in the world.

The Han period is universally regarded by China-men as one of the most glorious epochs in their history. They know no prouder title than that by which they delight to be called, the Sons of Han, and this is no doubt mainly due to the extraordinary revival of letters which took place under the new line of Sovereigns. It is true that Kaoti shared to some extent the suspicions entertained of the *Literati*

3

by the burner of the books, but his successors, taking
a truer view of the position, did all that lay in their
power to encourage the literary spirit of the nation.
So keen was the zeal of the people in the cause that
not only were the old texts restored, but a new and
scholarly school of letters was brought into being.
In every branch of literature the greatest activity was
displayed, and whereas it may be said that when
Kaoti ascended the throne in 206 B.C. polite literature
was non-existent, the fact remains that before the
dawn of the Christian era the Imperial library possessed upon its shelves 3,123 works on the classics,
2,705 on philosophy, and 1,383 on poetry. But not
alone in the peaceful paths of literature did the
Empire make giant strides at this period. The
nation's arms and diplomacy were carried far beyond
the frontier into the little known region of Central
Asia. In the second century B.C. the envoy Chang
Ch'ien visited the Court of Eastern Turkestan, and
two centuries later an army under General Pan
Ch'ao marched to Khoten, and even carried their
country's flag to the shores of the Caspian Sea. On
the southern and north-eastern frontiers, Cochin
China, and the Liaotung peninsula, which has figured
so prominently of late in Eastern politics, were conquered and reduced to the condition of feudatories,
while Yunnan was incorporated into the Empire.

But by no means the least momentous event of the
period was the introduction of Buddhism. The
histories affirm that one night the Emperor Mingti
(A.D. 58–76) saw in a vision on his bed a golden
image which bade him send to the western countries

to search for Buddha, and for books and images to illustrate the doctrines of the holy man. In obedience to this command he, without loss of time, despatched envoys to India, who after an absence of eleven years returned, bringing with them books, images, and drawings, together with an ordained priest of the new faith. This pioneer missionary was followed by others who, with extraordinary diligence, translated a number of the Sanscrit Sûtras into Chinese. But all these achievements failed to preserve the dynasty from that decadence which seems to be the natural fate of Chinese Imperial Houses. Towards the end of the second century of our era there occurred all those signs and symptoms of an impending political change to which the nation had now become accustomed. Three leaders arose. One in the state of Shuh, one in Wei, and one in Wu. Against these men Hsienti (190-221), the reigning sovereign, was unable to maintain his position, and having retired with a certain pusillanimity into private life, left his Empire to be contended for by the three chieftains. Then followed a period of bitter internecine strife, and the period is notorious in Chinese history for the more than usually savage wars which disturbed the peace and well-being of the people. Weary of the tumult under which they suffered, the nation welcomed the advent of a new dynasty, that of the Western Chin, in the year 265.

Buddhism, which had hitherto only received partial support, now gained powerful protectors in the sovereigns of the new line. It was during this period that the Chinese Buddhist Fa-hsien, made an expe-

dition to India to examine the sites sacred to the
sage, and to possess himself of such canonical works
as were still unknown to his country-men. After an
absence of fourteen years he returned by sea from
Ceylon, bringing with him a library of books and
notes which in subsequent years of leisure enabled
him to write the interesting record of his travels
which is known to European readers through the
fascinating translations of Remusat and Beal. At the
close of the Chin Dynasty in 419 the Empire again
suffered division, and for a hundred and sixty years,
six states fought for supremacy in the distracted
provinces. A short dynasty (about thirty years)
followed which was notorious only for the reign of
one sovereign, Yangti, who devoted himself with
laudable energy to the construction of canals in the
eastern and central portions of the Empire where
alone they were possible. On the ashes of this
dynasty rose the house of T'ang whose appearance
on the Imperial stage opened the period which is
well described as the Augustan age of Chinese
literature. The keynote of the great Emperors of
this line was to restore in their fulness the ancient
beliefs and traditions which had been consecrated by
the approval of Confucius. In pursuance of this
tendency many of them discouraged in every way in
their power the foreign religion which had been
introduced from India. Already monasteries had
sprung up in various parts of the country, and it is
possible that then, as now, these were occasionally
hotbeds of treason and sedition. But however that
may be, several decrees were issued commanding the

monks to range themselves as Benedicts, and to
rejoin the ranks of civil life, which in their mistaken
zeal they had deserted for the cloister.

But the chief glory of the dynasty was the literature which sprung up under the fostering care of the
rulers. Poets, essayists, and historians poured out from
their studies volumes which charmed their contem-
poraries as much as they delight students and scholars
of the present day. In every library in China will
now be found "The Complete Poems of the T'ang
Dynasty," while numberless volumes of the polite
literature of the period still hold unrivalled sway in
the opinion of the *Literati*. In the field of battle
the nation was as successful as in the arena of
literature. With skill and success the districts of
Hamil, Turfan, and the Ouigour country were added
to the Empire, and thus brought Far Cathay within
the cognisance of Western Asia, and even of the confines of Europe. The See of Rome, ever ready to
extend its influence and to gain converts to the faith,
took advantage of the opportunity thus offered to
despatch an embassy to the Chinese Court, where to
his astonishment the Papal envoy found assembled
envoys from Persia and Nepaul. Already the
Nestorian Christians had sent missionaries to proclaim
the truth, as they had received it, and though little is
said on the subject in the histories, it is plain that
considerable success attended their efforts. A striking
testimony to this is found in a monument which
stands at the present day in the city of Hsian Fu, on
which is inscribed a record of this first attempt to
introduce Christianity into China.

As time went on, however, the domestic affairs of the Empire fell into that disorder which always accompanies the declining years of dynasties. Twenty-three sovereigns of the line of T'ang sat in succession on the throne, and the reigns of many of these were marked rather by feeble administration than by any other characteristic. One exception to this criticism was the sovereignty of the Empress Wu who held the sceptre from 684 to 710. Having set aside the rightful sovereign, she usurped the throne, and by her wisdom and energy, secured a brief space of peace with honour for her distracted countrymen. This dynasty, which began by extending religious toleration to all beliefs, in course of time inaugurated that persecution of Christians which has been intermittently carried on ever since, and even laid heavy hands on followers of Mahomet and Buddha. It was during these restless days that Tu Fu and Li T'aipo wrote those poems on the beauties of nature and the pleasures of wine, which have made their names immortal—at least, within the frontiers of the Middle Kingdom. At length, in 907, the Imperial line, with all its glories and all its disgraces, passed away, and was followed by a succession of short dynasties, which did little more than keep alive the idea of Empire, until the rise of the Sung power in 960.

At the close of the T'ang dynasty, a tribe appeared on the frontiers of China which was destined to exercise a vast influence on the fortunes of the country. The Tartars, who had constantly raided the Northern Provinces, now appeared in force, and so successfully waged war on the Southern Empire that they secured for themselves the China of that day from the River Yangtsze northwards. These hardy warriors were known as K'itan, the word from which the mediaeval name of Cathay is derived, and which, under the form of K'itai, is still that by which China is known to the Russian people. The supremacy of these nomads was not, however, of very long duration. After a rule of less than two hundred years they yielded place to their congenitors, the Kin Tartars, the progenitors of the present ruling sovereigns, who in their turn divided with Sung the whole Empire.

II

BUT while constant war was being carried on between the Kin and Sung dynasties, yet another Power was rising on the Mongolian steppes destined to crush both under its iron heel. In the valley of the Onon, in the neighbourhood of the Karakorum hills, was fostered a Mongol chief, who in the near future was to be classed among the greatest rulers the world has ever seen. The parentage of Jenghiz Khan differed little from that of those about him, but from an early age Nature had marked him out as a leader of men. While yet young he was chosen as Khan of his tribe, and led his followers in a succession of campaigns against the neighbouring chieftains. Having humbled these rulers to the dust, and having swept their vanquished followers into his ranks, he braced himself up to more serious warfare.

The kingdom of Hsia, which consisted of the modern provinces of Kansu and Shensi, though not a fertile territory was, by comparison with the cold and bleak steppes of Mongolia, a land flowing with milk and honey. Without much difficulty Jenghiz Khan's

hardy warriors subdued this country under them, and, aspiring to fresh conquests, invaded the territory ruled over by the Kin Dynasty (1211). This campaign was partially successful, and at its conclusion Jenghiz, as was his wont, retired to his Ordu on the River Onon, to recruit his forces, and to collect his strength for a second onslaught. Two years later he again took the field, and, overrunning the modern province of Chihli, laid waste ninety of its fairest cities, including the Kin capital, which stood in the neighbourhood of the modern Peking. Leaving an occupying force to preserve his newly-acquired rights, Jenghiz turned his attention westward, and with marvellous speed and thoroughness, gathered within his borders the districts of Kashgar, Yarkand, and Khoten. Even such vast conquests as these failed to satisfy the lust for empire which had taken possession of the Mongol chieftain. On one excuse or another, he led his troops of nomad horsemen against the kingdom of Khuarezm, and having swept over its richest provinces, advanced into Georgia and Western Europe. With irresistible force, aided no doubt by the terror which, as the "curse of God," he inspired, he captured Moscow and Kiev, the Jerusalem of Russia, and did not draw rein until he had advanced as far as Cracow and Pesth. After having laid waste all these cities so that, as he boasted, he could ride over their sites without meeting an obstacle sufficient to make his " horse stumble," he returned to Mongolia, and there died in the year 1227. Meanwhile his generals had not been idle in China, but had advanced his conquests to the fertile region within the eastern bend of the Yellow River, thus securing a rich inheritance to his successor Oghotai.

It was during the reign of this monarch that the first Catholic missionaries carried the light of Christian civilisation to the dark regions of Mongolia. " It is worthy of the grateful remembrance of all Christian people," says the missionary Friar Ricold, of Monte Croce, as quoted by Colonel Yule ; " that just at the time when God had sent forth into the western parts of the world the Tartars to slay and to be slain ; He also sent into the east His faithful servants Dominic and Francis to enlighten, instruct, and build up in the Faith." Little or nothing is known of these messengers of the gospel, but in the years 1245–47 John de Plano Carpini presented himself before the great Khan, and has left us an account of his observations. Though he failed to reach China he saw a number of its subjects at the Mongol Court, and describes them as " heathen men," but "having a written character of their own. They seem," he says, " indeed to be kindly and polished folks enough. They have no beard, and in character of countenance have a considerable resemblance to the Mongols, but are not so broad in the face. They have a peculiar language. Their betters as craftsmen in every art practised by man are not to be found in the whole world. Their country is very rich in corn, in wine, in gold and silver, in silk, and in every kind of produce tending to the support of mankind."

Some few years later the Franciscan Friar Rubruquis followed in Carpini's footsteps, and as a result of shrewd observation supplements the very

graphic account left us by Carpini. In great Cathay
or China he recognises the land of the Ceres with
which we are made familiar by the writings of the
Latin poets of the Augustan age. "Those
Cathayans," he adds, "are little fellows, speaking
much through the nose, and as is general with all
those Eastern people, their eyes are very narrow.
They are first-rate artists of every kind, and their
physicians have a thorough knowledge of the virtues of
herbs, and an admirable skill in diagnosis by the pulse.
The common money of Cathay consists of pieces of
cotton paper about a palm in length and breadth,
upon which lines are printed resembling the seals of
Mangu Khan (the third in succession from Jenghiz
Khan); they do their writing with a pencil such as
painters paint with, and a single character of theirs
comprehends several letters so as to form a whole
word." These few lines describe with effective point
and great accuracy the leading characteristics of
the patient and laborious inhabitants of China.

But though these faithful emissaries of Pope Innocent saw much to interest them in the social manners
and customs of the Cathayans, they could only carry
back with them a depressing account of the condition
of Nestorian Christianity at the capital of the great
Khan (Mangu). Rubruquis states that when he first
attempted to explain the object of his mission to
the Khan, his address was considerably " marred by
the interpreter becoming incoherent from frequent
draughts of wine supplied him by Mangu, who
himself became maudlin before the friar retired,
from the same cause." The effect of the religious

services was much interfered with also by the indulgence of this infirmity. On high days and festivals
the sacred ceremonies ended in drunken orgies, and
on one occasion the Empress, who had a leaning for
Nestorian Christianity, "was carried home from
church in a state of intoxication, escorted by priests
who reeled after her, shouting out their chants and
hymns."

Meanwhile Mangu was still waging war against
the sovereign of the Sung Dynasty, and the enterprise was yet incomplete when he died in 1259,
leaving the still growing heritage of the Mongols to
his son, the Great Kublai, a grandson of Jenghiz
Khan. With indefatigable energy this sovereign took
in hand the conquest of China, which had been so
dear to the heart of the great founder of the race, and
it was while the fate of this venture was still in the
lap of the gods that the Venetian traveller, Marco
Polo, presented himself at the Court of the Great
Khan. Already the father and uncle of Marco had
made an adventurous journey in pursuit of commerce,
across Asia to the valley of the Onon, and it was on
the occasion of their second visit in 1571 that they
took the youthful Marco with them. "When the two
brothers and Mark," writes this last named, "had
arrived at that great city (the Mongol capital), they
went to the Imperial Palace, and there they found the
sovereign attended by a great company of barons.
So they bent the knee before him, and paid their
respects to him with all possible reverence, prostra-
ting themselves on the ground. Then the lord bade
them stand up, and treated them with great honour,

showing great pleasure at their coming, and asked
many questions as to their welfare and how they sped.
They replied that they had in verity sped very well
seeing that they found the Khan well and safe. They
then presented the credentials and letters which they
had received from the Pope, which pleased him right
well ; and after that they produced the oil from the
sepulchre, and at that also he was very glad, for he set
great store thereby. And next spying Mark, who was
then a young gallant, he asked who was that in their
company. ' Sire,' said his father, Messer Nicolo, ' 'tis
my son and your liege man.' ' Welcome is he, too,'
quoth the Emperor. . . . . There was great rejoicing
at the Court because of their arrival ; and they met
with attention and honour from everybody."

The pomp and splendour of the Oriental Court
struck the travellers with amazement. Never before
had they dreamed of such Imperial splendour. The
annual feasts and national commemorations were
celebrated with a magnificence that surpassed their
wildest imaginations, while the evidences of civilisation which they met with on all sides led them to
make comparisons as unfavourable to Europe, as
changed circumstances lead us now to make to the
disadvantage of China. One fact which especially
attracted their attention was the existence of bank-
notes at a time when as yet Europe was destined to
wait four centuries for a like convenient currency. A
Chinese bank-note of about a century later is now
exhibited in the King's Library of the British
Museum, which is noticeable from the fact that the
paper on which it is printed is almost black. The

explanation of this colour is given by Marco Polo:
"The Emperor," he tells us, "makes them (his subjects) take the bark of a certain tree, in fact of the
mulberry tree, the leaves of which are the food of the
silkworm,—these trees being so numerous that whole
districts are full of them. What they take is a
certain fine white bast or skin which lies between the
wood of the tree and the thick outer bark, and this
they make into something resembling sheets of paper,
but black." The Khan himself, he describes as being
of a good stature, neither tall nor short, and being
very shapely in all his limbs. If this were so the
Chinese artists who have left us portraits of the great
man have signally maligned him. According to them
he was stout almost to obesity, and far from possessing the shapely form described by the Venetian, whose
evidence, however, we should be inclined to accept
rather than the products of native studios.

Meanwhile Kublai was actively engaged in the
campaign against the reigning sovereign of the Sung
Dynasty, and it is even said that in this enterprise he
received useful help at the outset from the young
Marco. It is difficult, however, to reconcile this with
the dates assigned to Marco's arrival and the opening
of the campaign; but however that may be, Kublai's
first advance was made across the Yellow River, and
against the city of Hsiangyang, in the province of
Hupeh. It is remarkable in the history of these wars
to find how much stouter a resistance the Chinese
offered to the invading Mongols than the inhabitants
of Western Asia and Eastern Europe were able to
present. It was only after a long siege that Hsiang-

yang fell into the hands of the Mongols, and it required more than one arduous campaign to subdue the cities of Hanyang, Hankow, Wuchang, Soochow, and, finally, Hangchow, the Sung capital. With the fall of the capital the Sung Dynasty practically came to an end, though with fitful efforts the followers of the ruling house attempted to stem the tide of invasion, and by 1276 the whole of China acknowledged the sway of Kublai. At this time the Mongol sovereign ruled over an empire which was one of the largest of which the world's history has knowledge, and which claimed as its subjects the countless hordes occupying the vast territories which stretch from the Black Sea to the shores of the China Ocean, and from Northern Mongolia to the frontiers of Annam.

One of the most striking features of Kublai's campaigns was the ease and rapidity with which his forces were moved over vast stretches of territory. Whether the enemy to be assailed were the people of Persia or of Cochin China, his armies straightway marched against the foe, and with surprising speed gained striking distance. Those whose fortune it has been to travel through Western China, and to cross the many mountain ranges over which the only roads are narrow pathways, fitted rather for goats than for human beings, will well understand how formidable must, for example, have been the undertaking of moving an army from Peking to the frontiers of Burma. To the Mongols, however, it was enough to know that the work had to be done, and without loss of time they overcame the difficulties of transport, and succeeded in placing an army in the field on the plains of Yungchang. To Kublai's followers, accustomed to the warfare of northern latitudes, the Burmese arms and equipments presented new and alarming characteristics. For the first time in their experiences they were called upon to face troops of elephants—animals which they could never have seen before. Nothing daunted, the General in command dismounted his men, who fired such a storm of arrows into the huge monsters, that they turned and rushed through the Burmese ranks, causing disorder and panic among their masters. Taking advantage of the confusion thus caused, the Mongols charged home into the forces of the enemy, and gained a decisive victory. Alarmed at the swarming numbers and over-mastering power of the invaders, the King submitted himself to Kublai, and was allowed to return to his capital on the condition that he and his successors should pay a regular tribute to the Court of China. Up to the time of our taking possession of Burma this tribute was regularly paid; and unfortunately even after we were in possession of Mandalay one or two tribute-bearing missions were allowed to carry homage to Peking.

But while in the Burmese and other land campaigns Kublai was uniformly successful, he was, in his naval warfare, eminently unfortunate. In 1266 he sent two envoys in the direction of Japan, who, however, returned without having ventured to cross the intervening sea from the coast of Korea. The object of this mission was doubtless to put an end to the Japanese piratical raids which had long been occasioning panic and disorder on the coasts of China and

Korea; but, finally, having failed to arrive at a peaceful solution of the difficulty, Kublai despatched a fleet against the Japanese which suffered a fate similar to that which overtook the Chinese ships at the Yalu during the late war. A number of the vessels were captured, a number were destroyed, and only a remnant returned to carry back the news of the disaster. Some years later Kublai fitted out another fleet carrying 100,000 warriors in the hope of avenging the late disgrace, but no better fortune attended this second venture, and it is said that almost the whole fleet perished. Other expeditions against the islands in the China seas proved equally unsuccessful, and Kublai was compelled to recognise the fact that while invincible on land, his hardy warriors were no match afloat for the seafaring populations of the islands. It is not in man to command success, and Kublai the victor in so many hard fought fields could well afford to submit to these foreign rebuffs on a strange element. In matters of religion Kublai showed the same toleration which had been conspicuous in his predecessors ; with equal favour, or perhaps one may say, indifference, he showed an impartially friendly disposition towards Christianity, Buddhism, and Mohammedanism. He listened to the teachings of Christian fathers with the same attention that he gave to Buddhist priests and Mohammedan Mullahs ; if ever he showed special favour to any one form of faith it may safely be assumed that it was with the object of hunting the trail of policy by the concession. Thus when wishing to secure supremacy over the wild and little known regions of Tibet, he affected a strong leaning towards Buddhism, and gained such an ascendancy by so doing that on a vacancy occurring in the Pontifical Priesthood he was invited to appoint a Grand Lama to superintend the destinies of the country. Having thus secured the loyalty of the Chief of the State he became virtually its ruler, and added a new but profitless province to his already unwieldy Empire.

But his toleration extended beyond religions, and embraced foreigners of all nations and degrees ; the favour with which he regarded young Marco Polo on his first arrival at the Mongol capital was consistently extended to him during the whole of his seventeen years' residence in China. Recognising his zeal and ability he appointed him to office, and gave him, among other employments, a roving commission to go through the provinces of Shansi, Shensi, Szech'uan, and Yunnan, and to report on the condition of the districts through which he passed. So well did the Venetian acquit himself on this and other occasions that he was finally appointed Governor of the city of Yangchow. There he exercised rule for three years, and might have remained indefinitely had not a wish to return to his native land possessed him with overpowering desire. His father and uncle, who were still in the country, were also anxious to return to Venice, but to their repeated requests for leave of absence Kublai had invariably returned a negative, and it was by the merest chance that they ultimately succeeded in getting away from the country of their adoption. It happened that Arghun Khan of Persia, a great-

nephew of Kublai, who had been left a widower,
desired to wed, as his second venture, a lady of the
Mongol tribe, of which his first wife had been a
member. Kublai sanctioned the arrangement, and
made choice of a young lady whom he considered to
be a fit and proper person to fill the place of her
deceased relative. So far matters went smoothly,
but when the question came of her journey to Persia,
which was to be made by sea, Kublai found it more
difficult to provide a fitting escort than it had been
to find the lady. The Mongol officials, unaccustomed to the sea, shrank from the undertaking, and
as a *dernier ressort*, it was proposed and agreed to,
that Marco with his father and uncle should have
charge of the would-be bride. In 1292 they started
on their adventurous voyage, in the course of which
they met with not a few perils. However, at length
they reached Persia in safety, and Marco tells us that
the adieux on the part of the lady were more sym-
pathetic than probably her future husband would
have cared to witness. The lady, we are told, burst
into tears, and bade her escort farewell with many
lamentations. So long had been the voyage that it
was not until 1295 that the Governor of Yangchow,
with his father and uncle, appeared once more on the
Rialto.

It is beyond dispute that China enjoyed an unusual
share of prosperity during the reign of Kublai. With
the same wisdom that he showed in most concerns, he
exhibited towards the people marked consideration
and justice. He adopted their institutions and looked
favourably on their prejudices and leanings ; he was

a patron of their national literature ; and used every
effort to secure justice in the administration of the
laws. But he was a foreigner, and his dynasty had
never taken that hold on the country which might
make people forget that he was not a Chinaman.
Two years after Marco Polo had left the Great Khan
was gathered to his fathers, and was carried to his
tomb without any expression of regret on the part
of the people over whom he had reigned for five and
thirty years. His grandson Timur succeeded him
on the throne, but the ability which had enabled
Kublai to raise the Empire to the great height at
which he had left it was wanting in his successor.
Timur died in 1307, and after him followed in rapid
succession seven sovereigns, of whom little can be
said that is of good report, except possibly of the
second, Jĕn Tsung, who was an ardent follower of
Confucius, and who adopted the principle of distri-
buting offices more equally between Mongols and
Chinese than had hitherto been the case.

When Kublai Khan rose to supreme power, the
Mongols, who had no writing of their own, were
dependent on their more cultured neighbours for the
means of corresponding on paper. An acquaintance
with the cultured and literary people of China had
taught the great conqueror the necessity of remedying
this defect, and with the object of doing so, he
appointed a scholar of the name of Bashpa to devise
an alphabet which should give expression to the
thoughts of native writers in a national script.
Bashpa executed his task, and Kublai issued an
edict ordering that for the future all official docu-

ments should be written in the characters so invented.
No sooner, however, had the Mongols entered China,
than the new alphabet was discarded. As has been
said, "China is a sea that salts all the waters which
flow into it," and the Mongols having left their
dreary steppes, and their equally dreary scraps of
literature, became ardent admirers of the Chinese
scholarship. Under the influence of this new life
they forgot the results of Bashpa's ingenuity, and
adopted the learning and writing of their conquered
enemies. One branch of Chinese literature may
almost be said to have been the creation of the
Mongols; before their time puppet shows and
dramatic performances had been among the popular
amusements of the Chinese people. The patronage
which was extended to these scenic efforts by the
Mongols encouraged the production of more regular
plays, and the profession of playwright became in
consequence a popular one with such authors as had
more taste for holding the mirror up to Nature than
for discussing the sterner thoughts of the philo-
sophers. The dramas which were produced during
the Mongol period have never been surpassed in
China, and the "Plays of the Yuan Dynasty" are still
regarded as standard works in this department of
literature.

During the last reigns of the Yuan Dynasty the
usual precursors of revolution became prominent.
Rebellions and riots broke out on all sides, and
during the reign of Shunti, the last of the Mongols,
the disorders came to a head. The dynasty had
never been popular, and when its sovereigns ceased

to be powerful, the desire for the return to the throne of a Chinese line became intensified among the people. At the head of one of the risings in the south was one who was destined to wear the robes of sovereignty. Chu was essentially a man of the people, and his family having fallen on evil times, he was left on the death of his parents penniless and alone. To men in such a condition the cloister often offers a shelter from the storm. At all events this was Chu's anticipation when he shaved his head and took the vows of a Buddhist monk. But circumstances were too strong for the recluse, and the military spirit that was born in him having been awakened by a rebellion which broke out in the neighbourhood of his monastery, he incontinently cast aside his cowl and took the sword. A commanding presence, a strong will, and considerable ability, soon forced him to the head of the movement, and with such skilful tactics did he manœuvre his men on the battlefield that he was uniformly successful in his engagements with the enemy. With scarcely a check he marched on Nanking, and having captured that most important city after a short siege, he, like the T'aip'ing Wang of forty years ago, constituted it his capital. From this *point d'appuis* he succeeded in driving the Mongols out of the Province of Kiangsi.

The central provinces were not the only parts of the Empire where the fortunes of war declared against the Mongols at this time. In Korea, and in the western parts of the Empire, the rebellious forces claimed to have gained victories, and it was in the

midst of these clouds of disasters that Shunti was
gathered to his fathers (1370). Meanwhile Chu
despatched three armies for the conquest of the still
unsubdued districts. Two were commissioned to
subjugate the southern provinces of Fuhkien, Kwangtung, and Kwangsi, while the third, consisting, it is
said, of two hundred and fifty thousand men, was
ordered to overrun the northern portion of the
country. By this time the leaven of rebellion had
spread far and wide, and Chu's troops found little
difficulty in executing the commissions entrusted to
them. With scarcely any opposition Peking fell
before the rebel forces, and as a fitting climax to that
victory, Chu, at the bidding of his vast hosts, was
induced to accept the Imperial purple. He was well
aware, however, that the most difficult part of his
task still lay before him. At the head of an enthusiastic army, and in face of a disheartened foe, it
had been comparatively easy for him to overthrow the
Mongol power. He now had to justify the choice of
the people in placing him on the throne, and in this
trying position he displayed as far-seeing a judgment
as that which had already secured him temporary
success. He recognised the importance of fostering
that learning of which the nation was justly proud,
and one of his first public acts was directed towards
re-establishing throughout the country the schools
which had fallen into decay during the troublous
time which had marked the decadence of the House
of Jenghiz Khan.

During the halcyon period of the T'ang Dynasty
an Imperial College, known as the Hanlin or "Forest

of Pencils," had been established under Imperial patronage. Admittance to this palace of learning had always been regarded as the highest literary honour which could be obtained by the most erudite scholars. During the many dynastic changes which had taken place since its foundation its existence had been chequered by not a few periods of misfortune, and by none greater than that which had lately over-taken it. Hungwu—for such was the Imperial title adopted by Chu—determined to rehabilitate the institution. He rebuilt its shattered walls, refurnished its empty rooms, and showed his personal interest in the work by personally visiting the building, and super-intending the arrangements for its revival. It was fit and proper that the main building should be at Peking, but Hungwu could never forget that Nan-king had been the capital of his choice, and as evidence of this sentiment he built and endowed a sister institution at that city. Since the advent of power of the present Manchu Dynasty this last foundation has ceased to exist, though the college at Peking still maintains its high reputation. Like everything else, however, in the northern capital, with the exception perhaps of parts of the Imperial palace and of the foreign legations, the Hanlin College is fast hastening to decay. Its halls are deserted and its archives and library are covered thick with dust. It may sound paradoxical to say that a building in such a deplorable condition can represent an institution to which all men look up. But so it is. The highest literary honour that it is in the power of his Emperor to confer is admittance to the ranks of the chosen few who boast themselves as being Hanlin scholars, though it is probable that few of those who now bear that title have ever passed through the creaking gates of the Hanlin College.

Another great work undertaken by Hungwu was the codification of the laws of the Empire. During the Mongol Dynasty much laxity had been observed in the administration of justice. The Mongol rulers were men of action, and thought more of the weapons of their army than of the forms of the legal procedure. But an immense benefit was conferred on the nation at large by this peaceful achievement of Hungwu. History further tells us that, with the true instincts of a law-giver, he recognised that something more than forms, however excellent, was needed, and devoted much time and energy to promoting the practical administration of justice and equity in the local courts. There was unquestionably room for such an effort, but to cleanse so foul an Augean stable as the Chinese law courts was more than one man, however able and however well intentioned, could possibly accomplish, and unfortunately for the nation the officials ploughed up his good seed as soon as it was sown. More beneficial legislation in this direction would, however, undoubtedly have been effected had it not been that the Mongols, taking heart of grace after their defeat, took the field once again against their conqueror. Even in the home provinces of Shansi and Shensi they gained such victories over the Ming troops as put a considerable strain on Hungwu's resources, while in the promontory of Liaotung and the provinces of Szech'uan

and Yunnan they completely put the enemy to rout.
To meet this emergency Hungwu despatched one
army against Chungk'ing, and another against Ch'engtu
in Szech'uan, and having pacified those districts
marched across the border into Yunnan; and
ultimately recovered that province from the Mongol
yoke. In the midst of these victories, at a ripe age
and full of honours, Hungwu became a guest on high
(1399), leaving a rich inheritance to his successor. It
is noteworthy that recently the thoughts of a large
section of the Chinese people have been led back to
this period. It is by a comparison between the
present state of the Empire, and the condition of
things which existed under the first sovereign of the
Ming Dynasty, that the leaders of the Kolaohwei have
been able to enlist so many recruits to their banners.
Hung, the first syllable of the sovereign's name, has
now been taken as the second title of this very revolutionary Society. Time will show what is the extent
of the disaffection which is unquestionably now
brewing, and how far the existence of foreigners
in the country will serve as a check to any serious
disturbance of the political equilibrium. Already
within modern times the government has once at
least been saved from its own people by foreign
intervention, and it is possible that a like support
may again be required to bolster up the central
authority in times of future trouble.

Some years before Hungwu's death, his eldest son
having already succumbed to disease, he, by his last
testament devised his Empire and Throne to his grandson, who afterwards adopted the title of Chienwên. In

Eastern countries where primogeniture is not the invariable rule, some uncertainty as to the succession generally follows an Imperial demise. In this case each of the younger sons considered that he had a better claim to the Throne than his nephew, and to avoid the outburst of any unseemly violence between the disputants Hungwu before his death sent the malcontents to their provincial posts, keeping his grandson about his person at Court. The difficulty of the position was eventually accentuated by the obligation which Chienwên felt to be incumbent upon him of inviting his uncles to take part in the Imperial obsequies. With the exception of one, the Prince of Yen, they all with one consent declined to be present. Nor did the acceptance of the invitation by this prince by any means imply a feeling of loyalty towards his nephew. On the contrary, on leaving the Imperial presence he at once retired to Nanking to organise his forces of opposition. With as little loss of time as possible he took the field, and being a man of great energy, determination, and courage, he gained a series of victories over his kinsman, which were chequered only by some trifling defeats. At length, in 1402, his troops had so completely gained the upper hand that Chienwên determined to give up the struggle and to abdicate. So unusual a step led to the report that he had committed suicide, but possibly with a recollection of his grandfather's religious propensities he, instead, shaved his head and sought sanctuary in a monastery in Yunnan. For forty years he remained incognito in the cloister, but at the end of that time, perhaps weary of the monotony of his existence, he launched out into poetry, and published a volume describing his former trials and difficulties with such minute details that the authorship stood confessed. The fact of his being an Emperor's son, or possibly the fear that he might instigate a rebellion, induced the ruling sovereign to order him to Peking, where he was kept a state prisoner within the precincts of the palace until death put an end to his troublous existence. Meanwhile Yen was urged by his followers to usurp the throne. Nothing loth he accepted the crown, and for two and twenty years reigned with vigour over the Empire. During the Mongol period Peking had been the official capital, and Yunglo, as Yen had styled himself, determined so far to break the traditions belonging to his house as once again to transfer the seat of Government from Nanking to Peking. Further, for his own peace, and for the satisfaction of his followers also, he considered it wise that he should be handed down to posterity as the direct heir of Hungwu, and he therefore issued an edict commanding that Chienwen's reign should be obliterated from the annals, and that the four years during which he had held the Imperial sceptre should be added to the reign of Hungwu.

Under his able administration the country enjoyed comparative peace, and he had time to turn his attention from the "Eighteen Provinces" to the difficulties which were disturbing the political affairs of Tonquin. Compared with his predecessors' reigns his rule was in the happy position of having no history within the frontiers of the Empire. Beyond

the northern marches, however, war with the Tartars
was chronic, and though his generals gained repeated
victories over their restless adversaries, the system of
warfare which these practised made it impossible for
the Chinese to consolidate their triumphs. It is
always difficult to destroy a guerilla force which has
a boundless territory to which to retire. That he
inflicted serious losses on them is well established ;
and it was when on one of his expeditions against
these nomad marauders that his fatal illness overtook
him in 1425. Yunglo was more than a mere soldier.
He showed a wide and intelligent interest in the
literature of his country, and caused to be executed
one literary task which alone should make his name
famous. He appointed a commission of the leading
scholars of the time to compile an exhaustive ency-
clopædia on all subjects commemorated in Chinese
literature. After bestowing the labour of many
years on this gigantic compilation, the editors presented (1407) their Imperial Master with a work
consisting of no fewer than 22,877 books, besides the
table of contents, which occupied sixty volumes.

To Yunglo succeeded several sovereigns, the
history of whose reigns presents a dismal picture of
incompetence and anarchy. The historians, indeed,
delight to tell us that envoys from Central Asia,
India, and Malacca, came to pay homage at the
court of these Sons of Heaven. But these glimpses
of honour are set off in a background of open disorder
and successful rebellion. In 1428 Tonquin threw off
the Chinese yoke and the Tartars raided, almost
unchecked, over the northern frontier of the Empire.

At one great battle fought against these Mongol horsemen a hundred thousand Chinese are said to have been killed, and the victory was further emphasised by the capture of the Emperor Chêngt'ung himself. It is evidence of the abject condition to which the Empire was brought at this time, that though the Tartar chieftain offered to release his Imperial prisoner on the payment of a hundred taels of gold, two hundred taels of silver, and two hundred pieces of silk, the Chinese were unable to provide the ransom. Eight years Chêngt'ung remained in captivity, and during this enforced absence from Peking his throne was vicariously occupied by his next brother. In 1465 Chêngt'ung paid the great debt of nature, and made his death humanely memorable by an order that the barbarous Mongol practice of immolating slaves at the tombs of Sovereigns—a practice which had been adopted by the earlier Ming rulers—should not be followed in his case. A still more memorable record of his reign is found in the large geographical work on the Empire, entitled *Ta Ming yi t'ung chih*, or " A Complete Geographical Record of the Empire under the great Ming Dynasty." The example thus set has fortunately been followed by the rulers of the present line of sovereigns, under whose auspices the *Ta Ch'ing yi t'ung chih* in five hundred books, which describes in minute detail the geographical and political condition of the country, has been issued from the Press.

It was during the reign of Chêngt'ung's successor Ch'ênghwa, that the canal from Peking to the Peiho was made. This was the only public work for which there was either time or inclination in the midst of

the brigandage and seditious risings which disturbed
the Empire, more especially in the northern and
western provinces, with such constant persistency that
they may almost be said to have been endemic.

During the reign of Chéngté (1506-22) occurred
an event which led up, though at a long interval, to
the Treaties which now govern the relations of China
with the outer world. In 1511 the Portuguese, Raphael
Perestralo, arrived off the southern coast of China,
and six years later Don Fernao Peres D'Andrade
presented himself at Canton in command of a small
squadron. The object of these pioneers was the
extension of commerce, and D'Andrade having been
well received by the authorities at Canton, proceeded
to Peking, where he remained some years, acting the
part of an amateur ambassador. For some time his
relations with the central authorities were amicable,
but the outrageous action of his compatriots in other
parts of the Empire unhappily brought his mission to
an abrupt and unfortunate close. By order of the
Emperor he was arrested and imprisoned, and after
six years of confinement was summarily beheaded by
order of the succeeding ruler, Chiaching. Such a
reprisal was undoubtedly a high-handed measure, but
the Portuguese traders on the coast, notably at Ningpo
and Foochow, had rapidly filled up a large cup of
iniquity. They had been guilty of every form of
outrage, and at Ningpo had proceeded to such
excesses that on the occasion of a difference with the
people of a neighbouring village they had fallen upon
and massacred their opponents. When estimating
the conduct of an Oriental State in such circum-

stances, it is only fair that the opposite side of the shield should be seen, and it cannot be denied that the history of the early Portuguese settlements in China is stained by every form of iniquity.

In the Chinese histories no mention is made of D'Andrade's residence in Peking, and the first Portuguese visit on the coast is put down to the year 1535. At this time in the neighbourhood of Foochow a general massacre of the Portuguese took place in revenge for certain nefarious acts, and thirty only out of several hundred escaped to tell the tale to their countrymen in the neighbourhood of Canton. After numerous negotiations and much filibustering, the Canton officials allowed the Portuguese to settle on the peninsula of Macao in exchange for an annual rental. To say that the lives of these men were precarious would certainly not be over-stating the case. They were constantly engaged in conflicts with the forces of the Chinese Government, as well as with the pirates who ravaged the coasts, but, though they carried their lives in their hands, so lucrative was the trade in which they were engaged that as many as five or six hundred Portuguese were commonly to be found within the precincts of the new settlement.

It need not be a matter of surprise that the action of these pioneers of commerce rendered the Chinese disinclined to receive within their frontiers any foreigner whom they could conveniently keep out, and when the missionary Xavier, burning with a desire to carry a knowledge of Christianity to the people, asked for leave to be allowed to deliver this message of goodwill to all men, he was refused permission to land.

Unwilling to give up the enterprise he took up his residence on the island of Sanshan, within sight of the mainland, and there died in 1552 without having accomplished the yearning desire of his heart. The same inhospitality was offered to Michel Roger, the first of the Jesuit missionaries who attempted to gain a footing in the Middle Kingdom. The great Ricci who arrived at Macao in 1582 was more successful. He was a man with wide sympathies, great learning, and much Christian charity. He began his work in China by studying the language, together with the scientific and religious beliefs of the people, and he thought that he saw in the native ideas on the subject of the Supreme Being and the whole duty of man, a likeness, though deformed by superstition, but still a likeness, to the truths set forth in the gospel. He seized on all those passages in the Confucian literature which agree with the utterances of the inspired writers, and following the example of Saint Paul at Athens, he told his hearers that the God whom they ignorantly worshipped was the God whom he was sent to preach to them. The open-mindedness which thus characterised his sentiments gained for him consideration and respect among all classes alike, from the ignorant coolies to the educated mandarins. With such a reputation he was received with favour at Peking—a favour which was not diminished by his very practical knowledge of mechanics, which enabled him even to set to rights the Emperor's clocks and watches which, under the unwonted treatment to which they were subjected by the palace officials, had gone hopelessly wrong. Intent on interesting and at

the same time instructing the mandarins, he utilised
his knowledge of the language to translate the first
six books of Euclid into Chinese. At a later period
he published in Chinese a geometrical treatise on the
theory of astronomical measurement; and not to
leave the religious feelings of the people untouched,
he brought out a work on the character and attributes
of God. The scholarly style of these works commended them even to the punctilious taste of the
Literati, and their author enjoyed during his residence
in Peking the respect and friendship of the Court and
of the highest officials of the Empire. It is noteworthy that a movement is now on foot for inaugu-
rating a system similar to that of Ricci. Works of
scientific and general interest are being translated
into Chinese, and the attempt is thus being made to
reach those members of the upper classes who have
of late been so bitterly opposed to European intercourse. Ricci died in 1610, deeply regretted by all
with whom he had been brought into contact.

The reign of Chiaching (1522-67), which had been
disturbed from its beginning by domestic outbreaks,
was destined before its close to be imperilled by the
same enemy which has of late humbled Chinese
pride to the dust. It will be remembered that
Kublai Khan made several expeditions against
Japan, and though uniformly unsuccessful these
onslaughts none the less left a rankling feeling of
ill-will in the minds of the Japanese. As the
Mongol power declined the Japanese sought revenge for the injuries inflicted on them, by piratical
raids on the coast. Mr. Boulger, in his " History of

China," quotes a passage from a Chinese historian, who describes the Japanese of this period as being "intrepid, inured to fatigue, despising life, and knowing well how to face death ; although inferior in number, a hundred of them would blush to flee before a thousand foreigners, and, if they did, they would not dare to return to their country. Sentiments such as these, which are instilled into them from their earliest childhood, render them terrible in battle." This description is as true to-day as it was then, and their prowess appeared as conspicuously off the coasts of Fuhkien and Chehkiang in the sixteenth century as it did at the battles of Pingyang and Yalu. These lawless attacks on the Chinese coast were diversified with intervals of quiet, during which Japanese merchants reaped a rich harvest from the Chinese traders. But in 1552 a more serious campaign was undertaken, and a landing having been effected on the coast of Chehkiang, the invaders established themselves in a fortified post, and for a time defended their position against all comers. Some years later they even advanced and laid siege to Nanking, and though this attempt at conquest failed, the repeated onslaughts of the invaders paralysed the Imperial power, and kept the Eastern Provinces in a chronic state of disorder. In every naval engagement the Japanese were successful, and on land, though vastly outnumbered, they were never hopelessly defeated.

From time immemorial the pursuit of the philosopher's stone and of the elixir of life has been a favourite occupation with Chinese alchemists, and

though refuted over and over again by the cold hand
of death, it has never lost a certain fascination for the
ignorant seekers after the unknown. It is strange to
find that Chiaching, whose occupation of the throne
had been one long troublous struggle, should have
desired to perpetuate an existence which can have
afforded him so very little pleasure. But so it was,
and with ceaseless diligence he sought to snatch from
the professors of Taoism the secret which was to make
him immortal. As the approach of death proved
indisputably the folly of his ways, he owned his error,
and on his death-bed wrote a confession in these
words :—" Forty-five years have I occupied the
throne, and there have been few reigns as long.
My duty was to revere heaven, and to take care of
my people ; yet, actuated by the desire to find some
solace for the evils from which I have continually
suffered, I allowed myself to be deceived by impostors,
who promised me the secret of immortality. This
delusion has led me to set a bad example to both
my magnates and my people. I desire to repair the
evil by this edict, which is to be published throughout the Empire after my death." In 1566 he passed
into the land of shades, and his son Lungch'ing
reigned in his stead.

The only event of importance which occurred in
this reign was the submission of the turbulent
Mongol leader Yenta, who had long defied the
Chinese power. Yenta was now an old man, and
wishing to end his days in peace he entered into
negotiation with Lungch'ing, who, after the manner
of Eastern sovereigns when dealing with submissive

rebels, granted him the title of Prince, and so set at
rest a feud which had been of time-honoured existence. But though Lungch'ing's reign had ended in
peace and quiet, the general trend of the nation's
history was downwards, and it was unfortunate that
at this time, when a strong hand was needed at the
helm, a child should have succeeded to the throne.
As is usual in such cases the young Emperor's
mother was proclaimed Regent, and though for a
time the legacy of peace which had descended to
the Empire remained intact, it was not long before
disturbances again broke out. In Szech'uan, and on
the north-west frontier rebellions of considerable
dimensions afflicted the Empire. The important
town of Ninghsia fell into the hands of the Tartars,
led by the chieftain Popai, who added ingratitude to
the crime of rebellion by leading his forces against
the Chinese army in which he had at one time held
high rank. Fortunately the Imperialists were able
to recover the city, and at the same time to crush the
rebellion.

But while thus successful in the north-west, the
same foe appeared on the eastern coast who had
lately proved to be a formidable antagonist to the
Chinese. Many years of peace and of successful
raiding on the Chinese mainland had introduced an
era of prosperity into Japan, and the people having
waxed fat began to kick. They had long been
associated with Korean politics and rivalries, and
seizing on the present opportunity (1592) when
Korea, as has not been uncommonly the case in her
history, was distracted by internal feuds, they landed

a force at the port of Fusan under the command
of the celebrated general and subsequent Shogun,
Hideyoshi. Without meeting with much opposition
Hideyoshi advanced across the peninsula and made
himself master of the capital, Seoul. Until the
recent war the Chinese have always acted as the
suzerain power in Korea, and in this emergency the
King, as in duty and interest bound, appealed to the
Chinese Emperor for assistance. The appeal was
at once acknowledged, and a large Chinese force
marched into Korea by way of the Yalu district.
In anticipation of this movement the Japanese
advanced northwards to meet the attack, and, as in
1894, took up their position in Pingyang, where they
were received without opposition by the inhabitants.
The Chinese attack was delivered in force, but
Hideyoshi commanded and disposed his men so
ably that they had little difficulty in beating off
their assailants.

The efforts which had been made for the campaign
by both nations had, however, so far weakened their
resources that neither was much inclined to continue
the struggle at once. The Chinese, therefore, waited
for reinforcements, and the Japanese slowly retired
on their base at Fusan. Desultory engagements
ensued, and the Chinese gained one decided victory
near Pingyang, where they succeeded in burning a
depôt of warlike stores on which Hideyoshi had
depended for the army. Negotiations for peace
followed, and it is noticeable that the Chinese
adopted precisely the same tactics as those which
they practised in 1895. They sent ambassadors of

inferior rank to represent the Emperor, and by this course so outraged the feelings of Hideyoshi, who in the meantime had become Shogun, that he prepared a fresh expedition for the renewed conquest of the country. Before, however, anything could be effected, the news reached Fusan of his death. This catastrophe put an end to the war, and peace was once more restored between the two countries. Of the spoils carried off by the Chinese we hear nothing, but the Japanese returned to their islands laden with trophies, among which were the ears of ten thousand Koreans who had been butchered in the frays.

It was during this reign that the Spaniards reached the Philippine islands, where they found a congenial climate and a fertile soil. They, however, were not the only people who recognised these advantages. They had no sooner settled themselves on the islands than Chinese emigrants followed their example, and in the quiet, persistent way common to the race, poured into the country. At first the Spaniards were well pleased to have such willing and handy craftsmen, but as the number of them increased by leaps and bounds they soon began to fear for their dominion. Threats and persuasions were freely used to induce the intruders to return to their native land, and these proving unavailing an order was given for the massacre of the strangers. Twenty thousand Chinamen are said to have been slaughtered at this time, and had these been subjects of any other state than China a war would have been inevitable. But until recent years, when international law has been made a subject of study at Peking, the

Chinese Government has troubled itself very little, if at all, about the welfare of its subjects in foreign lands. In this case, however, a more immediately direct reason caused the Emperor Wanli to overlook the outrage. Disturbances had broken out within the Empire which, to hold in check, required the services of every available man at his command. To subdue these completely was plainly beyond his power, and to the day of his death, in 1620, wars and rumours of wars were endemic in the country.

Meanwhile, under the skilful guidance of Ricci, Christianity had made considerable progress, even amid the disorders which had disturbed the reign of Wanli. Hsü, one of the *Literati*, and a man of high scholarly attainments and standing, having been converted by Ricci's influence, threw himself heart and soul into the missionary work. It was mainly due to the help of this man that Ricci was able to publish the scholarly treatises which have made his name immortal in connection with Chinese Missions, and Hsü's granddaughter, baptized under the name of Candida, ably seconded his influence with money and energy. Thirty churches are said to have been built by her means, besides ninety buildings for the use of the missionaries. Unfortunately for the peace of the Empire, Wanli left no son by his Empress to succeed him, and at his death he was compelled, therefore, to nominate as his heir the eldest son of one of his concubines. A younger brother of this fortunate youth, being a favourite with his father, had been led to expect that in default of a son by the Empress, he would have been chosen as successor to the Purple. In his anger at what he considered to be his supersession, he raised the standard of revolt, and embittered the last few months of his father's life by creating a conflict within his own household. Three

CHINESE BARROWMAN GOING HOME.

Emperors in succession to Wanli completed the list of Ming rulers, and in 1644 the first Sovereign of the present Ta Ch'ing Dynasty ascended the throne.

Though it cannot be said that science and art

flourished under the Ming rulers, yet the artistic taste, at least, of the people was not entirely neglected. Numerous artists painted landscapes, flowers, and birds, with all the skill that had guided the pencils of the artists of the T'ang and Sung Dynasties, and to them the Japanese owe and acknowledge a deep debt of gratitude for the examples which they set to the contemporary painters of Miako and Osaka. The works of no artists are more admired in Japan than those of Sesshiu and Kano, both of whom drew their inspirations direct from China during this period. The landscapes of Ma Yuan, and the flowers and birds of Ting Yüch'uan are artistic creations which must at all times and in all places command admiration, and these are but two of a host of painters who delighted and still delight all connoisseurs of art. The wood-engraving of this period is famous for beauty of design and skilful treatment, and is eagerly sought after for the adornment of houses by those to whom the god of wealth has been propitious.

In several important points scientific teaching improved considerably during the same period owing to the arrival of Western missionaries in the country. Ricci, as we have seen, instructed the *Literati* in geometrical and astronomical knowledge, which happily was not allowed to perish with him. In 1628 John Adam Schall arrived in China, and proceeded to Peking, where, under Imperial patronage, he was appointed Astronomer-Royal, and was deputed to rearrange the Imperial Calendar. Under the three last Emperors of the Ming Dynasty, and the two first of the present dynasty, Schall was

treated with all the respect and honour to which he
was entitled. But at the beginning of the reign of
K'anghsi he fell on evil days. Jealousy was aroused
against him, and on a charge of law-breaking brought
by his enemies, he was thrown into prison and loaded
with chains. From this evil strait he was liberated
by death in about 1666. During the years of his
ascendancy he had worked with single-hearted zeal
in the cause of the faith, and it is said that between
the years 1660 and 1664 a hundred thousand converts
were claimed by the Church through the instrumentality of Schall and his co-workers. At one time the
Emperor K'anghsi showed a disposition which tended
towards conversion. But this wished-for consummation was never achieved, though the Emperor's
mother, wife, and son all received baptism, which rite
was also sought and received by fifty ladies of the
Court.

As men of science the missionaries received every
consideration from the Emperor, and though they
were disposed at times to consider that his attitude
towards Christianity was satisfactory, it is plain that
in his heart of hearts he viewed the subject with
all the perfect indifference of a faithful follower of
Confucius.

"Why do you so much trouble yourselves," he
asked on one occasion of a spiritual adviser, "about
a world which you have never yet entered?" and
adopting the, to him, canonical view, he expressed his
opinion that it would be much wiser if they thought
less of the world to come, and more of the present
life. It is possible that when he said this he may

have had in his mind the dying word of Ferdinand de Capillas, who suffered martyrdom in 1648. " I have had no home but the world," said this priest, as he faced his last earthly judge, " no bed but the ground, no food but what Providence sent me from day to day, and no other object than to do and suffer for the glory of Jesus Christ, and for the eternal happiness of those who believe in His Name."

It is possible also that the dissensions which broke out among the Roman Catholic missionaries in China during the last half of the seventeenth century may have had something to do with the cynical attitude adopted by K'anghsi towards them. In 1651 a party of Dominicans arrived in China to supplement the work being done by the Jesuits. These latest arrivals had no sooner landed than they became shocked at the wise latitude allowed by the Jesuits in matters of religious forms. With the wisdom of the serpent, and, as it had hitherto proved, with the harmlessness of the dove, the Jesuits, in their desire to gain intellectual dominion over the people, had granted admission into their services of practices which savoured somewhat of the superstitious rites of the natives. The ancient and respectable worship of Ancestors received their approval on the plea that it was rather a civil than a religious service. They had adopted also the abstract term T'ien, or Heaven, for the Christian God, and made no objection to the exhibition in their churches of scrolls bearing the inscription, "Worship Heaven." The Dominicans, fresh from Rome, and unaccustomed to the casuistry which by long practice had become part of the Jesuit character, at once set their faces against these practices. The Jesuits, firm in the inherited wisdom of Ricci, refused to listen to what they considered to be the carping criticism of their opponents, and declined to make any alterations in their practices. The Dominicans appealed to Rome, and after much doubt and controversy, a papal decree was issued proclaiming the worship of ancestors to be a heathenish practice, and one which was not to be for a moment sanctioned by the Holy Mother Church.

III

THE RISE OF THE MANCHUS

WHILE yet the influence of Ricci was supreme at Peking, and while yet Wanli sat on the throne, the Manchu power was rising in the north-east, which was destined ultimately to bring all China under its yoke. After the defeat of the Kin Tartars by the Mongols in the thirteenth century, scattered bands had made their way back to their original haunts in the neighbourhood of Moukden. Many of these men had added military skill to their warlike natures, and thus formed a formidable though small body of warriors in the midst of the various tribes of Manchus who inhabited the surrounding territories. Among these wandering and superstitious people a miracle was proclaimed. While a Manchu maiden was seated on the shores of the lake whose waters lap the sides of the Long White Mountain, a magpie dropped a red fruit into her lap. The maiden ate the fruit and straightway conceived a son, whose name was called Aisin Gioro, the Golden. Such a birth entitled the infant to the highest honours,

and with one consent he was elected to the chieftainship of the clan. To this chieftain succeeded in

A MONUMENT AT MOUKDEN.

course of time his son, whose grandson, Nurhachu,
born in 1559, was destined to justify his miraculous

6

origin by vanquishing for himself and his successors the ancient Empire of China.

As Nurhachu reached manhood he took an active part in the affairs of his tribe, and by virtue of his

A MANCHU OFFICIAL AND LADY.

descent was, in the natural order of things, proclaimed chieftain of it. His appearance is said to have indicated the future that lay before him. Native writers love to dwell on his dragon face and phœnix eyes, his enormous chest, his large ears, and his deep-toned voice. These features, by common belief, belong to leaders of men, and if they graced the frame of Nurhachu they were certainly truer omens than are most signs and forecasts. At this time the Manchus were divided up into numberless small clans which were scattered in the wide district which divides the great wall from the Amur, and the first task to which Nurhachu devoted himself was to weld these scattered tribes into one confederacy. Good fortune attended his efforts, and the extent of his success may be estimated by the jealousy with which he was viewed by rival chieftains. At first the Chinese, who considered themselves the lords paramount over the Manchurian tribes, regarded the movement as being too insignificant to require their attention. Besides, at this time local riots and somewhat serious rebellions were disturbing the peace of several of the provinces of the Empire. At length Wanli, who still sat on the throne at Peking, was roused to action by such complaints as the defeated are always ready to bring against a successful foe, and he took up the cause of a certain Nikan, who was of all others Nurhachu's chief opponent. Like other people, the Chinese often make the mistake of despising their enemies, and in the campaign which followed they suffered the penalty of their misguided folly. In 1591 Nurhachu had so far advanced his cause as to be able to annex the Yalu district. Such an obvious proof of his success was gall and wormwood to those neighbouring chieftains who had held aloof from his confederacy, and seven of these dis-

contented rulers banded themselves together to rob
him of the legitimate rewards of his wisdom and
foresight.   At the head of thirty thousand men they
marched out to meet the four thousand who fought
under his banners.   But Nurhachu, who had all the
military ability of a Napoleon, defeated the allies in
detail and slew four thousand of their chosen warriors.
This success tempted him to further ventures, and as
a preliminary step he opened his plan of campaign
by an assault on the Liaotung peninsula.   This was
a direct attack on the Empire of China, and to justify
so extreme a measure he drew up a statement of
the seven grievances which he brought against his
powerful neighbour, the first of which described in
general terms the grounds of his several indictments.
" Though my ancestors," he wrote, " never took a
straw from, nor injured an inch of earth within, the
Chinese boundary, the Chinese were unceasingly
quarrelling with them, and without just reason abetted
my neighbours to the great injury of my ancestors."
    The other six complaints described in detail the
specific acts of which he complained.   In the following year (1618) he opened the campaign by crossing
the Chinese frontier and capturing the cities of Fushun
and Chingho.
    The Chinese were now fully alarmed ; but as has so
often happened in the history of the Empire, they had
so overlooked the beginning of the evil that by the
time they took the field they found themselves face to
face with a large and well-equipped army, instead of
the roving bands of banditti which had represented
the original force of the movement.   The saying that

Providence is on the side of large battalions is one of
those aphorisms which does not apply to Chinese
battlefields. We have lately seen how, though
numerically inferior, the Japanese defeated, put to
flight, and destroyed the huge masses of troops
which the Chinese were able to bring against them in
Korea and in those districts over which Nurhachu
in his day manœuvred. And in this instance it was
as inapplicable as during the late war. A hundred
thousand Chinese troops marched against the 60,000
who followed the Niuchi chieftain, and if in executing
his tactics the general commanding had desired to
place himself and his men in the hollow of his adversary's hand, he could not have acted better than he
did. With fatal consequences he divided his army
into three forces, and thus gave Nurhachu the opportunity which he desired. With unerring instinct he
recognised his opponent's mistake, and by a series of
rapid movements he fought the three armies in detail,
and practically annihilated them. It is said that in
these engagements 310 general officers and 45,000
soldiers were slain. The baggage of the vanquished
also fell into the hands of the Manchus, who thus
became possessed of welcome stores with which to
replenish and supplement the very defective supplies
of their men.

It so happened that just when the news of the first
reverses reached Peking the Portuguese Envoy, Gonsalvo de Texeira, arrived at the capital on a mission
connected with the settlement at Macao. Finding
the Government in a dire strait, the Envoy, on the
principle of *Do ut des*, offered to supply a Portuguese

contingent to help the Imperial forces against the
invader. Chinese pride has never been able to resist the
offer of help in times of emergency. The mandarins
may profess to despise the foreign barbarians and all
their works, but whether against the invading Manchus
or the rebellious T'aip'ings they have always shown a
readiness to avail themselves of any assistance which

A STREET SCENE IN MOUKDEN.

foreigners have chosen to offer. In this case they instantly accepted the Envoy's proposal, and a corps of two
hundred Portuguese arquebusiers, with an equal number
of drilled and equipped natives, were enrolled for the
service. With a certain amount of parade this small
force travelled from Macao to Peking. But by the
time they reached the capital, however, the Emperor's

alarm had subsided, and his zeal having consequently diminished, the Portuguese commander was politely requested to leave his guns, and to march his men back to Macao. It is on record that the guns so borrowed eventually did good service against the enemy.

But though effective these weapons failed to check the march of the Manchus, who, after a difficult siege, captured the city of Moukden, and marched to the attack of Liaoyang. Here a vigorous defence was offered, and the city yielded only when the entire garrison had been put to the sword. After the capture of this city the native historians mention incidentally that the townspeople acknowledged allegiance to their new masters by shaving their heads. This is the first reference to be met with of the custom of shaving the head and wearing the pigtail, which is now the universal custom in China. Such a subject is generally beneath the notice of Chinese writers of history, who never trouble themselves to chronicle anything but the events occurring in court and camp during the period of which they write. Their silence on this point leaves the origin of the practice obscure, and whether it was a Manchu custom or one which was only then adopted as a sign of conquest, we have no means of ascertaining.

Meanwhile disturbances of a serious nature broke out in the Province of Szech'uan, and in the existing distracted state of the country the Emperor's forces would have had great difficulty in re-establishing order in this outlying district, had not a native heroine stepped into the breach. Tsinliang, the female

chieftain of one of the aboriginal tribes in the Province, like another Joan of Arc, raised a large force
on the outbreak of hostilities, to supplement the small
army which the Emperor was able to put into the
field. Success attended Tsinliang's efforts and the
Province was recovered for
the Imperialists. But this
rising was only one symp-
tom of the evil which was
germinating in the body
politic. In Yunnan and
Kweichow leaders arose,
who led the unruly and
disaffected after them, and
at the same time an equally
serious outbreak occurred in
the North-eastern Province
of Shantung, where, before
the prowess and skill of a
chief named Shu, a number
of cities yielded themselves
to his arms. Shu, however,
with all his ability, had not
the makings of a permanent
leader of men, and at his
first reverse his followers
deserted him.

A CHINESE GENERAL.

But the cloud which was really charged with danger
to the dynasty lay over the north-eastern portion of
the Empire, where Nurhachu was still threatening the
frontier. In his various raids and expeditions he was,
with one exception, uniformly successful; but it

chanced that at the city of Ningyuan to the north of
the Great Wall, there was stationed a general whose
eminent ability and cool courage enabled him for a
time, at least, to turn back the tide of war. Against
this fortress Nurhachu made two vigorous attacks, and
on both occasions was defeated with heavy loss. Had
the defenders of the walls been dependent on native
arms alone the result may possibly have been different. But the guns which the Portuguese had
brought from Macao, and which were supplemented
by others cast under the superintendence of the
Jesuits at Peking, stood on the battlements, and
against these destructive weapons the Manchus failed
even to hold their own. Nurhachu was now an
elderly man, and this second failure was more than
his declining energies could enable him to withstand.
With a sense of his impending doom upon him, he
withdrew his troops to Moukden, where in 1626 death
brought to an end a great and memorable career.
The mantle of the deceased warrior fell on his fourth
son, T'ientsung. At first this new sovereign showed
some inclination to come to terms with China ; but
if his desire was genuine he, to say the least, made
his advances in a most unfortunate fashion : " There
is only one sun in the heavens and only one Emperor
beneath the sky," is the Chinese saying, and so far as
the extreme east of Asia is concerned there is some
justification for the boast. When, therefore, T'ientsung addressed the Emperor on equal terms, the
Imperial advisers were taken aback at his audacity.
Nor was their irritation diminished when news
reached the capital that the Manchus had invaded

Korea, and had crushed it beneath their heels. Negotiations for peace, therefore, did not prosper, and T'ientsung determined, in default of successful negotiations, to take up arms against his foes. But the city of Ningyuan still stood between him and his prey, and his forces fared no better before its walls than had his father's legions. While the Manchus were thus

A MANCHURIAN THEATRE.

being held at arms' length by this faithful city, the Chinese Emperor, T'iench'i, became a guest on high (1627), and was succeeded by his younger brother, T'sungchêng. The renowned skill and valour of the defender of Ningyuan were, as the Manchus were well aware, rare qualities in Chinese generals, and T'ientsung knew with equal certainty that if he could once

pass this invincible fortress he might achieve easy
victories in the fertile plains of Northern China. It
is a common axiom of war that it is unsafe to advance
into an enemy's country while leaving a strong uncon-
quered fortress in the rear of the invading force. There
are, however, exceptions to this dictum, and T'ientsung
rightly considered that this was one. Acting on his
instinctive perception, he proposed to his generals that
he should mask Ningyuan and march at once on
Peking. The idea was so bold that it met with opposition, which, however, finally yielded to argument,
and the order of march was given. Assisted by his
Mongolian allies T'ientsung led his troops southward through the Ta-an and other passes. By these
routes the Manchu army poured into the plains,
leaving a small force to represent the main body
before Ningyuan. Chunghwan, the defender of Ningyuan, was not long deceived by this manœuvre. He
felt that he was out of touch with his adversary, and
his suspicions were confirmed by his scouts, who
brought him news of the adventurous advance of the
enemy. Without a moment's hesitation he determined on the course to be pursued. He knew the
capital was insufficiently garrisoned, and he resolved
at once to march to its relief. Then began a race
between the two armies, and though the Manchus had
some days' start the delay occasioned by the necessary investment of cities by the way, enabled Chunghwan to reach Peking first. The presence of this very
formidable opponent convinced T'ientsung that his
chances of taking the city by fair means were very
considerably diminished, and he therefore entered into

a plot to bring about the downfall of the great Chinese general. The scheme he adopted was as mean as it was successful. He induced some of his officers to hold a conversation within earshot of two of the palace eunuchs whom he had taken prisoners. The burden of their conversation was that Chunghwan had turned traitor, and had agreed to open the gates of the city

TRAVELLING IN MANCHURIA.

to the Manchus. So soon as the subtle poison had entered the ears of the eunuchs the prison doors were left unguarded, and the captives were allowed to escape to tell their Imperial master of the supposed treachery of the man in whom he trusted. Fully believing the truth of the story, the Emperor summoned Chunghwan to his presence, when, without giving him

any opportunity of defending himself against the
slander, he condemned him to prison and to the execution ground.   But even without the strength which
Chunghwan's presence had added to the garrison
T'ientsung felt unable to carry the city, and being
unwilling to continue engaging in the constant
encounters which merely tended to harass his troops,
he raised the siege and retired northwards.   The
Chinese, who always prefer following a retreating
rather than facing an advancing enemy, hung on his
line of march and recaptured several cities which had
previously yielded to the Manchu attack.

In this direction the Imperial prospects had improved, but the advantage was only momentary.   The
Emperor had scarcely ceased to congratulate himself
on the retreat of the Manchus when news was brought
him of the outbreak of a more than usually formidable rebellion in the province of Shensi.   This revolt
was headed by the two powerful rebel leaders, Chang
and Li, who, at first, according to the historians, fared
badly at the hands of the army sent against them.
But Chinese reports from battlefields are not
always to be trusted.   On one occasion, however, it is
certain that the Imperialists gained a victory.   But
this advantage they, with a folly which would be in-
conceivable except on the ground of treachery, turned
to their own detriment.   Having driven the rebel
force commanded by Li into the mountains they demanded an unconditional surrender.   To this they
were plainly entitled, for so impossible did escape
appear to be that Li at once agreed to lay down his
arms, though with a certain effrontery he added the

condition that he and his men should be allowed to go their way in safety. To these extravagant terms the Chinese general agreed, and the army had the mortification of seeing thirty-six thousand rebels, who had been completely at their mercy, march off scot free.

The retreat of T'ientsung into Manchuria was by no means indicative of an intention to give up his great enterprise ; rather, it was with the idea of preparing for another spring at the prize which was destined to fall into his country's hands. It was at this crisis that the Manchus, for the first time, provided themselves with artillery, having learnt by experience that the god of battles was in the habit of lending his countenance to the destructive guns of the foreigners. As a preliminary plan of campaign they overran the districts in Mongolia bordering on the Great Wall, and then turned their attention to the strongly-fortified city of Tungchow, which, after resisting their attack for some time, fell into their hands, together with the fortified position of Sungshan. But in T'ientsung's opinion these advantages availed him little so long as Ningyuan, which was now commanded by the celebrated general Wu Sankwei, held out against him. With this fortress in his rear he dared not advance in force against Peking, and pending its capture he was obliged to content himself with raiding expeditions into some of the northern provinces of the Empire. But the fates were adverse to him, and in their wisdom had decreed that, though in sight of the promised land, the possession of the goodly heritage should be left to other hands than his. At the early age of fifty-two death overtook him at Moukden, in 1643, not, however, before he had assumed the Imperial Purple and had given to his dynasty the name of Ta Ch'ing, which it still bears.

Meanwhile the Li and Chang rebellion had been making way in the provinces. In Shensi, Shansi, and Honan the first named had become all powerful, and to Chang's lot had fallen considerable success in Hupeh and Kiangnan. At Hsiangyang one of those curious coincidences which occasionally befall adventurers occurred to Chang. On entering the city he, by chance, discovered his wife and children, who had been captured by the Imperialists some ten months before, living quietly among the people. That they had not met the common doom of the relatives of rebels is probably to be attributed less to the mercy of their captors than to the idea that they might be held as hostages to tempt Chang to return to his allegiance. Though generally victory sided with Li he met with failure before K'aifêng. What Ningyuan had been to T'ientsung, that city was to Li. His repeated attacks on the fortress were as vain as the washing of the waves against a rock, and after numerous assaults, in one of which he lost an eye, he determined to adopt a desperate expedient such as is happily unknown in civilised warfare. Within a short distance of the city walls flows the sluggish stream of the Yellow River between high banks which rise up at a considerable elevation above the plain. All that was necessary to effect the ruin of the city was to make a breach in the embankment so as to flood, as has often happened in the history of the Empire, the neighbouring districts,

The breach was made, and the water swept over the plain and into the city, devastating the country and destroying both Imperialists and rebels alike. A million people are said to have perished in this fearful catastrophe, Li himself losing ten thousand men in the waters. But his object was gained, and what Li's soldiers could not effect the Yellow River accomplished. When the breach was filled in and the flood had subsided the rebel banners floated on the ramparts of the stronghold.

Li now felt his position to be sufficiently strong to justify him in proclaiming himself king, a title which satisfied his ambition for one year. At the end of that time his taste coming with eating he took to himself the title of Emperor and named the dynasty which he hoped to found, the T'ai Shun. Further, in imitation of the existing system of government, he appointed six Boards of office, and satisfied the cravings of his followers by establishing ranks of nobility to which he freely admitted them.

Having thus placed himself on the throne it only remained for him to make himself master of the capital, and to accomplish this object he undertook an adventurous expedition towards Peking. By the way he captured T'aiyuan, the capital of Shansi, and then led his triumphant warriors against the stronghold of Ningwu. This fortress was strongly garrisoned and valiantly held, nor was it taken until ten thousand of the besiegers had licked the dust, and the city had been given to the flames. The resistance which the Chinese had here offered gave Li a pause which, however, was of short duration. Unexpectedly, while

7

musing on the possibilities of a retreat, news reached
him of the surrender of the cities of Tat'ung and
Hsunhwa. The road to Peking was thus open to
him, and with as little delay as possible he presented
himself before the walls of the capital.

Numerically the garrison of Peking was quite large
enough to defend the city, but it is safe to assert that

MINING IN SHANSI.

no Chinese army is ever so numerous and powerful as
it appears to be on paper. Even, however, with the
army as it was, it is possible that a stout defence might
have been made, and that the city might have been
held until a relieving force had come to the rescue.
But other influences were at work, and the commander
of the southern gates, a man " composed and framed

of treachery," opened his gate to the enemy. A faint-hearted defence of the palace was made by men who were more concerned for their own safety than for the preservation of the dynasty, and the Emperor, instead of placing himself at the head of his troops, and either losing his life or saving his throne, took to flight. From the top of a hill which stands in the northern portion of the city, he looked down upon a scene of bloodshed and conflagration such as is the common fate of captured cities in the East. Finding that escape on the northern side was impossible he returned to the city, hoping to find a way open to him in some other direction. But the rebel forces on all sides barred his exit. Thus confronted with difficulty he returned to the hill and, having written a letter imploring the rebels to spare his people, he hung himself on a tree. It is a curious illustration of the Chinese reverence for a royal race that by order of the first Emperor of the present dynasty this tree was loaded with chains in token of the crime it had committed in being instrumental to the death of a Son of Heaven.

Li was now in possession of Peking, and in obedience to the usual custom in such cases, the magnates of the capital who had survived the siege presented themselves at Court to pay their homage to him. Among these was a certain Wu whose son, Wu Sankwei, had succeeded Chunghwan in the command at Ningyuan, and had held that fortress with all the courage of his predecessor. On the approach of Li's army the Emperor had ordered this officer to march to the relief of the capital. While on the way thither news reached him of the fall of Peking and the death

of the Emperor.   Almost simultaneously a messenger
arrived bearing a letter from his father urging him to
offer his submission to Li, and enforcing his entreaties
by the news that the lives of himself and the other
members of the family at Peking depended on his
giving in his allegiance.   At first Wu Sankwei was
inclined to consent, but while he was yet wavering the
messenger informed him of an event which at once
induced him to take the opposite course.

In not a few instances in the world's history a
woman has changed the fates of Empires, and in
this case a young slave girl was indirectly the cause of
the ultimate triumph of the present Manchu dynasty
in China.   Before he had left Peking to take up the
command of Ningyuan, Wu Sankwei had been presented by a friend with a young slave girl who added
great beauty to her many virtues.   It was possibly
with the thought of saving her from the general massacre which, as a Chinaman, he knew would overtake
the inhabitants of Peking if surrendered to Li, that at
the first summons he had marched with alacrity to
the relief of the capital.

He now learnt from the messenger that Ch'enyuan,
as the lady was called, had been given as part of the
spoil of the city to a rebel officer.   After this outrage
submission to the guilty powers was impossible, and
he obviously had no compliments to exchange with
the triumphant rebel.   In his anger he wrote two
notable letters, one upbraiding his father for yielding
the lady to the embraces of a rebel, and another to
the regent of the Manchus, inviting him to combine
with him in an attack upon the new ruler of Peking.

This startling turn of events made it incumbent on Li to march against the allies. At the approach of the

A MANCHU LADY.

rebel legions, Wu Sankwei, who had returned to the fortress of Shanhai Kwan, made every preparation to

oppose the advancing host. Thinking it possible
that the sight of his father might cause Wu Sankwei
to relent and submit, Li ordered that the old man
should be led out within sight of the walls. With
tears and entreaties the father implored his son to
save his life by submitting. But the recollection of
the slave girl at Peking was too fresh in his memory
to allow him to yield, and in a few words he declared
that no power on earth would induce him to surrender
his command to rebels, and to rebels who had inflicted
such a wrong upon him. The duty of filial obedience
is the first moral law recognised by the Chinese, and
in any other circumstances Wu Sankwei would
doubtless have submitted. But his affections out-
weighed his sense of duty, and he did not hesitate a
moment in virtually sentencing his father to death.
Seeing that it was hopeless to expect to win over so
determined an enemy, Li gave the order for the
execution of the elder Wu, and in the sight of the
two contending armies the old man suffered death by
decapitation.

It was plain that there was now a breach between
the two commanders that nothing could bridge over,
and Wu Sankwei determined to take what revenge
he could by marching against the enemy. It is said
that Li's force numbered 220,000 men. But nothing
awed by these huge battalions, the Imperialist general
marched out from the cover of the fortress and gave
battle. So fierce was the onslaught of the Imperialists that the rebel cavalry were driven back on
their supports. These joined in the engagement,
and but for the undaunted courage of Wu and his

men would certainly have overwhelmed them. As
the day wore on it became plain that their ruin was
inevitable had not the Manchu Regent, Durgun,
prepared a seasonable relief. A large force of his
men who had been disposed in secret and difficult
passes in the mountains suddenly assailed the rebels,
who were already rejoicing in the belief that the
victory was won. This favourable change in the
conditions was improved by the valour of Wu. He
revived the courage of his troops, and pressed the
rebels on every side. The Regent's manœuvre was
completely successful. The rebels, taken by surprise,
reeled under the shock of the charge of the Manchu
cavalry, and after a short and half-hearted stand
turned and fled. For fourteen miles the allies
followed the flying enemy and slaughtered them in
hecatombs. To Wu was assigned the duty of
following still further in pursuit, while the Manchu
Regent returned to Shanhai Kwan to rest his troops,
who were already exhausted by their long and hurried
march from Manchuria.

Li fled to Peking, where, having possessed himself
of everything valuable that was portable, and having
ordered the execution of the family and dependents
of Wu, he set fire to the Palace and continued his
flight westwards. With the dogged tenacity of a
sleuthhound Wu followed at his heels, and,
strengthened by the prestige of victory, inflicted a
series of defeats on the disheartened rebels. There
is always a tendency to desert a falling cause, and
more especially is this true in China, where success is
the national test of merit. Li's men were now

suffering the dire consequences of an unsuccessful rebellion, and they deserted his banners in whole battalions. With but twenty followers, and destitute of both food and clothing, the wretched band of discomfited rebels were driven to supply their wants by plundering the poverty-stricken peasantry of Shensi. Unfortunately for them their numbers were insufficient to overawe the pillaged rustics, who, seizing the implements of their toil, turned on their oppressors, and cut them down one by one. When Wu's troops reached Li's final halting place they found nothing but the bodies of the arch rebel and his dwindled following.

Meanwhile the Regent Dorgun, who held the reins of government for his infant nephew and sovereign, entered Peking in triumph (1644). The city was well-nigh burnt to the ground, for Wu Sankwei's beautiful slave girl had, like another Helen, fired another Troy. In these circumstances Dorgun recognised that his first duties, if he was to establish a dynasty, were to reassure the people by establishing order, and to calm, so far as possible, the proud susceptibilities of the upper classes by showing regard to their prejudices. He therefore issued a proclamation which was more conspicuous for its policy than for its truth. He assured the people in it that his one object in marching into the capital was to save them from the pillage and violence of the rebel Li; and he urged them to rebuild the ruined city, promising to protect their goods and property against all comers. At the same time he conferred the posthumous title of " The sedate and heroic Emperor " on the

Sovereign who had put an end to his existence on the hill above Peking. By a stroke of the pen he

MANCHU WOMEN AND CHILD.

proclaimed the removal of the capital from Moukden to Peking, and directed that his nephew, who was

then but six years old, should join him at the latter
city. The revolution was now complete, and the
new Dynasty established which still holds possession
of the throne. The young Emperor adopted the
title of Shunchih.

During the reigns of the Ming Emperors the
palace eunuchs, as has often happened in the history
of the Empire, acquired additional power as the
hands which held the reins of government became
increasingly nerveless. The danger of such a
shameful usurpation of authority is sufficiently
obvious, and was fully recognised by Dorgun, who
issued an order that henceforth no eunuch should be
allowed to hold any official office under the crown,
and to the present day this law holds force. So
generally conciliatory, however, to all ranks was
Dorgun's attitude that the upper classes in the
neighbourhood of the capital readily gave in their
adhesion to his rule. So far all was well, but in the
Provinces a very different state of things prevailed.
The inhabitants of the central provinces had had no
knowledge of the exactions and cruelties of Li and
his confederates, nor had they experienced the relief
that had been felt at Peking by the substitution of a
settled government for a rebel tyranny. The fact
also that for the most part they were free from the
taint of Manchu blood naturally inclined them to
take a line against the invaders. For this last reason
it has always been that among the people of the
South, the Ming Dynasty has found its strongest
supporters. In modern times it will be remembered
that the T'aip'ing rebellion, which had for its proposed

object the restoration of the Chinese rulers, first took shape in Kwangsi, and the very powerful secret Society, the Kolaohwei, which has its strongest base on the shores of the Yang-tsze-kiang, has for its motto, " overthrow the Ch'ing and restore the Ming."

At this time in the old capital of the first Sovereign of the Ming Dynasty, there arose a scholar Shih K'ofa, who adopted, in principle, the motto of the Kolaohwei, and aroused his compatriots in defence of the expiring line of Sovereigns. So formidable was the movement that the Regent Dorgun thought it wisest and best to open negotiations with the rebel. But Shih declined to listen to the appeals made to him, and declared that matters had reached such a crisis that the decision of their quarrel must be left to the arbitrament of war. Meanwhile, on the death of the Ming Emperor Ts'ungchèng, it had become necessary to elect a successor to the throne, and the choice fell on Fu Wang, a son of the prince of that name, who had been Wan Li's favourite son, and who had returned the kindness shown him by his father by rebelling against him. A more unfortunate choice could not have been made. For such an emergency a Sovereign was required who should be a man endowed with wisdom, courage, and energy. In all these qualities Fu Wang was signally wanting, and he spent in lust and riot time which should have been devoted to furthering his cause, and consolidating his forces. In the campaign which followed on the marching of the Manchu army to suppress the revolt, Fu Wang was rather an encumbrance than otherwise, and the whole conduct of the war fell upon Shih.

On the lower waters of the Yang-tsze-kiang, and
close to the junction of the Grand Canal with that

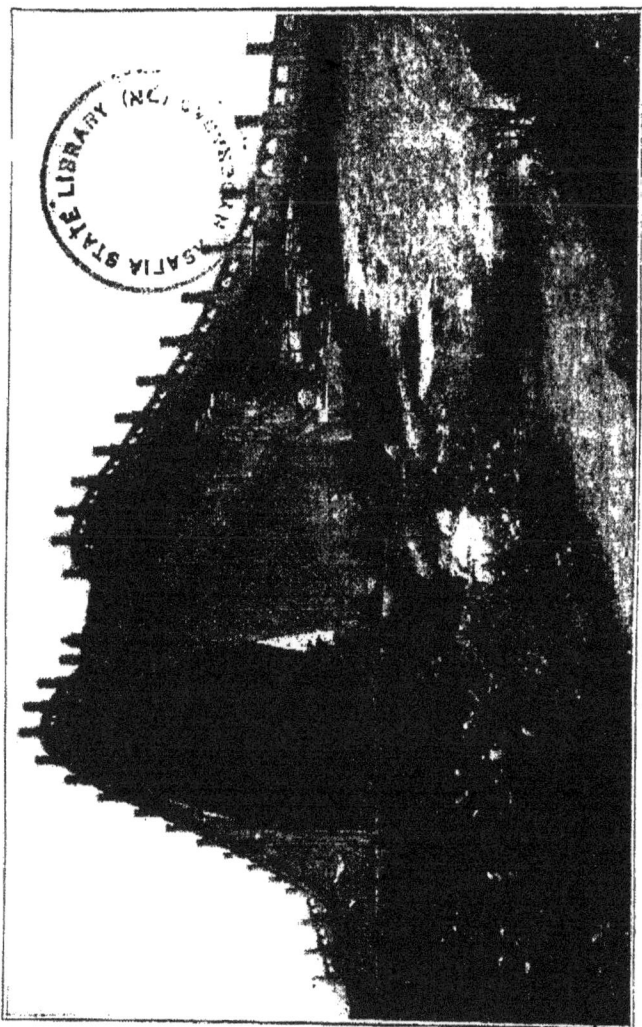

A "CAMEL-BACK" BRIDGE

river, stands the ancient city of Yangchow, which
commands the approach to Nanking from the north

Here Shih took his stand, and awaited the attack of
the enemy. Nor was this attack long delayed.
Accustomed to lengthened marches, and constant
fatigues, the Manchus passed rapidly over country
which represented leisurely marches to less nomadic
troops, and appeared suddenly before the walls. For
seven days the fighting lasted around the doomed
city, and at the end of that time the Manchus rushed
to the assault. The exhausted garrison failed to
withstand the terrible onslaught, and in the midst of
awful bloodshed the city fell. The diary of a
contemporary inhabitant of Yangchow has lately
been published, and from it it is easy to gather both
that the arrival of the Manchus before the walls was
quite unexpected, and that the slaughter of the
inhabitants even after the city was taken was carried
out with brutal cruelty and thoroughness. Shih was
cut down as he was attempting to make his escape
by way of the north gate, and his troops were
slaughtered almost to a man. Leaving a garrison
within the walls the Manchu leader marched on to
Nanking, where the puppet Fu Wang was indulging
in all the vices and follies common to Oriental
sovereigns of the baser sort. In the midst of a
drunken carouse the news was brought him of the
approach of the Manchus. To men of Imperial
calibre such a juncture would have suggested that he
should place himself at the head of his troops and
march against the enemy. But the only idea which
occurred to Fu Wang was to fly from his capital,
leaving it a prey to the advancing hosts. His flight
availed him nothing, for he was speedily overtaken by

a mounted force sent in pursuit, and was brought a prisoner into Nanking, where after a short shrift he was beheaded.

For three days Ch'ang Wang, who succeeded Fu Wang, enjoyed the empty title of Emperor and held court for that brief period at Hangchow. But the valour of the early Ming Sovereigns had long exhausted itself, and instead of attempting to defend the city he opened the gates to the enemy on the understanding that they should spare the lives of himself and of the inhabitants. Oriental leaders are bad people to treat with in such emergencies, and though in this case the people were left unmolested, the first act of the Manchu leader was to order the execution of the occupier of the Ming throne. The next to assume the Imperial purple was T'ang Wang, a descendant of Hungwu, the first Sovereign of the Ming Dynasty. Though this man showed more of the royal spirit than his immediate predecessors had done, all his efforts to oppose the Manchus proved fruitless, and the whole of the rich and fertile district embracing the cities of Ningpo, Shanghai, Wênchow, and T'aichow fell into the hands of the invaders. At Tingchow T'ang Wang was captured, and there the usual fate of defeated sovereigns overtook him.

But though defeated everywhere on land, hopes were still entertained that the immense fleet commanded by Chêng Chihlung might yet turn the tide of war. Admiral Chêng was a native of the maritime Province of Fuhkien, and had in early life come under the influence of the Roman Catholic missionaries who laboured in the cause of their faith in that province. Being of a restless disposition and probably attracted by his Portuguese fathers in God, he migrated to Macao and thence drifted to Manila, and subsequently to Japan. Like most foreign visitors to Japan he fell under the charm of the women of that country, and eventually took one to wife by whom a son was born, who was named Chêng Kung. Chêng's early years had been passed in poverty, and, following the instincts of his race, his one absorbing desire was to court the god of wealth. When, therefore, an opportunity presented itself for laying the foundation of an enormous fortune, which, however, any honourable man would have disregarded, he seized on it without a scruple. Having wormed himself into the good graces of a Japanese merchant he induced his employer to entrust him with a rich cargo for the China markets. On arriving at Foochow he, without the slightest compunction, appropriated the cargo, and with the proceeds fitted out a fleet of piratical junks, with which he harried the coast and plundered the merchant shipping. So successful was he in these enterprises that he quickly amassed colossal wealth, and with it gained considerable power and importance. Following a time-honoured precedent, the Emperor, fearing to combat him, made overtures to the successful pirate, on whom, at his submission to the throne, he conferred the rank of Admiral. With honeyed words the new commander was invited to Peking, and once there was placed in the position of a state prisoner. So long as the Emperor Shunchih reigned he was allowed to live at ease within the city walls, for the

Emperor, like another David, had promised that no
harm should befall him while under his protection.
But whether with or without the treacherous message

DECAPITATION.

addressed to Solomon with which David sealed
Joab's fate, the Emperor had no sooner become a
guest on high than the Regents appointed during the

minority of his successor, threw the late pirate into prison, and eventually sent him to the execution ground. The son born to Chéng by his Japanese wife had at an early period attracted the attention of the Emperor. At the extraordinarily youthful age of fifteen this scion of the pirate took his degree at the competitive examinations, and as a reward for his eminent ability the Emperor conferred on him his own surname of Chu, and further honoured him by expressing a regret that he had no daughter to bestow upon him in marriage.

From the circumstance of his having received the Imperial surname he was designated Kwosingye ("Possessor of the National Surname"), which has been corrupted by foreigners into Koxinga. When Admiral Chéng was invited to Peking the Emperor hoped that Koxinga would have accompanied him. But the young man feared the Imperial messengers with their gifts, and instead of journeying with his father northwards, carried off a fleet which he had collected and sailed to the Pescadores, where he fortified himself against all comers.

Meanwhile the rebellion in the provinces continued with varying success. At one time Kwei Wang, who had succeeded to the Ming throne on the death of T'ang Wang, appeared to be gaining ground. In Kiangsi and Kwangtung his generals were victorious, and the great prize of Canton fell into his hands. But once more the tide turned, and the people of the provinces and cities had scarcely yet learned to pronounce again the shibboleth of the Ming Dynasty when such of them as survived again passed under the Manchu rule. On the recapture of Canton, Koxinga, who had favoured the Ming cause in so far as it chimed in with his piratical instincts, gave refuge on board his ships to the fugitive population. With an immense force he subsequently attacked the Tartar detachments on the coast of Fuhkien, and gained considerable advantages over them. He then proceeded northwards, and even ventured to undertake the siege of Nanking. This, however, was a venture beyond his power, and while, as it is said, his troops were revelling in anticipation of the assault on the city, which they were to have made on the following morning, the Manchu leader delivered an attack which utterly discomfited Koxinga's host. Three thousand men of the besieging army were slain, and Koxinga, with the remnants of his fleet and army, sailed to the more congenial regions of the south. The Manchus have never been good sailors. To them the sea is a foreign element, and so long as there was an effective Chinese fleet they were always subject to disaster on the coast. In other parts of the Empire victory followed their standards, and Kwei Wang's fortunes reached their lowest ebb.

We have seen how Wu Sankwei followed the flying footsteps of the rebel Li until he ran him to earth, and now with the same ruthless tenacity he chased Kwei Wang through the Provinces of Kweichow and Yunnan, and even over the border into Burma. On arriving at the Burmese capital the Imperial fugitive had been hospitably received by the King, who, however, at the sight of Wu Sankwei's large and threatening army, thought it wise to forego the pleasure of hospitality. He therefore handed his guest over to the Chinese general, in whose custody he, either by

A MANCHURIAN LANDSCAPE.

his own hands or by those of executioners, met his fate. Hitherto the fortunes of the Manchus had been

guided by the Regent Dorgun, but about this time
the young Emperor was by an adverse fate deprived
of his counsel. During a hunting expedition which
he had undertaken into Manchuria death overtook
him, much to the grief of the youthful sovereign, who
granted him an Imperial funeral, and eulogised his
virtues in an Imperial edict. But while the memory
of his services were yet green, a charge of intended
rebellion was brought against him. Inquiries, the
value of which may fairly be doubted, having proved
to the satisfaction of the boy Emperor that this
charge was well founded, the honours which had
been conferred upon him were cancelled and his
name consigned to oblivion. It is evidence of the
supremacy which the Manchus had acquired at this
time (1664) that two European embassies arrived at
Peking with the design of opening diplomatic relations with Shunchih. Though they came by different
routes—the Dutchman by sea and the Russians overland through Siberia—the reception which they met
with was the same, and was not such as to encourage
others to follow in their footsteps. As a preliminary
they were told that on entering the presence of the
Emperor they would be expected to " k'ot'ow." The
Dutchman yielded, and got very little for his pains.
After lengthy negotiations and a liberal distribution
of presents the Imperial answer to his petition was
couched in these words : "You have asked leave to
come to trade in my country, but as your country is
so far distant, and the winds on the east coast so
boisterous and so dangerous to your ships, if you do
think fit to send hither I desire it may be but once

every eight years, and no more than one hundred men in a company, twenty of whom may come up to the place where I keep my court." The Russians, as a reward for their contumacy, were not even granted these doubtful privileges, but were dismissed no richer than they came, and returned by Siberia to report their failure to the Czar. These were the first European embassies which reached Peking (1656), and their receptions taught lessons which happily were not altogether lost upon their successors. While affairs were thus settling down in the Empire Koxinga was pursuing his piratical course with varying success. That he harried the coast is conclusively proved from the fact that the Emperor thought it necessary to issue an edict commanding the natives of the littoral provinces to retire four leagues inland —a command which, strange to say, was strictly enforced.

It was while the Empire was in this unsettled state that the Emperor Shunchih was gathered to his fathers (1661) after a reign of eighteen years. Before his death he nominated his second son as heir to the throne. No choice could have been happier. K'anghsi was in every way qualified to rule. From his youth up, as it proved, he was straightforward, honest, and of good report, and after a reign of sixty-one years, during which time he ruled his subjects with firmness and justice, he died regretted by all. He was only eight years old when he ascended the throne, and his earlier years of sovereignty were guided by the advice of four Regents appointed by his father. After the death of Kwei

Wang the most important rebellious force in the Empire with which the Regents had to contend was that commanded by Koxinga, and they at once took steps to crush their dangerous opponent. In 1663 a Chinese fleet, in conjunction with some Dutch ships, whose co-operation had been secured, attacked the pirate in his haunts at Amoy. Victory attended the allies, and Koxinga, finding it no longer possible to retain his hold on the mainland, took ship to Formosa, where he established himself as king, and where he subsequently died in a fit of madness. The Empire may now be said to have reached a time of peace, a formidable rebellion which had broken out in Szech'uan having previously collapsed. This move-ment furnishes so apt an illustration of the fiendish cruelty which too often governs the action of Orientals when fighting for a failing cause, that it deserves mention. Being anxious to secure the support of the learned for his enterprise, Hsi Wang, the rebel chief, induced thirty thousand *Literati* of the province to take up their residence at his capital at Ch'engtu. On some slight provocation the tyrant ordered the slaughter of every one of these Confu-cianists, and subsequently massacred six hundred thousand of the inhabitants of the city on the bare suspicion that they were disaffected towards him. But his culminating crime was yet to come. As is the case with most rebel armies, his enormous forces had been kept together by the prospect of the plunder to which he had hitherto been able to lead them, and among the spoils taken from the conquered districts had been immense numbers of women and girls, several of whom had been given as prizes to each of the soldiers. In the easy times of success the existence of these camp followers, though burdensome, was readily sanctioned, but in the face of danger and difficulty, of rapid movements, and of fierce attacks, their presence was plainly inconsistent with the efficiency of the army. Hsi Wang felt therefore that they were to be got rid of, and he knew of only one way of accomplishing his object. In pursuance of it he issued an edict commanding every soldier to bring his women on to the parade ground at a certain hour, and then at a given signal the tyrant himself set the example which he desired should be followed, by slaying his handmaids with his own hands. It is said that on that day four hundred thousand women were slaughtered. In dealing with such facts it is fortunate that we are not bound to accept the figures mentioned as being accurate. Orientals delight in round numbers, and it should in fairness be remembered that the accounts we have of these transactions come from the pens of Imperialist chroniclers, who certainly would not be inclined to understate the crimes of their opponents.

The position of a Regent in an Oriental country is one which is always surrounded with difficulties. Every act is liable to be misconstrued, and every mistake is apt to be visited with undue censure. If this is the case when one Regent holds the reins of power, it is easy to see that when four co-equal potentates reign supreme, there must inevitably be abundant opportunities for jealousies and heart burnings. Such was eminently the case at the present time, and to such lengths did the consequent disagreements go, that the Emperor by a stroke of his pen dissolved the Regency and assumed the government (1667). To no section of the community was this change more welcome than to the Roman Catholic missionaries and their converts. During the reign of Shunchih every consideration had been paid them, and high honours had been conferred on their most eminent member, Père Schaal, who had even held the lofty and responsible post of tutor to the young Emperor. No sooner, however, were Shunchih's eyes sealed in death than the Regents, who, in the true spirit of Chinese conservatism, had cherished a bitter resentment at the favour which had been shown to the foreigners and their faith, threw Schaal into prison under one of those charges which are so easily trumped up against unpopular personages in eastern countries, and sentenced him to death by *Lingch'ih*, or the slow and lingering process. Fortunately even the Regents were wise enough to abstain from putting this cruel sentence into execution, and Schaal was left in prison until death released him in the seventy-eighth year of his age.

Unfortunately this consummation was reached before K'anghsi began to rule. But no sooner had he taken the reins than he did all in his power to redress the balance which had of late been so unfairly turned against the missionaries. It is curious to see, however, how strong the opposition was to any extension of privileges to that body. The half-hearted measures of relief accorded to them by K'anghsi sufficiently mark the difficulties with which he had to contend. He issued an Imperial edict granting leave to the missionaries who had been driven into hiding by the Regents, to return to their churches, but forbade them to proselytise. "As we do not restrain the Lamas of Tartary," so ran the edict, " or the bonzes of China, from building temples and burning incense, we cannot refuse these having their own churches, and publicly teaching their religion, especially as nothing has been alleged against it as contrary to law. Were we not to do this we should contradict ourselves. We hold therefore that they may build temples to the Lord of Heaven and maintain them wherever they will ; and that those who honour them may freely resort to them to burn incense and to observe the rites usual to Christianity."

Meanwhile Père Verbiest, a Dutch priest, had succeeded Père Schaal at Peking. The young Emperor, who was greatly interested in philosophy and science, and who had found the Father proficient in both subjects, appointed him his tutor, and listened with eager attention to his discourses on the intricate subjects of Christianity and philosophy. It so happened that at this time doubts arose as to the accuracy of the Calendar issued by the Astronomical Board. In this difficulty the Emperor turned to Père Verbiest, who demonstrated to his Majesty's complete satisfaction that an egregious mistake had been made by the native astronomers. As a reward for his knowledge and sagacity the Emperor made the priest President of the Board, and dismissed the native Presidents from their offices, at the same time commanding the new President to issue a revised Calendar. The disgraced officials, fearful lest their ignorance should be made public throughout the Empire, begged Verbiest not to expose the mistake into which they had fallen. He, however, refused to listen to their pleadings, and possibly with a self-righteous satisfaction at the consciousness that he was right and that they were wrong, refused in any way to blink their error. The wisdom of this course was open to doubt, and in the persecutions that followed it may well be imagined that a recollection of this passage of arms may have added virulence to the aspersions of the *Literati*.

During the campaign against the Ming rebels which had ended in consolidating the Imperial power it had been deemed wise to confer the rank of Prince on the three generals who had contributed most to the success of the cause. The leader of these three was the redoubtable Wu Sankwei who by virtue of his office was practically in possession of the provinces of Kweichow and Yunnan. The other two Viceroys presided over the destinies of Kwangtung and Kwangsi; and of Fuhkien and Chehkiang. All these three were Chinamen, and, therefore, were not bound by racial ties to the new dynasty. Their careers, also, had not displayed any fixed loyalty to any given cause, and K'anghsi felt that it was dangerous to leave them in undisputed possession of their vice-royalties. Of the three he had reason to dread Wu Sankwei the most, both from his character and from

the influence which he wielded, and though he held
Wu's son as a hostage for his father's loyalty, he
deemed it only prudent to put the views of the veteran
to the test. It has always been usual for high
dignitaries to visit the Court at varying intervals,
and there was nothing unusual, therefore, in the
summons which K'anghsi issued inviting Wu to
present himself at the capital. But the younger
Wu, who was connected by marriage with the Court,
being aware of the course which the Imperial
suspicions were taking, despatched a messenger to
his father warning him not to accept the invitation. Acting on this hint, Wu pleaded old age and
begged the Emperor to excuse his undertaking such
a long journey. This implied refusal confirmed the
Emperor's suspicions, but being unwilling immediately to drive so powerful a man into open
enmity, he commissioned officials to inquire whether
decrepitude really debarred Wu from presenting
himself at Peking. Wu received these by no means
welcome visitors with a show of cordiality, but when
they broached the real object of their visit and urged
him to comply with the Emperor's desire, he felt that
it was time to speak plainly. "Yes, I will come to
Peking," he said, "but it will be at the head of eighty
thousand soldiers."

This declaration made further negotiations unnecessary, and the envoys returned to Peking to
report their want of success. Meanwhile, Wu
Sankwei raised the standard of rebellion, and proceeded to form a separate State of the provinces
under his control. He had on a former occasion

sacrificed his father to his political leanings, and now
his action was destined to send his son to the execution ground.   The historians tell us that the
younger Wu had embarked in a plot to murder the
Emperor and his surroundings.   This possibly may
have been so, for Oriental courts are fit scenes for
"treasons, stratagems, and spoils," but the reported
crime so closely synchronises with his father's rebellion, that there appears to be a likelihood that the
charge, if ever preferred, was trumped up to justify the
extreme measures which the Emperor took against him.

The news of the death of his son added intensity
to Wu Sankwei's hatred of the usurping dynasty, and
in 1674 he killed the Governor of Yunnan, and virtually conquered that province together with Kweichow, Szech'uan, and Hunan.   Being still willing,
however, to arrive at a peaceable solution K'anghsi
once more attempted to open negotiations with him,
but the veteran was irreconcileable, and so potent
was his influence that his two fellow princes threw in
their lot with his, and thus the whole of the west and
south of China were in arms against the Manchus.
To add to the complexity of the position an outbreak
occurred within the walls of Peking, and at the same
time the Mongol chieftain, Satchar, threatened the
northern frontier with a hundred thousand men.   The
emergency was one which may well have tried the
stoutest courage.   But K'anghsi was equal to the
occasion.   By the aid of troops drawn from the
Liaotung peninsula he crushed the Mongol movement, and brought Satchar with his family as
prisoners to Peking.   Having thus disposed of the

difficulty in his rear he marched his armies against the southern rebels. Success attended his arms. The provinces of Fuhkien and Chehkiang were recovered without striking a blow by the submission of the Viceroy, and Wu was driven out of Hunan and Szech'uan. To inspire his troops with zeal K'anghsi proposed to place himself at their head, and while preparing to leave Peking for the front the welcome news reached him of the death of Wu (1678). With the disappearance from the political stage of this veteran, the back of the rebellion may be said to have been broken. Wu's grandson who succeeded to the command, though brave, failed to preserve the frontiers committed to him. By the relentless and persistent Manchu he was driven from city to city, until he reached Yunnan Fu, where he made his last stand. The city, however, was taken, and to avoid submitting to the tender mercies of the Imperialists the rebel chief committed suicide. With Oriental barbarity the Manchu leader beheaded the lifeless corpse, and sent the head as a trophy to Peking ; but even this did not satisfy his cruel humour. With an excess of brutality he disinterred the body of Wu Sankwei, and so scattered the bones over the provinces which had owned his sway in life, that no one should be able to say " this is Wu Sankwei." The year in which these events took place had been a distressful one to China. As if in sympathy with the disturbed political conditions an earthquake shook the foundations of Peking, and destroyed three hundred thousand within the city and neighbourhood.

Peace, however, having been once more restored
within the "eighteen provinces" K'anghsi had an
opportunity of attacking Koxinga's successor who
held a rebellious sway in the Pescadores and Formosa.   At the head of three hundred ships containing twelve thousand men the Manchu commander
sailed to attack the island fastnesses of the rebels in
the first-named group.   With this imposing force he
advanced to the attack, but was met by a determined
resistance on the part of the pirates.   The battle
lasted all day, and at the close the Manchus were
completely successful.   Twelve thousand rebels are
said to have been slain, and the majority of the
survivors taking ship fled to Formosa.   Thither the
Manchus followed them, but their ships being of
considerable draught they were, at first, unable to
approach the shore.   An unusually high spring tide,
however, carried the vessels over the shallows in precisely the same way as that, remembered by the
rebels, in which Koxinga's ships had been brought
within striking distance of the shore.   The similarity
of the two incidents deeply impressed the superstitious natives, who, readily accepting the superficial
belief that the increased depth of water was due
entirely to the interposition of providence, submitted
without a struggle to the invaders.   Koxinga's son
was sent to Peking, where the Emperor varied the
usual practice of decapitation by creating him a
Duke, and, at the same time, lavished honours on
the victors in the fray.

The wide extent of the Chinese Empire, and the
number of peoples who are actually, or theoretically,

subject to Peking, enforce on the country an almost chronic state of war. On the north and west the Empire is bounded by mountain ranges which are inhabited by hardy and warlike tribes, to whom the Empire's difficulty is their opportunity. And thus it was not, probably, a surprise to K'anghsi to receive news of hostilities on his northern frontier, while yet he was crowning with laurels the generals who had vanquished Wu Sankwei, and had recovered Formosa. It had always been difficult to trace the beginning of the many tribal wars outside the northern marches, and Central Asia had been so long and completely shrouded from observance that, at this time, little was known at Peking of the progress of events beyond the Great Wall. The first intimation which reached K'anghsi that mischief was brewing was the irruption across the frontier of bodies of Khalka Tartars into Chinese territory. These men brought news that the Eleuths, a Kalmuck tribe occupying a territory in the neighbourhood of Ili, had declared war against their countrymen who, as they took pains to remind K'anghsi, owned allegiance to China. This was practically a declaration of war against the Middle Kingdom, but Galdan, the chief of the Eleuths, was not unnaturally anxious to enjoy the advantage of peace with China while he fought with his Tartar neighbours. He therefore sent ambassadors to Peking, who reached the capital just at the time when Wu Sankwei's rebellion was absorbing K'anghsi's attention. So disastrous at this crisis appeared to be the state of the Empire that the envoys were induced to suppose and to expect, that, as had been the case in many other royal lines, the Ch'ing Dynasty was tottering to its fall. Galdan therefore carried on his invasion of the Khalka country free from any dread of reprisals from the suzerain State.

At this juncture a new power appeared on the banks of the Amur river. With that steady step which is characteristic of the Russians, they had been gradually extending their frontier eastward, and had erected fortifications and entrenchments at Albazin on the upper course of the Amur. Galdan recognising the superior weapons and organisation of the Europeans, offered them an alliance which he was quickwitted enough to see would impart strength to his ambitious designs against China. Rumours of these intrigues having reached Peking, K'anghsi despatched envoys to the Khalka country, and sent with them the two Jesuit missionaries, Gerbillon and Pereira. These men had won the confidence of the Emperor by their straightforward conduct and scientific knowledge, and had secured his gratitude by, on one occasion, curing him of a severe attack of fever by the use of quinine. They possessed also the unusual qualification of a knowledge of both his Mongolian and Russian languages.

The accounts which these envoys brought back made it plain to K'anghsi that if he was to maintain his hold over the Khalka country, and check the advance of the Russians, who showed a decided tendency to encroach on the fertile lands south of the Amur river, it would be necessary for him to

send a force to overawe the Tartars and to drive the
European invaders across the frontier. It may well
be supposed that the Russians felt themselves secure
from an attack in a region so remote from Peking,
and doubtless their surprise was great when they
found a Chinese army advancing against them.
Though behind entrenchments and in possession of
superior weapons, they were unable to withstand the
attack of K'anghsi's hordes. Their fortifications were
demolished, and those of the garrison who survived
were taken prisoners and were marched to Peking,
where a small quarter in the northern part of the city
was appropriated to their use. The descendants of
these men, who for the most part married Chinese
wives and settled down as citizens of the capital, still
occupy the same streets and houses as their ancestors
did in the seventeenth century, and even now among
them a European type of face is sometimes to be
noticed, though the large mixture of Chinese blood
which must necessarily run through their veins may
well have obliterated all traces of their Caucasian
origin. The ruin which had overtaken Albazin did
not, however, prevent the Russians from again
occupying the dismantled forts and entrenchments
of that town. So long as the country was disturbed
by war's alarms, Pères Gerbillon and Pereira had had
no opportunity of opening negotiations, but in 1689
they succeeded in coming to terms with the representative of the Russian Government, and finally
signed a treaty at Nerchinsk on the Amur by which
it was arranged that Russia should be bounded as to
her ambition by the river northwards, and should

9

cease to disturb the peace of its southern shores. This was the first treaty that the Chinese ever concluded with an European power, and was the precursor of the many conventions which have since been concluded between the two Empires.

Though foiled in his endeavour to enlist the help of Russia in his ambitious career, Galdan yet felt himself strong enough to renew his campaign single-handed against the Kalkas. With a certain amount of effrontery he complained that the Chinese had accepted as subjects the Kalkas who had fled over the southern frontier to escape from his troops. As the Kalkas were already Chinese subjects the complaint was preposterous; but, strange as it may seem, it met with the support of the Dalai Lama of Tibet, of whom it may be said that if his religious instincts were not truer than his political ideas the spiritual condition of the people under him must have been in a parlous state. Wisely K'anghsi refused to listen to this misguided prelate, and prepared to take the field against his northern enemy. Meanwhile Galdan suffered a defeat which was as disastrous as it was unexpected. While yet a young man he had, after the by no means uncommon manner of his countrymen, murdered his elder brother, for no other reason than that, as he rightly thought, he was a bar to his succession to the chieftainship. The son of the murdered man had, under the influence of K'anghsi, assumed the command of a portion of the Khalka territory, and between him and his uncle there was, as may well be imagined, a deathless blood feud. In an engagement

fought between the forces of the two relatives the
son of the murdered man partly avenged the assassination by inflicting a crushing defeat on his uncle's
troops. But, though discomfited, Galdan was by
no means vanquished, and gained respect among
his compeers by an act which in Western countries
would be deemed infamous. K'anghsi had sent
envoys to Galdan in the vain hope that even yet
further hostilities might be averted. These men
Galdan arrested, and held as hostages for the
peaceable action of the Chinese. So soon as the
news of this outrage reached Peking, K'anghsi
resigned all thoughts of peace, and marched three
armies against the recalcitrant Mongol. After an
arduous march through the dreary wastes which
separate China proper from the Mongolian pastures
the Imperial armies faced their enemy at Wulanpu-
tang. After the manner of his kind, Galdan, seeing
the immense forces with which he had to contend,
attempted to avoid the impending evil by opening
negotiations; but K'anghsi rating these overtures at
their proper value, answered him by marching to the
attack. By a most mistaken strategy Galdan surrounded his men by a huge lager composed of
countless camels, and awaited the onslaught. It will
be remembered that in Wu Sankwei's campaign
against the Burmese the Burmans made the mistake
of placing their elephants in the front rank, with the
result that when tortured by the Manchu arrows the
huge monsters turned and ran among the ranks of
their masters, throwing them into hopeless confusion.
A similar fate overtook Galdan's troops. The fire

from the Chinese guns so frightened the camels that
they trampled through the Mongol soldiers, and left
them an easy prey to their enemies. It often happens
in Eastern warfare that an incompetent general fails
to reap the full results of victory by not following up
his defeated foes, and on this occasion the want of
warlike energy displayed by the Chinese gave a new
lease of life to Galdan. Illness had made the return
of K'anghsi to Peking absolutely necessary, and his
generals, deprived of his wisdom and energy, instead
of pursuing the shattered forces of the enemy,
withdrew their troops, and allowed Galdan to
reorganise his broken forces.

For a time political and military matters remained
in a state of suspended animation. War, however,
was in the air, and while yet a sort of armed truce
was existing Galdan committed an act of profligate
wrong which precipitated action. K'anghsi desiring
to be in touch with passing events in Central Asia,
had sent envoys to Galdan's nephew, the Khalka
chief. On their way to the Khalka capital these
emissaries were attacked, robbed, and murdered by
Galdan's troops. Such an act in Western countries
would place the doer beyond the pale of civilisation.
But in Asia events of the kind are not so uncommon
as to arouse unusual indignation. K'anghsi, however,
waxed wrath at the outrage; but still being unwilling
to make reconciliation impossible, he wrote the
offender a letter, in which, with a certain magna-
nimity, he gave him room for repentance. " I learn
that, notwithstanding your oaths," he wrote, " you
and Tsi Wang Rabdan cannot live at peace with

one another; the instant I was informed of your disagreements I took steps to remove them. I sent one of the officers of my tribunal to be the bearer of words of peace, and your people, like mere savages, have committed the inhuman act of massacring him. . . . What ought I to think of conduct which proclaims you false to both your oath and your allegiance? I now finally desire to warn you that unless your repentance follows close upon your fault I shall come with arms in my hands to exact from you the fullest reparation for these outrages."

But though K'anghsi was placable, Galdan, with all the restless combativeness of a tribal leader, threw peace to the winds and prepared for war. To strengthen his position he sought for alliance among the neighbouring Mongol tribes, and even went the length of becoming a Mahommedan in the hope that by so doing he might the more readily enlist the sympathies of the followers of the Prophet. Distinctive faiths sit lightly on Orientals, and, though in earlier life he had visited Lhasa, and had formed a close alliance with the Dalai Lama, he now found no difficulty in professing to accept the Kuran as his guide to Heaven.

As soon as the news of these intrigues reached Peking, K'anghsi set his battalions in array, and appointed General Fei Commander-in-chief (1695-96). Circumstances had invested this campaign with peculiar importance, and to infuse enthusiasm into his army and officers K'anghsi held a high court ceremony at Peking which was intended to be as inspiriting as it was impressive. Surrounded by all the gorgeous

trappings of the East, and, above all, in the midst
of a crowd of officers of all ranks from the Commander-
in-chief down to the youngest subaltern—

> " Aloft in awful state
>   The god-like hero sat
>   On his Imperial throne."

So soon as the pageant was complete General Fei
advanced and knelt before his Sovereign, who, with
his own hands, presented him with a cup of wine,
which the warrior drank as a pledge of his loyalty,
and as an omen of future success. In due accordance
with their ranks, the other officers partook of a
similar honour, and from the presence of their
Emperor marched to the head of their regiments.
Upwards of thirty thousand men followed Fei's
banners, and these had scarcely left the capital
when K'anghsi put into the field two more hosts
of equal number, of one of which he took the
command in person. Before leaving his capital he
presented himself before his God at the Temple of
Heaven, and there, in the centre of the highest of the
terraces which beautify those splendid precincts, he
offered up a propitiatory prayer to Shangti, the
supreme Deity. " Receive my homage," he prayed,
"and protect the humblest of your subjects, Sovereign
Heaven, Supreme Ruler! With confidence but respect I invoke your aid in the war that I find myself
compelled to undertake. You have already showered
favours upon me. . . . I admit in silence and respect
your benefits. . . My most ardent desire has ever
been to see the peoples of my Empire, and even

foreign nations, enjoy all the advantages of peace. Galdan destroys my dearest hopes ; he sows disorder everywhere ; he tramples underfoot your laws, and despises the commands of his Sovereign who holds your place here on earth ; he is both the most false and the most wicked of men. . . . I hold from you the right to make war upon the wicked. In order to fulfil this duty I am about to march at the head of my troops. Prostrate before you, I implore your support, and I offer up his sacrifice animated with the hope of drawing down upon myself some of your most marked favours. But one vow I most resolutely formed, and that is to bestow the blessing of peace throughout the vast territory over which you have placed me."

The sought-for blessing was granted in full measure. As the Chinese armies approached Galdan's lairs he retreated before them, possibly in the hope that, like Napoleon's army before the retiring Russians, they would be reduced to defeat by cold and starvation. At last, however, he made up his mind to give battle, and victory was still hanging in the balance, when, by an ingenious though inhuman artifice, Fei turned the scales in his favour. He noticed that on a neigh-bouring height a large crowd of apparently non-combatants stood watching the fight. Rightly assuming that these were the women and children of Galdan's soldiers, he opened a heavy fire upon them. The result was exactly that which he had anticipated. The Mongols, seeing their wives and children mowed down by the Chinese fire, broke their ranks and rushed to their protection. With

well-directed energy Fei charged into the disordered
host, and after a short struggle gained a complete
and crushing victory. Galdan escaped from the field,
but his career was over, and while yet the Chinese
troops were preparing to follow in pursuit the news
was brought in of his death. Towards the memory
of the arch-traitor K'anghsi showed no consideration.
He demanded the remains of his foe as well as the

A STREET SCENE IN PEKING.

surrender of his son and daughter. With these
pledges of his victory he returned to Peking. What
dishonour was placed upon the bones of Galdan we
are not told, but with rare generosity the Son of
Heaven gave official rank to the son and an
honourable marriage to the daughter. As the spoil
of conquest he divided the territory lately ruled over
by Galdan between himself and Tsi Wang, giving to

this chieftain all the country to the west of the Altai Range, and keeping the eastern districts in his own hands.

The benevolent desire for peace expressed by K'anghsi at the Temple of Heaven was however denied fulfilment, and the Chinese armies had scarcely returned to Peking when Tsi Wang, waxing fat with conquests, developed all the restless proclivities of his late uncle. On the plea of giving a safe escort to his daughter, who was betrothed to a Tibetan grandee, he marched with six thousand men against Lhasa. With little or no opposition he presented himself before the walls of that city, and, having taken it, delivered it up to the predatory instincts of his followers. This raid was an equivalent to a declaration of war against China, Tibet being a dependency of that Empire. For the third time, therefore, K'anghsi sent an army into Mongolia, and, though the campaign was long protracted, it ended in victory to his banners, and in the annihilation of Tsi Wang's forces. This much-wished-for consummation was reached in the year 1721, when K'anghsi celebrated his Diamond Jubilee on the completion of the sixtieth year of his reign, and formed a fitting climax to the gorgeous pageant with which that far-famed occasion was commemorated.

Not long after this manifestation of popular rejoicing, and before the enthusiasm of his subjects had died away, the great Emperor who had ruled his vast possessions for more than sixty years, became a guest on high (1722). His illness was short, lasting only thirteen days, but was long enough to enable him to make arrangements for the administration of future affairs, and to appoint his fourth son, Yung Chêng, to succeed him on the throne. Few emperors have ruled the destinies of China as successfully as K'anghsi. He loved justice, and aimed at doing what appeared right in his eyes. He was learned in all the knowledge of his countrymen, and was a munificent patron of literature. He was himself an author, and his numerous writings both in prose and verse filled many portly volumes. Two works which were compiled at his instigation would alone be sufficient to make his name memorable in the annals of Chinese literature. The splendid dictionary of the language, which is known as " K'anghsi's Dictionary," is a monumental work, and was compiled at the order of the Emperor by a Commission of Scholars especially appointed for the purpose. It has ever since been recognised as the standard dictionary of the language, and in the ordinary editions fills thirty-six volumes. The other, which owes its initiative to him, is the huge encyclopedia known as the " *Ch'inting t'ushu chi ch'êng*," which issued from the press in five thousand and twenty volumes. The subjects included in this publication are divided into thirty-two grand categories, with countless subdivisions, each of which is illustrated by quotations from works of authority arranged in chronological order. So that the student has placed before him in due succession the opinions of every native scholar of weight on the subject of his study. But K'anghsi was also the author of the " Sixteen maxims " which form part of the initial studies of every Chinese boy.

These maxims were annotated and enlarged upon by his son and successor, Yungchêng, who considered himself at liberty, in the case of one maxim at least, to give a bias to K'anghsi's words, which probably was never intended by their author. "Avoid strange sects in order to exalt orthodox doctrines," wrote K'anghsi, and among these "strange sects" Yungchêng chose to include Roman Catholicism, and further warned his subjects to have no relations with the followers of the "Lord of heaven," adding, for the information of the people, that the missionaries attached to the Court at Peking owed their position entirely to their very useful knowledge of mathematics.

The support and favour accorded to the missionaries during the lifetime of K'anghsi, makes it improbable that he would have warned his people so pointedly against them, unless, indeed, he may have penned the words when vexed and perplexed by the unseemly quarrels which broke out in their ranks. It will be remembered that after the death of Ricci the arrival of Dominican and Franciscan missionaries gave rise to acute disputes and dissensions, the new arrivals considering that the earlier Jesuits had carried their principle of being all things to all men to an extent which bordered on sacrilege. This cleavage between the Jesuits on the one hand, and the Dominicans and Franciscans on the other, was to a great extent national as well as religious, the Portuguese representing the Jesuits, and the French and Italians their detractors. For some years the question between them took no public

shape, but in 1645 a reference was made to the
Propaganda, which was answered by a decree of
Innocent X. One of the main questions put in this
reference was "whether, in regard to the frailty of
the people, it could be tolerated, for the present, that
Christian magistrates should carry a cross hidden
under the flowers which were presented at the
heathen altars, and secretly worship that, while they
were in outward form and appearance worshipping
the idol." The answer was a direct negative, as it
was also to the inquiry whether the presence of
Christians in the temples of the idols, and their
attendance at the worship and sacrifices, were to be
sanctioned.

Though disappointed the Jesuits were not crushed,
and at a later date a second reference was made to
the Propaganda, which met with a different response.
The congregation under Alexander VII. upheld the
views of the Jesuits on the matter in dispute. They
drew a distinction between the political and religious
rites of the people, and included among the former
the worship of ancestors ; and added "that Chinese
converts should be permitted to perform the ceremonies towards the dead even with the unconverted,
superstitious objects alone being prohibited ; that
they may also assist in their worship when they are
performing superstitious rites, having protested their
faith, and not being in peril of subversion, and when
otherwise they could not avoid hatred and enmities."

The arrival in China of Bishop Maigrot added a
new element of discord to the already divided bodies
of missionaries. The bishop was a man with strong

views, and though, as events proved, no match for the Jesuits, he was yet one who could express himself with force. In a decree which he issued on the questions in dispute, he forbade the use of the expressions *T'ien* and *Shangti* for God, and ordered that the Deity should always be spoken of as *Tien Chu*, or "Lord of Heaven," the term universally used among Roman Catholics. He condemned the questions proposed to Alexander the VIIth as not having been truthfully set forth, and he prohibited missionaries from being present at the festivals or sacrifices connected with heathen worship. K'anghsi, who still showed symptoms of being under the influence of the Jesuits, took umbrage at the appearance of this declaration, and summoned the Bishop to an audience in the wilds of Tartary, whither he had gone on a hunting expedition. The Bishop's knowledge of the country was slight, and of the language little or nothing. These imperfections were eagerly taken advantage of by the Emperor, who, after the interview, thus wrote of his guest. "I have ordered Bishop Maigrot to come hither, that I might examine him. He knows a little Chinese, but cannot speak so as to be understood, he is consequently obliged to have an interpreter. Not only does he not understand the meaning of the books, but is even ignorant of the characters. A native who should show such ignorance would not dare to speak in public, and if he did so would move his hearers to laughter. Not understanding the sense of the books, he is not in a position to say what they contain, as he professes to do."

The inference thus drawn by the Emperor, that the Bishop's ignorance of the language rendered him incapable of forming a right judgment on the subject of the term for God, had considerable force. In the Imperial eyes, also, it was presumption on his part to offer an opinion on the question, inasmuch as the Emperor had traced with his vermilion pencil a statement to the effect that *Tien* was understood by the Chinese to be both the material Heaven and the Supreme God. These differences in China were reflected at Rome, and in the exercise of his wisdom Clement XI. appointed a legate to proceed to China to settle the differences between the contending missionaries. This appointment was a rock of offence to K'anghsi, who was annoyed at the idea of a visitor being appointed when he, the Emperor, was there to superintend the conduct of the Fathers. He, however, granted the Legate, Charles Maillard de Tournon, an interview, and treated him with marked courtesy. During the audience Pereira, who was in attendance on the Emperor, showed by a variety of approving gestures that the Emperor's address had been dictated by himself, and that the entire scene had been got up rather as an exhibition of the influence of the Father than as a complimentary recognition of the Pope or of his representative.

The Legate soon found out that the friendly expressions used by K'anghsi at this interview were merely complimentary, and that an occult influence was being exercised against him. The Emperor had promised him a house at Peking, and had prepared complimentary gifts for presentation to the

Pope, but on one excuse or another the house was never conveyed and the gifts were never sent. The religious difficulties had, as we have seen, been productive of much mischief and dissension, but a further matter was destined to emphasise the quarrel. It came to the knowledge of the Legate that the Jesuits were in the habit of lending money to the natives at a rate of interest which in Europe would be considered usurious, but which in China was less than the extreme legal rate. The Jesuits considered that they were moderate in charging 24 per cent., when native money-lenders were entitled to receive thirty-six, and from the source thus temperately utilised, it was affirmed that the three Jesuit houses at the capital derived an annual income of 180,000 taels. But this profit was " nothing in comparison with that which they drew from the commerce in manufactures, wines, clocks, and on other industries, by which these Fathers amassed enormous treasures, which rendered them richer in the Indies than the King of Portugal." These statements induced the Legate to take a strong step. He issued a solemn decree denouncing this practice of the Jesuits as being unworthy of Christians, and ordered them to suppress and annul all dealings of the kind.

An incident which occurred immediately on the promulgation of this Decree led to a serious suspicion being entertained against the Jesuit Fathers. After a solitary repast consisting of a stewed pigeon served up with broth and bread sauce, the Legate was seized with a sudden and dangerous illness, which bore some resemblance to the effects of poison. So strained were the relations between the two sides in the controversy, that the friends of the Legate did not hesitate to express their belief that the Fathers had attempted to rid themselves of the visitor by violent means. But whether this suspicion was well or ill founded, certain it is that the quarrel from this time became bitterly intensified. It is always easy to find Orientals ready and willing to bring charges against unpopular personages. The tide was now running against the Legate, Bishop Maigrot, and their friends. It was natural, therefore, that Chinamen should lay indictments against them, and that, with considerable worldly wisdom, the disregard shown to the decision of the Emperor with reference to the term for God, should be placed in the fore-front of the indictment. For this misdemeanour Bishop Maigrot and his allies were summoned to Peking, and after the form of a trial judgment was pronounced against them by the Emperor in person. The Bishop and others were sentenced to be exiled from the Empire as turbulent and disorderly men. No European was to be allowed to remain in China unless he had letters patent from his Imperial Majesty, and all coming after that date were to present themselves at Peking and to apply for the said letters.

The Legate felt now that nothing he could say or do would mitigate either the wrath of the Emperor, or the enmity of the Jesuits. He therefore felt moved to issue a decree enjoining all the missionaries who should present themselves at Peking "to give a distinct negative on all the questions which formed the Imperial test, to abjure all the rights and observances

which the Chinese law enjoined, . . . and to declare
the incompatibility of all these doctrines and practices
with the Christian law." Irritated by this opposition
to his will and decisions, K'anghsi sent two Jesuits
to Rome to represent to the Pope the unfortunate
position to which the quarrels of the missionaries
had reduced the affairs of the mission. Meanwhile,
he banished the Legate to Macao, there to await the
return of the envoys. On arriving at his destination
De Tournon was virtually put under arrest. His
house was surrounded by a guard of soldiers, who
allowed no one to pass except those who carried the
authorisation of the Portuguese Governor. Even food
was admitted with difficulty, and his condition was
aggravated by mental anxiety as to the result of the
Emperor's reference to Rome. Under this cruel persecution, his health broke down, and in 1710 death
released him from the ill-will of his enemies. That
the Jesuits conferred great advantages on the Chinese
it cannot be denied. As engineers, architects, and
surveyors they did much useful work, and by the
books which they translated, they opened a door for the
admittance of Western learning into the schools of the
country. Gerbillon and Bouvet translated Euclid and
other mathematical works, Thomas taught the people
algebra, Brocart instructed them in the arts, and
Pereira in music. Men learned in all the knowledge
of the West gave up home and country for the good
of the people ; while scientists of the first rank
thought it not degrading to mend clocks and make
musical boxes for the Emperor and his mandarins.
But to the cause of religion the dissensions which

they fomented did infinite harm, and exposed the Fathers to the taunt of K'anghsi, that instead of propagating the faith in China, they were ruining it.

IV

THE REIGNS OF YUNGCHÊNG AND CH'IENLUNG

THE son to whom the Imperial purple had descended was the fourth among K'anghsi's numerous progeny. He was a man of fine bearing and good abilities. As his father said of him, "Yungchêng is a man of rare and precious character," and, with perhaps pardonable pride, he added, "he has a great resemblance to myself." The new Emperor was forty-four years of age when he ascended the throne, and his first care was to remove beyond the reach of temptation those of his brothers whom he considered to be politically dangerous. The fourteenth prince, who at this time held a command in Central Asia, was first attacked, as being the most prominent possible aspirant to the Throne. He was therefore ordered to Peking, where, with his son, he was imprisoned in the garden of "Perpetual Spring." On other princes various kinds of repression were exercised, and one was banished to Hsining on the western frontier, where he, together with his brothers, embraced Christianity. The conversion of these banished members of his family added fuel to Yungchêng's wrath against them, and resulted in a sentence of perpetual banishment on all members of that section of the Imperial clan.

The new Emperor's attitude towards Christianity chimed in so naturally with the feelings of the *Literati* that it was plain that the new faith had fallen on evil days. A largely and influentially signed memorial was presented to the Emperor, calling upon him to banish all foreign priests from the Empire, and to permit the conversion of their churches to other and " better " uses. In accordance with the usual practice this memorial was referred to the Board of Rites, who recommended that all missionaries except those in the service of the Emperor, should be sent to Macao, and should be forbidden, on pain of death, to make any attempt to proselytise. As a result of the measures thus recommended and approved, upwards of three hundred churches were destroyed, and over three hundred thousand converts were left spiritual orphans.

The political horizon meanwhile was no clearer than the religious one. The Mongols, who had kept K'anghsi in a perpetual state of warfare, again gave evidence of their turbulent disposition, and a formidable rebellion broke out in the district of Chinghai. The duty of suppressing this revolt was entrusted to General Nien, who so well played his part that the rebels were severely punished and offered their submission, pleading with every appearance of sincerity to be allowed once more to live under the benign rule of the Emperor. For this service Nien was made a Duke, and was fêted by Yungchêng on his return to

Peking. On the occasion of this feast, Nien's officers
were entertained in the outer courtyard of the Palace,
while he alone was admitted into the Imperial
presence. Intoxicated by their success his officers,
in the enjoyment of the feast, so far forgot their
respect for their surroundings as to become riotous in
their cups. The Emperor repeatedly sent out to
enjoin silence, and, on his orders being disregarded,
his guest, jealous of the credit of his men, blew the
whistle with which he had been accustomed to guide
his troops to victory on the fields of battle. The
effect was instantaneous. The riot ceased as by
magic, and not a voice was heard. Yungchêng was
greatly alarmed at this evidence of the influence which
Nien had acquired over his staff, and seeing that
where he was impotent Nien was all powerful, he
felt that the existence of so potent a leader might
constitute a danger to the State. It is possible, also,
that the consciousness of his might may have made
Nien self-asserting in the presence of his sovereign.
At all events the decree went forth that he was to be
crushed; and instantly memorials were presented to
the Throne accusing the successful general of not
having even been in Chinghai, the reported scene of
his triumphs, but of having amused himself at a safe
distance from the field, where his soldiers were facing
the enemy. It was further roundly asserted that he
had adopted the emblems and insignia of royalty;
that he had worn robes which none other than the
Emperor should wear; and that he had ordered the
streets of towns and cities through which he had
passed to be cleared before him. Bribery and corrup-

tion on a gigantic scale were also laid to his charge, and the man who was yesterday an all-powerful general, was next day cast into prison, and after a brief trial was sentenced to be sliced to pieces. Humanity, however, induced the Emperor to mitigate this barbarous sentence, and the fallen victim was allowed by Imperial clemency to strangle himself in his prison cell.

All this time the tide had been flowing steadily against the Christians, and even the arrival of foreign embassies, instead of giving them a much needed support, gained for them nothing but disaster. In 1727 Count Sava Vladislavitche arrived at Peking at the head of a mission from the Czar, and was especially deputed to arrange with the Chinese Court a revision of the treaty of Nerchinsk. Two events made this mission noticeable. One was the fact that it served to establish a permanent Russian footing in Peking in the persons, firstly of a number of youths who were destined by their Imperial master for the study of Chinese; and secondly, of persons of authority over the students on whom were conferred certain plenipotentiary powers, which enabled them when occasion required to act as diplomatic agents at the Chinese capital. The other was an incident which occurred when Count Sava presented his credentials. Up to this time all foreigners to whom Imperial audiences had been granted, had been bidden to deposit their credentials on a table placed in front of the Emperor. Deeming this form to be derogatory, Count Sava overlooked the table and placed the documents in the hands of his Majesty.

A little later in the course of the same year a Portuguese Mission arrived at Peking and Don Metello Souza y Menzès, the Envoy, having heard of the action of his Russian colleague, and desiring to emulate it, informed the Court officials that it was unnecessary to place a table in front of his Majesty as he intended to hand his credentials to him *in propia persona.* At this avowal the Court dignitaries were much disturbed, and accused the Jesuits, who had interpreted for Count Sava, of having prompted the Portuguese to follow his example. The Emperor, however, took a more reasonable view of the question, and gave Don Metello Souza permission to follow the course which he proposed.

In the difficulties which these and other circumstances had brought upon them, the Jesuits deemed it wise to ask leave to appear by deputation before the Emperor. Their request was granted, but without listening to their representations His Majesty addressed them in a speech especially prepared for the occasion, and which at least displayed an intimate knowledge of the missionaries and their doings. "The late Emperor my father," he said, "after having instructed me during forty years, chose me . . . to succeed him on the throne. I make it one of my first objects to imitate him, and to depart in nothing from his manner of government. . . . You tell me that your law is not a false one. I believe you; if I thought that it was false what would prevent me from destroying your churches and from driving you out of the country? . . . But what would you say if I were to send a troop of bonzes and lamas into your

country in order to preach their doctrines? How
would you receive them? . . . You wish that all the
Chinese should become Christians, and indeed your
creed commands it. I am well aware of this, but in
that event what would become of us? Should we
not soon be merely the subjects of your kings? The
converts you have made already recognise nobody
but you, and in a time of trouble they would listen to
no other voice but yours. . . I permit you to reside
here, and at Canton, so long as you give no cause for
complaint; but if any should arise, I will not allow
you to remain here or at Canton. I will have none
of you in the provinces. The Emperor my father
suffered much in reputation among the *Literati* by
the condescension with which he allowed you to
establish yourselves. . . . Do not imagine, in conclusion, that I have nothing against you, or on the
other hand that I wish to oppress you. . . . My sole
care is to govern the Empire well."

It will be observed that in this speech the Emperor
dwelt especially on those points which have ever
since formed the bones of contention between the
missionaries and the ruling powers in China. It is
beyond question that the missionaries, in their
righteous zeal, have often unduly interfered on behalf
of their converts in the native courts. This applies
to both Roman Catholics and Protestants, though it
must be confessed that the Roman Catholic Fathers
have tried to arrogate to themselves administrative
powers in a more open and palpable way than their
Protestant brethren have ever attempted.

There is a natural disposition in men who are

persecuted for their religion's sake to regard any misfortunes which happen to overtake their persecutors as being specially designed by Heaven to avenge their wrongs. Deprived of their political privileges, and of the Court favour in which they had so long basked, the Jesuits found some consolation in the indulgence of this weakness of humanity. And truth to tell they had many occasions for the gratification of this consoling reflection. Pestilence, floods, and earthquakes, dogged the steps of the repressive Emperor. Death was rife within the Palace, whole districts in the northern portion of the Empire were flooded by the bursting of the banks of " China's Sorrow," the Yellow River, and, as if to emphasise the special iniquity of the Imperial Court, Peking was shaken to its very foundations by an earthquake (1730), which is said to have destroyed upwards of a hundred thousand people, while Providence which seems to have been guided by the same instinct which directed the allies when they destroyed the Palace of Yuan-ming-yuan in 1860, caused the earthquake to inflict overwhelming havoc on the same Imperial buildings. About the same time riots broke out at Canton, and the whole Empire appeared to be tottering on the verge of a catastrophe.

In China, as in England, there has always been a party who have advocated a policy of withdrawing from conquests beyond the national frontier. K'anghsi and later again Ch'ienlung with truer insight had seen that the only way of establishing peace on the Mongolian frontier was to overawe that indestructible element of disloyalty and violence which had always to be reckoned with when Mongols were concerned. Yungchéng however failed to realise this, and accepting the advice of his councillors withdrew his army from beyond the northern frontier. Happily for the Empire but a short time was allowed for the ill effects of this experiment to develop themselves, for on the 7th of October, 1735, the stroke of fate fell upon the Emperor. Early in the day he had granted the usual audiences, and was almost immediately afterwards seized with a sudden illness which ended his career on the same evening. Yungchéng was not a popular Sovereign, although he possessed that quality which is more highly esteemed than any other by the Chinese, the love of literature. He was a voluminous writer, but it is to be regretted that throughout all his works there is noticeable a strong anti-foreign feeling, which is happily wanting in the writings of both his predecessor and successor. His death was so sudden that he was unable to nominate his heir, and, as is usual in such cases, his eldest son, who adopted the title of Ch'ienlung, ascended the throne.

V

THE REIGN OF CH'IENLUNG

CH'IENLUNG succeeded his father at the age of twenty-five, and with an engaging modesty which is unusual in the case of "Sons of Heaven," he appointed four Regents to guide and direct his faltering steps in the administration of the Empire. His first exercise of Imperial power was in the direction of that quality which blesses those who give and those who take. He released the brothers of his late father from the confinement to which Yungchêng in his jealous fear had consigned them, and opened the prison doors to many casual offenders. The founder of the dynasty had divided the members of his family into two branches, distinguished by the colour of their girdles or belts. To himself and his direct heirs he reserved the use of the yellow girdle, while the collateral branches were entitled only to wear one of a red colour. The princes who had fallen under the displeasure of Yungchêng had been deprived at their fall of their right to either of these distinctions, but the restoration to favour accorded them by Ch'ienlung restored to them the privilege of again wearing the girdle of their great ancestor.

The missionaries were not so fortunate as these scions of the Imperial race, since, though Ch'ienlung at that time showed no personal animus against them, the Regents to a man were their bitter opponents. At the instigation of these potentates an edict was issued forbidding the missionaries to propagate their faith, and directing them to prosecute with all humbleness the mechanical callings in which they had shown themselves proficient. The province of Fuhkien has always been a troublesome one so far as foreigners are concerned. Some of the greatest outrages that the Jesuits had to submit to occurred in this province, and a long series of enormities has since been perpetrated within the district ending in the last wholesale murder of English missionaries in 1895. In 1746 persecutions of a particularly savage nature broke out in Fuhkien. Several Spanish missionaries were imprisoned and tortured, while those who attempted to shield them from their enemies were strangled in spite of the intercession of the Jesuits at Peking. The unhappy prisoners were only released from their miseries by the sword of the executioner.

Meanwhile a rebellion broke out in South-western China and spread to the provinces of Hunan and Kwangsi. As has so often happened in Chinese campaigns, the generals who had been entrusted with the suppression of this revolt had so mismanaged matters that the Imperial troops could make no headway against the rebels. The Chinese have a rough-and-ready way of dealing with men who either from their own faults, or by some mischance, are

unlucky enough to meet with disaster. A short shrift
and a sharp sword, unless the prisoner should happen
to be a *persona grata,* when a silken cord is sent to
him, is commonly their fate. In this case such a lot
was meted out to the unsuccessful leaders, and a certain
General Chang Kwang was appointed in their place.
The new general justified his appointment. In a
short time he subjugated the rebels and pacified the
disturbed districts. If we are to believe the native
historians we must accept the facts that he slaughtered
in the field eighteen thousand of the enemy, and
sent to execution almost as many prisoners. Shortly
afterwards an insurrection broke out in the province
of Szech'uan, and Chang Kwang again took the field.
But success no longer waited on his footsteps. He
was surrounded by the enemy's spies, so that the
words which he spake in his bedchamber were told
to the chiefs of the rebels. In this way all his plans
were forestalled, and to him was decreed a like fate
to that which had overtaken the generals whom he
had superseded. His successor, General Fu was
more successful, and recovered the revolted province
to his master's rule. The tender mercies of Chinese
victors are almost invariably cruel, and Ch'ienlung
was in no melting mood when the captured rebel
chief and his family were brought before him. Following the traditional usage adopted towards hardened rebels, he passed sentence of *Ling Chih* upon
them all, with the exception of one little girl who was
tranferred to the palace.

For the first ten years of Ch'ienlung's reign the
chieftain Tséning had ruled over the Mongols in

peace and quiet. His death however in 1745 let
loose all the elements of violence which he had
hitherto been able to hold in check. After some disturbance and many acts of violence, one of the sons
of the late chieftain, Dardsha by name, assumed the
reins of power, but his supremacy was not long left
undisputed. A restless relative named Davatsi, with
an ally as truculent as himself in the person of
Amursana, a neighbouring chief, took the field
against him. The fortunes of war are always uncertain, and in border warfare they can seldom be
counted on with surety. In this instance success
passed now to one side, and now to the other, with
perplexing fickleness. To follow the fortunes of each
army would be as difficult as it would be unprofitable,
but in the end Dardsha was defeated and slain,
leaving to the allies the possession of his territory.
" When thieves fall out honest men come to their
dues," and in this case the quarrel which sprung up
between the two allies resulted eventually in Ch'ienlung recovering the possessions which his father had
so weakly receded from. The war which raged
between the two usurpers ended in the defeat of
Amursana, who fled to Peking desiring to enlist the
sympathies of Ch'ienlung on his behalf. The fugitive
was received with honour and an army was sent to
chastise Davatsi. At the conclusion of the campaign
Amursana was left in the recovered territory as the
representative of Ch'ienlung, but with the consistent
faithlessness of a Mongol, he no sooner found himself
in the possession of an inch of power than he took
an ell.

The news of his unauthorised assumption of
monarchical rights having reached Ch'ienlung's ears,
the deputy was ordered to Peking to answer for his
conduct. His reply was in keeping with his character.
He put to the sword the small Chinese garrison left
with him, and prepared for war. Nor had he long to
wait. Ch'ienlung at once mustered his battalions
and issued a manifesto to the Empire explaining the
call to arms. In this document he said with pardonable pride, "My Empire is larger than any in the
world; it is more populous; it is richer. My coffers
overflow with silver, and my granaries are full of all
kinds of provisions." After this exordium he explained the cause of the quarrel, and justified to his
entire satisfaction the course which he was about to
take. For Amursana's treachery he had no words of
condemnation strong enough, and as for the arch-
traitor himself he was to be regarded "as a wolf"
which flies at the approach of an enemy and has to
be hunted down as vermin. Strict orders were given
that the rebel was to be brought to Peking dead or
alive, and Generals Chao Huei and Fu were commissioned to lead their troops to the attack. Ch'ienlung's description of the rebel's tactics was true to
the letter. Amursana instinctively avoided general
engagements, and, when worsted in skirmishes, rode
off with as many of his men as could follow him to
fresh woods and pastures new. General Fu who was
specially deputed to follow on his tracks, hunted him
down with ceaseless pertinacity. Eventually, deserted
by his followers, and discredited as a chieftain, Amursana fled for refuge to Russian territory, and implored

the protection of the Czar. Here he was safe from his human pursuers, but unconsciously he had walked into the jaws of death. A violent epidemic of small-pox was desolating the country at the time, and to that dreadful disease he speedily fell a victim. On receiving the news of his death General Fu demanded his body, that Ch'ienlung might have the gratification of gazing on the remains of his adversary. To this the Russians very naturally declined to accede, but invited Fu to send messengers to identify the features of the rebel.

The brilliant success which had attended the Chinese generals left them dissatisfied so long as Eastern Turkistan remained as a possible hotbed of discontent on their western frontier. Chao, therefore, determined to move against Kashgar and Yarkand, and in the first instance despatched a certain General Ma at the head of the invading force. Ma blun-dered in the execution of his task, and met with more than one serious reverse. As we have seen, there is only one rule in China for the treatment of unsuccessful generals. In this case it was not departed from, and Ma being beheaded, Chao took the matter into his own hands. The impetus given to the campaign by his skill and energy was such that before long he was able to report to his sovereign the capture of both the objects of his attack. The prestige thus acquired by the Chinese arms so impressed the ruler of Khokand that he immediately made his submission to the "Son of Heaven," an example which was followed by several of the neighbouring chiefs. As the victors entered the city of Kashgar the inhabitants, as we learn by a letter from General Chao to Ch'ienlung (1759), surrendered with every demonstration of joy. They lavished refreshments on the troops, and covered the generals with honour. As the procession advanced the people threw themselves on their knees and cried aloud, "Long live the great Emperor of China!"

Having established some form of administration in the conquered provinces, Chao and Fu returned to Peking to receive the rewards of their services. As they approached the capital Ch'ienlung went out half a day's journey to meet them, and graciously placed palaces within the city at their disposal. Chao was raised to the highest rank of nobility, and Fu to that of the next grade. Chao who was already advanced in years remained at Peking until his death, resting on his laurels, and eventually died in the odour of Court favour. It is said that after his decease the Emperor visited him and in support of a strange fiction directed that the dead man should be seated in a chair as though still alive. "I command you to remain as you are," said the monarch. "I come to see you for the purpose of exhorting you to leave nothing undone towards the re-establishment of your health. A man like you is still necessary to the Empire."

But though war's alarms were frequent during the reign of Ch'ienlung peaceful celebrations were mingled with the echoes of distant strife. Nearer home the prosperity of the country advanced by leaps and by bounds, and the favour of Heaven was reflected in the well-being of the Imperial family. An inte-

resting ceremony took place in the year 1752 when
the Dowager Empress attained her sixtieth year.
The whole route from Yuan-ming-yuan, some seven
miles from Peking, to the Imperial Palace within the
city walls, was made one long festive pageant, while the
sides of the road were lined with extempore pavilions
and theatres, where musicians and actors did their
utmost to add harmony and amusement to the scene.
It had been originally intended that the Imperial
cortège should have been carried in barges along the
course of the river to the city walls, and though the
season was winter when in the ordinary course everything is hard bound with frost, every effort was made
to keep the river open. But the attempt failed and
sleighs were substituted. Within the city walls the
decorations were even more elaborate than by the
highways. Artificial mountains with Buddhist temples and monasteries dotted on their sides, arcades
and restaurants bordered the streets, while for the
amusement of the Imperial party children dressed as
monkeys climbed artificial trees and gathered with a
variety of grimace every kind of artificial fruit. At
other places gigantic pears and apples opened at
intervals displaying children in their hollow interiors.
Never was there a more gorgeous scene, but it was
robbed of more than half its value and significance
by the law which obliges, on such occasions, the
inhabitants of the neighbourhood to remain indoors
with closed shutters to prevent them gazing on the
Dragon countenance. Like Frederick the Great who
was wont to form the solitary spectator of theatrical
performances in the Royal Theatre in Berlin, the

A CHINESE BARROW RIDE.

Emperors of China are accustomed to traverse the streets of their capital unseen by those who have prepared for their delight the decorations of the streets and buildings.

As interludes between the higher duties of State, the artistic labours of the Jesuits, Castiglione and Attiret, formed an endless source of interest and amusement to the Emperor, and he was even induced by the excellence of their painting to honour Attiret by sitting for his portrait. So delighted was he with the result that he was minded to confer on the artist the high distinction of a mandarin's button. This honour, however, Attiret declined with many expressions of gratitude, but he and others continued to devote themselves to amusing and astonishing the Emperor by all kinds of mechanical contrivances without reward or recompense. In the construction of one piece of mechanism they surpassed themselves. With much elaborate and ornate detail they constructed a clock representing a courtyard, from the pavilion in which, at the stroke of the hour, the figure of a mandarin advanced carrying a banner bearing the words, "Long live the Emperor!" As the automaton bowed low, four attendants appeared who, with short batons, beat out a chime representing the particular time of the day. The Chinese have always had a taste for this kind of mechanical contrivance, and when the Allies took possession of the Summer Palace in 1860 a number of clocks of a construction similar to that just described were found among the Imperial treasures.

At this time Ch'ienlung may be said to have

reached the zenith of his power, and to have extended his fame throughout the length and breadth of Asia. A notable instance of the confidence which was reposed in his rule is afforded by one of the strangest migrations which even the East with its manifold caprices has ever witnessed. While the tribes on the Mongol frontier had been in a state of ferment the Tourgots, under the leadership of their chief Ayuka, fled from the ever-recurring turmoil across the Steppes of the Kirghez into Russian territory. At first their sudden incursion caused the Governor of Orenburg some alarm, but on becoming better informed as to its cause and object, he placed at the disposal of the wanderers a fertile territory lying between the Volga and the Yaik. Here they remained, pursuing their avocations for half a century, not without some provocation from their new government, but in the enjoyment of a tranquillity which, compared with their former harassed existence, was as a haven of rest. It is true that the Russian drill sergeants decimated their young men for the service of the Czar, and that taxes were levied upon them such as in their more primitive state of society had been entirely unknown. But these were grievances to which, so long as their former habitat remained the scene of constant strife, they were content to submit. After the defeat and death of Amursana, however, and the complete pacification of the districts over which he had been in the habit of raiding, the Tourgots turned their eyes towards the lands where they had originally dwelt, and desired to offer their submission to the " Son of Heaven," who had been instrumental in producing order out of chaos. Having satisfied themselves that their reappearance within the Chinese frontier would be welcomed as a return to their fold, they in all secrecy made preparation for their return march across the dreary deserts of Central Asia. On one of the first days of January, in the year 1771, the Tourgot men, women, and children, to the number of 600,000, started on their ill-starred journey in the direction of their ancient home.

The choice of winter for this great adventure was directed by the fact that their settlements were situated on both sides of the river Volga, and that it was thus necessary to wait until a frozen surface should afford a means by which the western portion might at any moment join their *confrères* on the eastern shore. Absolute secrecy was observed by the Khan and his colleagues as to their intentions, and the ignorance of the Russian Government on the point was preserved and heightened by the apparent zeal with which the Tourgots offered themselves for military service under the banners of the Czaritza in the war in which the Empire was engaged against the Turk. It was proposed by the Khan and his confederates that on a signal being given, the settlers should set fire to their dwellings and crops, and, if possible, include in the conflagration the neighbouring Russian cities and villages.

When the momentous day arrived, and the signal was given, the western settlers, alarmed by the presence of Russian troopers, who were, by a strange accident, in their neighbourhood, refused to move,

and by this coincidence not only were the Russian
riverine towns saved from destruction, but the
amount of misery entailed by the march was lessened
by one-half. As one person, the men, women, and
children dwelling on the eastern bank, moved eastward at the bidding of the Khan. The first stage of
three hundred miles was covered in seven days with
the aid of horses and camels. But already the
Cossacks were following at the heels of the fugitives,
and one division of the huge crowd of wanderers was
cut to pieces by these merciless pursuers. Harassed
by their enemies and tortured by famine, thirst, and
disease, the Tourgots, in spite of every obstacle,
pushed on towards their goal. For eight months
they marched through the steppes and deserts of
Asia, and the small remnant were rejoiced at the end
of that time to re-enter the Chinese frontier on the
shores of the Lake of Tengis. To this point Ch'ienlung
had despatched a force of cavalry to receive the
wanderers, of whose approach he had been apprised.
One morning the Celestial troopers "reached the
summit of a road which led through a cradle-like
dip in the mountains right down upon the margin
of the lake. From this pass elevated about two
thousand feet above the level of the water, they
continued to descend, by a very winding and difficult
road, for an hour and a half; and during the whole
of this descent they were compelled to be inactive
spectators of the fiendish spectacle below. The
Kalmucks (Tourgots) reduced by this time from
about six hundred thousand souls to two hundred
thousand, and after enduring the miseries we have

previously described—outrageous heat, famine, and
the destroying scimitar of the Kirghizes and the
Bashkirs—had for the last ten days been traversing
a hideous desert, where no vestiges were seen of
vegetation, and no drop of water could be found.
Camels and men were already so overladen that it
was a mere impossibility that they should carry a
tolerable sufficiency for the passage of this frightful
wilderness. On the eighth day, the wretched daily
allowance, which had been continually diminishing,
failed entirely ; and thus, for two days of insupport-
able fatigue, the horrors of thirst had been carried to
the fiercest extremity. Upon this last morning, at
the sight of the hills and the forest scenery, which
announced to those who acted as guides the neighbourhood of the Lake of Tengis, all the people
rushed along with maddening eagerness to the
anticipated solace. The day grew hotter and hotter,
the people more and more exhausted; and gradually,
in the general rush forwards to the lake, all discipline
and command were lost—all attempts to preserve a
rearguard were neglected. The wild Bashkirs rode in
amongst the encumbered people, and slaughtered them
wholesale, and almost without resistance. Screams
and tumultous shouts proclaimed the progress of the
massacre ; but none heeded, none halted ; all alike
pauper or noble, continued to rush with maniacal
haste to the waters—all with faces blackened with
the heat preying upon the liver, and with tongue
drooping from the mouth. The cruel Bashkir was
affected by the same misery, and manifested the same
symptoms of his misery, as the wretched Kalmuck.

The murderer was oftentimes in the same frantic
misery as his murdered victim. Many, indeed (an
ordinary effect of thirst) in both nations, had become
lunatic; and in this state, whilst mere multitude
and condensation of bodies alone opposed any check
to the destroying scimitar and the trampling hoof,
the lake was reached; and to that the whole vast body
of enemies rushed, and together continued to rush,
forgetful of all things at that moment but of one
almighty instinct. This absorption of the thoughts
in one maddening appetite lasted for a single minute;
but in the next arose the final scene of parting
vengeance. Far and wide the waters of the solitary
lake were instantly dyed red with blood and gore.
Here rode a party of savage Bashkirs, hewing off
heads as fast as the swaths fall before the mower's
scythe; there stood unarmed Kalmucks in a death-
grapple with their detested foes, both up to the
middle in water, and oftentimes both sinking together
below the surface, from weakness or from struggles,
and perishing in each other's arms. Did the Bashkirs
at any point collect in a cluster for the sake of giving
impetus to the assault, thither were the camels driven
in fiercely by those who rode them, generally women
and boys; and even these quiet creatures were forced
into a share in this carnival of murder by trampling
down as many as they could strike prostrate with the
lash of their forelegs. Every moment the water
grew more polluted; and yet every moment fresh
myriads came up to the lake and rushed in, not able
to resist their frantic thirst, and swallowing large
draughts of water, visibly contaminated with the

blood of their slaughtered compatriots. Wheresoever the lake was shallow enough to allow of men raising their heads above the water, there, for scores of acres, were to be seen all forms of ghastly fear, of agonising struggle, of spasm, of convulsion, of mortal conflict—death, and the fear of death—revenge, and the lunacy of revenge—hatred, and the frenzy of hatred—until the neutral spectators, of whom there were not a few, now descending the eastern side of the lake, at length averted their eyes in horror. This horror, which seemed incapable of further addition was, however, increased by an unexpected incident. The Bashkirs, beginning to perceive here and there the approach of the Chinese cavalry, felt it prudent, wheresoever they were sufficiently at leisure from the passions of the murderous scene, to gather into bodies. This was noticed by the governor of a small Chinese fort built upon an eminence above the lake, and immediately he threw in a broadside which spread havoc among the Bashkir tribe. As often as the Bashkirs collected into 'globes' and 'turms' as their only means of meeting the long line of descending Chinese cavalry, so often did the Chinese governor of the fort pour his exterminating broadside, until at length the lake, at the lower end, became one vast seething caldron of human bloodshed and carnage. The Chinese cavalry had reached the foot of the hills ; the Bashkirs, attentive to their movements, had formed ; skirmishes had been fought ; and with a quick sense that the contest was henceforward rapidly becoming hopeless, the Bashkirs and Kirghizes began to retire. The pursuit was not as vigorous as the Kalmuck hatred would have desired ; but, at the same time, the very gloomiest hatred could not but find, in their own dreadful experience of the Asiatic deserts, and in the certainty that these wretched Bashkirs had to repeat that same experience a second time, for thousands of miles, as the price exacted by a retributary providence for their vindictive cruelty, not the very gloomiest of the Kalmucks or the least reflecting, but found in all this a retaliatory chastisement more complete and absolute than any which their swords and lances could have obtained, or human vengeance could have devised." [1]

With merciful foresight Ch'ienlung provided food and garments for the wretched remainder of the wanderers that had reached his frontier. Lands were also placed at their disposal, and on the shores of the lake a pillar was raised to commemorate the hardships endured, and the engagements fought on this great and notable march.

But while peace and quiet were established on the northern frontiers of the Empire, the relations with Burma had become strained to the point of war. The histories do not describe clearly the causes of the rupture between the two countries. In Oriental states there are constantly occurring causes of hostility, and the probability is that incursions of Burmese marauders may have taxed the patience of the Chinese to breaking point. But, however that may be, certain it is that in 1768 Ch'ienlung ordered his troops to take the field. At first success attended the Chinese arms. The Burmese who had

[1] "The Flight of a Tartar Tribe," by De Quincey.

rashly invaded the province of Yunnan, were completely defeated, and were compelled to retreat across
the frontier.   Flushed with victory the Chinese
general followed in pursuit, and again inflicted defeat
on the Burmese within their own territory.   But no
one who has traversed the mountain ranges which
separate Western China from Burma will be surprised to hear that the difficulty of getting provisions
from China considerably hampered the movements
of the Celestials.   Meanwhile the Burmese had
summonèd every available man to their standards,
and had marched with overwhelming numbers against
the invaders.   Destitute of supplies and surrounded
by the enemy the Chinese position was desperate.
In a moment of despair the general ordered a
sauve qui peut, and only those few who were not
slain by the victorious Burmese escaped through the
mountain passes to China.

On receipt of the news of this disaster, Ch'ienlung
ordered Generals Alikun and Akwei to take command of another army to avenge the defeat.   Again
the Chinese troops crossed the dizzy heights which
separate the two Empires, and established themselves
in a fortified camp at Bhamo.   Starting from this
point d'appui, Alikun at the head of a considerable
force, marched towards the capital.   At his approach
the King of Burma lost heart, and though possessed
of forces which might well have opposed successfully
the advance of the Chinese troops, he proposed terms
of peace.   Alikun, nothing loth, being in the face of a
numerically superior army, and with ranges of mountains and narrow defiles in the rear, readily agreed to

discuss a treaty of alliance. It cannot be denied that as diplomatists the Chinese are not to be surpassed, and though on the present occasion at a disadvantage in the field, Alikun succeeded in completely over-reaching the Burmese Ministers in conclave. By the terms of the treaty which was then signed, perpetual peace was proclaimed between the two Empires, and the King agreed to pay a triennal tribute to the Court of Peking. The tribute then provided for was regularly paid up to the time of our taking possession of Upper Burma, and even afterwards, for by a most mistaken and unfortunate belief in the power of China, and the importance of her alliance, we agreed, after establishing ourselves at Mandalay, that the tribute should still continue to be paid by the highest Burmese authority in the country. The leading principle of our policy in China since the war of 1842 has been to establish by every art and form the equality of our government with that of Peking. By this mistaken step, however, we became generally recognised as tributaries of China, and by our own act and deed laid ourselves open to impertinences similar to those perpetrated on Lord Macartney, when the flag on the boat which carried him to Peking was made to bear the inscription, " Tribute Bearers to the Imperial Court." Peace was no sooner secured on the south-western frontier than distur-bances broke out among the Miaotzŭ tribes on the borders of Szech'uan. The Miaotzŭ are an interest-ing people, and are the descendants of one of the aboriginal tribes who inhabited China before the advent of the Chinese. As the primitive Chinese

settlers advanced over the country and possessed
themselves of the plains and valleys, the aboriginal
tribes were driven to take refuge in the mountain
ranges of Western and South-western China. These
dispossessed tribes have never been entirely subdued,
and the Chinese with that tolerance which in some
regard characterises their government, have refrained
from interfering with the internal affairs of the
mountaineers, unless compelled to do so by aggres-
sion on their part. The Miaotzŭ, who are by nature
joyous and independent, have thus followed their
own customs, and have preserved their form of
civilisation in entire independence of the more
cultured people by whom they are surrounded.
In the mountain valleys where they dwell they
still preserve old-world customs, which are found
only in the most backward portions of the earth's
surface. That strange custom of couvade still
exists among them, and their marriage customs
carry us back to the time when the world was
indeed young. Small in stature and badly armed,
they can never have been a match for Chinese
soldiers ; but like the Afridis of the North-West
Frontier of India, their true strength lay in the
intricate and difficult nature of the country which
they inhabited.

At various times wars have broken out between
these people and their Chinese neighbours, and so
far as it is possible to judge, the outrages which
have led up to these hostilities have as often been
committed by one side as the other. A few skirmishes on the Szech'uan frontier led on this

occasion to a war which was intended to be one
of extermination. In these engagements the
Miaotzŭ were generally successful, and in ordinary
circumstances it may well have been that a peace
would have been patched up between the disputants.
But Ch'ienlung had been long fed on victory, and
his troops by constant warfare had reached a high
standard of combativeness and efficiency. He was
unwilling therefore to submit to defeat at the hands
of the Miao barbarians, and made immediate preparations for the despatch of a punitive expedition. But
being ready to give the rebels one more chance
of repentance, he, before sending an army into
the field, despatched two envoys to the rebellious
tribes bearing an Imperial letter offering terms of
peace. The chief, however, flushed with victory, and
barbarously unmindful of the hospitality due to
plenipotentiaries, murdered the two envoys, and
scattered the letter of peace to the four winds of
heaven. The die was now cast, and a strong force
was at once sent to punish the recalcitrant rebels.
The chief command of this army was given to
General Wên Fu, with Akwei and Feng Shênê as
Lieutenant-Generals. The Emperor's orders were
stringent. The two fortified camps of the enemy
were to be captured at all costs, and an iron heel
was to be placed on the necks of the rebels. The
district over which the army had to deploy was
mountainous in the extreme. The roads were
nothing more than mountain tracks, and except in
some places where suspension bridges crossed the
rivers, passages across the torrents had to be made

in skin boats. The three generals at the head of as many separate forces converged by different ways on the Golden River district. General Wên Fu, at the head of ten thousand men, took the main route, and having arrived within striking distance of the enemy, fortified himself in an entrenched camp. Like many Chinese generals he seems to have been of the opinion that the presence of his master's big battalions, and the sight of a forest of flags would strike terror into the hearts of the hillmen. But he was mistaken. He had no sooner established himself than he was rudely awakened by a sudden and furious onslaught of the enemy. The attack was so unexpected, and the manner of warfare was so little understood by the Chinese officers and men, that hardly any show of resistance was made, and the invaders were cut down like grass before the scythe. General Wên Fu was killed and only a small remnant of his force succeeded in effecting a junction with the other detachments.

The news of this disaster reached Ch'ienlung as he was enjoying his ease at Jehol, his hunting palace in Mongolia. Without a moment's delay he called together a council, by whose advice he promoted Akwei to the supreme command, and ordered him to prosecute the war with all despatch. Akwei lost no time in obeying these orders, and after a battle which lasted five days and five nights, so completely defeated the Miaotzŭ that they came forward with humble petitions for peace. Ch'ienlung would, however, make no terms with rebels who had so flagrantly defied his authority, and Akwei again pushed his advantage to the utmost. At last every stronghold but one was taken, and at this remaining fortress the Miaotzŭ offered an heroic defence. So bravely did they fight that Akwei, with all the force at his command was unable to capture the place. Famine, however, brought the defenders to their knees. The stronghold was yielded, and the chief with his wife and children surrendered to the Chinese general on condition that their lives should be spared. General Gordon had some experience of the value of such a promise as that made by Akwei on this occasion. It will be remembered that when the Wangs of Soochow surrendered to Gordon on the express condition that their lives should be granted to them, Li Hungchang treacherously put them to death. In the same way Ch'ienlung acted towards the Miaotzŭ chief and family. With great pomp and circumstance Akwei presented his captives to the Emperor, who in spite of the plighted word of the general, sentenced the chief, Sonomu, and his family to death, and transported the men of the garrison to Ili, where they were condemned to labour as military convicts for the rest of their lives.

The conquest of the Miaotzŭ was one which fostered the Imperial vanity of Ch'ienlung. They were a tribe within his own frontier, and had never before suffered at the hands of the Chinese such crushing defeats as had now overtaken them. A dukedom was conferred on Akwei, who was further graced with a yellow girdle to replace the red one which had hitherto marked his rank, while abundant honours were showered on his subordinates. For some reason, which does not plainly appear, General Fu Tê, who had been second in command, was left out in the cold, or, at least, considered that he had been so treated. He was a rough soldier, and was not accustomed to conceal his feelings. The elevation of Akwei was, in his eyes, excessive, and he was incautious enough to express his views on the subject. In the East it is not wise to denounce a Court favourite when in high honour, and the friends of Akwei took occasion to bring to light certain peccadillos which during his career had been committed by Fu Tê, and which were probably far less important than those which might have been laid to their own charge. But the tide was in their favour, and the Emperor sentenced the general to death. Fu Tê had served his country well in Mongolia and in South-western China, and had received signal instances of his Imperial master's favour for the skill with which he had seconded the efforts of Chao Huei in the pacification of the tribes in Central Asia, and one cannot, therefore, but regret that so stern a fate should have overtaken him. In narrating the incidents connected with the Miaotzŭ war, the Imperial Chronicler states that the cost of the expedition amounted to 30,000,000 taels.

In an Empire extending over such a wide area as that ruled by Ch'ienlung, and in a country where the administration from its decentralised nature has never been thoroughly effective, it is impossible that there should not be constant outbreaks and disturbances in the outlying districts. Formosa has always been a difficult possession. The ranges of mountains which fringe its eastern shores form the homes of savage

tribes who have never submitted to the Chinese yoke ;
while the Chinese settlers on the western plains have
acquired a rough and independent habit from the lack
of all official restraint. It will be remembered that
Koxinga found a congenial refuge in its harbours
from the attacks of the Manchus, and it has been at
all times an Alsatia to which the lawless and the
vagabonds have naturally gravitated. In 1786 a local
official took upon himself the responsibility of
arresting a man named Lin on the charge of disloyalty. It must be confessed that the arrest was
fully justified. Lin was one of those men whose
personality was such as enabled him to exercise a
powerful influence on his fellow men. By establishing
a secret society he had succeeded in drawing many
thousands of his fellow-subjects to his banners ; and
the local mandarin not unnaturally thought that if he
were not quickly lodged in prison he might possibly
seat himself on the throne. But he did not count
the cost, and the news was no sooner bruited about
that Lin was a prisoner than his followers rose, murdered the venturesome mandarin, and released his
prisoner. Here were undoubtedly the makings of a
very pretty quarrel, and Ch'ienlung was not the man
to submit to be browbeaten. An army was sent to
the scene of strife, but like so many first movements
in Chinese campaigns the efforts of the force were
doomed to complete failure. The troops had no
sooner touched the shores of Formosa than they were
attacked by Lin's banditti and utterly destroyed, the
general in command saving himself only by a hasty
flight to the mainland. On receipt of this news

Ch'ienlung, after an usual custom, offered the rebels terms of peace. What the nature of these were does not appear, but that negotiations were carried on is plain from the fact that Lin made counter propositions to those presented to him by Ch'ienlung's envoys. He demanded first of all that the mandarin who after his release had attempted cruel measures of repression should be put to death; (2) that he should not be called upon to present himself at Peking; and (3) that the administration on the island should be of a milder form than had been the case hitherto. It was said that upwards of twenty thousand soldiers had fallen in battle, and though it is not incumbent upon us to accept this as an accurate statement, yet there can be no doubt that the loss of life had been very great. The recollection of this death roll, coupled with Lin's repudiation of his Imperial terms, determined Ch'ienlung to send an overwhelming force to crush the movement.

An army of one hundred thousand men, under the command of General Fu K'angan, was shipped across the straits which divided Fuhkien from the scene of strife, and though Lin's troops fought bravely against the invaders, they were no match for the seasoned Imperial soldiers, many of whom had learned the art of war in Burma, and had helped to carry the fast-nesses of the Miaotzŭ tribes. In these conditions there could be but one result, and before long General Fu was able to return to Peking with the news that the island was thoroughly pacified. The loss of life among the natives in this campaign is frightful to contem-plate, and as a matter of fact Fu's triumph was achieved by making a desert and calling it peace. At the present time Formosa is presenting to the Japanese the same administrative difficulties that it has always offered to the Chinese since its incorporation into the Empire. The people are not readily handled, and the neighbourhood of the mountain tribes adds an ever-impending terror to the occupation of the more habitable and less inaccessible parts of the island.

At this time Ch'ienlung was not only master of his own Empire, but was also the arbiter of the fates of the surrounding countries. His battalions were so vast, the civilisation which he represented was, comparatively speaking, so advanced, and the weapons used by his troops were so superior to those employed in other Eastern lands, that his name was one to conjure with ; and in disputed successions, whether in Tibet, Mongolia, or Cochin China, he was commonly appealed to as judge. Shortly after the conclusion of the Formosan war a revolution broke out in Cochin China, headed by an ex-Minister named Yuan, which ended in the deposition of the King. In this emergency the defeated potentate appealed for help to Ch'ienlung, who ordered the Governor of the neighbouring province of Kwangsi to reinstate the dethroned monarch. This the Governor successfully effected. On his return towards the Chinese frontier, however, he was suddenly attacked by the rebel leader who, by force of arms and by clever strategy, inflicted a humiliating defeat upon him. On the occasion of this reverse Ch'ienlung appointed the veteran Fu K'angan to avenge the outrage. Probably the fame of this noted general impressed Yuan with the consciousness that further resistance was useless. At all events he made the most abject submission to the Imperial forces, and so persuasive was he in his pleadings for a favourable consideration that Ch'ienlung not only forgave him his offences, but placed him on the throne of the now, for the second time, dispossessed king. To display his gratitude Yuan, taking advantage of Ch'ienlung's eightieth birthday, presented himself at Jehol, and, as a reward for his loyalty, was invested with the title and authority of a tributary sovereign.

The reign of Ch'ienlung was throughout a period of wars and rumours of wars, and he had no sooner settled the Cochin China difficulty to his satisfaction than his attention was directed to the extreme western part of his subordinate dominions. It happened that a short time previously the Panshen Lama of ulterior Tibet had made a pilgrimage to Peking, in order to implore the Seven Weeks of Blessings on the aged Emperor. In the presence of his Imperial Majesty, the Lama displayed Buddhist relics so numerous that, as the native historian states, they " might have filled the sea, and when piled up were as high as mountains." While glorying in these religious trophies he was seized with small-pox and died after a short illness. His valuables and treasures, which seem to have been as plentiful as his relics, were handed over to his elder brother, the Hut'ukht'u, or Saint Tsungpa, to the exclusion of his younger brother, who was further excommunicated as a heretic for belonging to the " Red Religion " rather than the orthodox yellow phase of the Faith.

Shémarpa, the younger brother, could have put up with the excommunication, but to be disinherited was

THE LAMA TEMPLE AT PEKING.

more than he felt inclined to endure, and, with a notable want of patriotism, he, by way of revenge for

the treatment he had received, invited the Gurkhas
of Nepal to enrich themselves by plundering the
immense wealth which Tsungpa had appropriated to
himself. Ever ready for either fighting or plunder,
the Gurkhas easily yielded to the temptation, and
having collected an army crossed the frontier into
Tibet. Generals Pa Chung, Go Huei, and Chêng Tê,
the Chinese Wardens of the Marches, being well
aware that the troops at their command were quite
insufficient to withstand the invaders, compounded
with them by offering them a bribe on behalf of the
Tibetans of 10,500 ounces of gold to be paid annually
by the abbots of the Lamaist monasteries. At the
same time the gallant generals reported to the throne
that the Gurkhas had tendered their allegiance to the
Empire, and had presented tribute as an offering of
peace.

When the time for the first settlement arrived the
Gurkhas addressed a letter to the Chinese Resident,
requesting payment of the sum agreed upon. By
skilful manœuvring the Resident evaded, for the time
being, this demand, but when the second year's
subsidy became due, his blandishments failed, and
the Gurkhas invaded the country in force. The rich
city of Tashilumbo, or "Mountain of Blessings,"
where resided the Saint Tsungpa, was their objective.
The position of the city is by nature strong, being
protected on one side by the "Much-winding" River,
and on the other by a range of precipitous mountains.
If the Lamas, who numbered several thousand, had
seriously undertaken the defence of the sacred city,
they would, without question, have been able to hold

it against the assault of the Gurkhas. But these holy
men being debilitated by their religious calling, and
being disinclined to fight, discovered that the omens
were favourable, and that the fact of the " Mother ot
Heaven " having taken the city under her special
protection made it unnecessary for them to bestir
themselves. The result was that Tashilumbo fell an
easy prey to the invader, and that those who should
have defended it were either dispersed or slain. The
news of this defeat completely upset the proverbial
calm of the Dalai Lama, who not unnaturally feared
that the same fate which had overtaken the " Mountain of Blessings " might be shared by the holy city
of Lhasa. The gods not having interfered for the
protection of the divine soil of Tibet he, in his difficulty, turned to Peking for help, and it so happened
that at the moment when his appeal reached Ch'ienlung, Pa Chung was commanding the escort which
was accompanying the Emperor to Jehol. The
position was further complicated, from Pa Chung's
point of view, by the fact that a revelation was at
the same time made of the compact entered into
between him and the Gurkhas. Feeling incapable
of facing the inevitable inquiry he escaped from the
dilemma by committing suicide, and his mouth being
thus closed his two late colleagues promptly disclaimed all participation in the arrangement which
had been come to, and denounced Pa Chung as
an arch traitor. The answer to these disclaimers
was an order to those who made them to
march at once into Tibet and to drive out the
invaders. In order to make victory certain, how-

ever, General Fu K'angan was appointed Commander-in-chief, with directions to collect Manchu troops and trained colonists to attack the enemy. A considerable share of blame was attached by the Emperor to the late Resident in Tibet, who, to expiate his offences, was sentenced to march at the head of the troops, wearing on his neck a Canque, or heavy wooden collar.

Meanwhile the Gurkhas, who had taken part in the corrupt negotiations of peace, had returned to Nepal with their plunder, leaving only a thousand men to guard the frontier. So pusillanimous were the Chinese generals on the spot that they neither interfered with these "gorged vagrants" as the Chinese historian calls them, nor attacked the insignificant force left to oppose them. In the following year, however, General Fu entered ulterior Tibet from Kokonor, and having defeated the Gurkha frontier force, invaded Nepal. For strategic reasons he divided his army into three columns, the centre one being under his personal command. The generals commanding the right and left columns had orders to push on and turn the flanks of any force that might be opposing the main advance. But from the first the Gurkhas showed rather signs of retreating than of advancing, and as they retired they sought to impede the enemy's movements by destroying the suspension and other bridges which crossed the mountain torrents in those highland districts. Though these tactics delayed the Chinese advance, General Fu pushed persistently on, and inflicted several severe defeats on the enemy. The Gurkhas were now thoroughly alarmed, and sent messengers to beg for peace. But Fu was inexorable, and in spite of the stubborn opposition of the Gurkhas at points of vantage, he succeeded in reaching within striking distance of the capital, Khatmandu. This advance completed the demoralisation of the Gurkha army, and the approach of winter, when a retreat through the mountain passes of Nepal and Tibet must necessarily have been attended with difficulty and danger, inclined General Fu to listen to renewed pleading for peace. Finally, this was granted, and Fu retired, after having received the submission of the Gurkha chiefs, who declared their country to be tributary to China. From that day to this tribute missions in compliance with this treaty have without fail wended their weary way through the wastes of Tibet to Peking, at the stated intervals agreed upon.

VI

THE OPENING OF DIPLOMATIC INTERCOURSE
WITH CHINA

THE reign of Ch'ienlung was now drawing to its close, but before he abdicated, in 1796, an event occurred which opened new relations between the West and China. Up to this time the relations of foreigners with the Chinese Government had been in a most unsatisfactory condition, although England had attempted on many occasions so to open diplomatic intercourse as to secure to her subjects at least the rights and privileges belonging to traders in foreign lands. So long ago as the reign of Queen Elizabeth an expedition was sent out under John Mildenhall to open trading relations with the Celestial Empire. The mission was a failure, but, nothing daunted, Charles I. granted a Charter to a body of English merchants empowering them to form an official company to promote commerce with the Chinese. In pursuance of this right, Captain Weddell in 1635 reached Macao in command of a small trading fleet. The Portuguese, whose Government had promised to support the British venture, threw, however,

every obstacle in the way of the English captain, who
at length wearied out by the obstructions offered by
the Portuguese, and the subterfuges of the mandarins,
determined to advance in his boats to Canton. When
passing the Bogue Forts on his way up the river,
a battery suddenly opened fire on his flotilla, upon
which he at once determined to inflict punishment on
the authors of this attack. Having moved his ships
into position opposite the forts, he hoisted a red
flag, and opened fire on the batteries. The Chinese
gunners, unaccustomed to such reprisals, soon ceased
to reply to the English guns. Weddell thereupon
landed a force, took possession of the forts, and hoisted
the British colours over them.

This kind of argument had the effect which it
always has had upon the Chinese. Negotiations were
opened at once, and the right to trade was granted on
condition that the guns captured from the Bogue
Forts should be returned. Very little however resulted from this agreement. The exactions imposed
by the Chinese on all imports and exports were so
excessive that the Company felt it almost useless to
attempt to carry on a trade. During the piratical
rule, however, of Koxinga's son at Formosa and
Amoy, some privileges of value were granted to
English traders, and in 1678 the trade at the two
places was valued at something like 60,000 dollars.
Three years later, however, the Company withdrew
from these ports, and established a single factory at
Canton. Subsequently Mr. Catchpoole was appointed
Consul in China, and in 1701 succeeded in inducing
the Chinese to allow ships to trade at Ningpo. But

again the extortions of the mandarins destroyed the expected profit of the venture, and at Canton equally grievous burdens were tending to make trade impossible. The duty on imports was increased to 16 per cent., and heavy exactions were demanded in exchange for the right of provisioning the ships. An appeal against these disabilities was made to the Governor of Canton in person, but though some temporary relief was granted, the system which had been adopted of farming out the foreign trade to a small company of native merchants had proved so convenient to the authorities that, though it practically entailed the evils complained of, it was again reverted to, while an additional duty of 10 per cent. upon all exports was further imposed. Such was the position of things when Ch'ienlung ascended the throne, and one of the first acts of his long and glorious reign was the remission of this extra burden. The Emperor, however, coupled the concession with the demand that the foreign merchants should listen to his gracious message on their knees, and should give up all the arms which they possessed on board their ships. Happily the merchants refused to buy the Imperial favour by such observances, and they neither bowed the knee nor gave up their guns at Ch'ienlung's bidding. Though hampered by vexatious regulations and impoverished by extortions, the foreign trade at Canton made some headway, and it is stated that in the year of Ch'ienlung's accession there were anchored at that port four English, two French, two Dutch, one Danish, and one Swedish vessel. In 1742 H.M.S. *Centurion*, commanded by Commodore Anson, the first British man-of-war which had ever visited China, arrived at Macao. With an even hand the Chinese sought to inflict on the Commodore the same petty annoyances as those to which the merchants were accustomed. He was refused provisions for his ship, an unfriendly act which he met by demanding an interview with the Governor, and by refusing to leave the river until he had been supplied with all necessary requirements.

With the shortsighted policy which has always distinguished the conduct of the Chinese towards foreigners, the authorities at Canton, instead of trying to foster the trade which was already enriching the native officials and merchants, continued to heap burdens upon it, until they nearly succeeded in starving out the European traders. As at present is the case with the Likin duties, the mandarins, at that time, were · risking, for the sake of an immediate temporary gain, the future and increasing profit which might legitimately be expected to accrue to them. So discouraged were the foreigners at this attitude of the Canton anthorities, that they again attempted to open a trade with Amoy and Ningpo. In neither case, however, was the enterprise successful, and, in 1759, Mr. Flint, who had been sent to Ningpo as a pioneer of commerce, finding commercial relations impossible at that port, took ship in a native vessel for Tientsin, from which place he communicated a memorial to the Emperor, showing the position of affairs. So enterprising a foreigner was evidently one to be got rid of, and by way of an answer he was ordered to return to Canton in the company of a mandarin appointed to escort him. Ostensibly, however, he had gained much that he had sought for. All duties over 6 per cent. were remitted, and illegal exactions were forbidden.

According to the Chinese custom in such matters, the Governor of the city desired to communicate the Emperor's orders to Mr. Flint in person. Fortunately for that gentleman he was accompanied on the occasion by some of his own countrymen, for, to the extreme astonishment of himself and his friends, they were, without notice, forcibly hurried into the Governor's presence, where the official myrmidons tried to compel them to do homage on their knees after the Chinese manner. The Englishmen resisted this violence, and with such determination that, at length, the Governor ordered his men to desist from what seemed likely to prove an unsuccessful struggle. He then bade Mr. Flint advance, and showing him a paper which purported to be an Imperial edict, he informed him that he was to be banished to Macao, and subsequently to be deported to England as a punishment for having endeavoured to open a trade at Ningpo contrary to orders from Peking. This sentence was carried out in its entirety, and the Chinaman who had written the petition which had been presented to the Emperor, was beheaded for having traitorously encouraged a foreigner.

It is difficult to understand how the foreign residents at Canton could have put up with the insults to which they were now daily subjected. " The barbarians are like beasts, and are not to be ruled on the same principles as ordinary men," said the Chinese ; and, to give them their due, they certainly acted up to their opinions. The handful of foreigners, who were constantly threatened by the millions of natives by whom they were surrounded, were powerless to resist successfully the indignities which were heaped upon them, and some lamentable instances occurred in which gross injustice resulted to individuals from the inequality of the opposing forces. In 1784, on the occasion of a salute being fired from an English ship, a Chinaman was accidentally killed by a shot which had been carelessly left in the gun. The authorities immediately demanded that the man who fired the gun should be handed over to them for punishment. Having a shrewd suspicion that this demand would be refused, the Chinese strengthened their hands by the adoption of a subterfuge. They seized the supercargo of another vessel, and gave formal notice that his release could only be obtained by the surrender of the gunner. The supercargo was well treated in his confinement, and, believing that the object of the mandarins in desiring the gunner's presence was merely to arrive at a full understanding of the case, he wrote urging that the man should be sent. Unfortunately this was done. The supercargo was instantly released and the gunner was strangled. Happily this is the only case in which an Englishman, under similar circumstances, has been handed over to the tender mercies of the Chinese, and it may be safely assumed that it will be the last.

Enough has been said to show how extremely unsatisfactory were the relations between China and the East India Company during the last century. The whole position was so derogatory to England,

and was so full of profitless difficulties to the merchants themselves, that the serious attention of the
English Government was directed to the situation,
and it was finally decided to send a special Ambassador to the Court of Peking to arrange terms on which
the natives of the two countries might live together
in peace and amity.   In 1788 Colonel Cathcart was
appointed to this office.   Unhappily, however, he
died before reaching China, and four years later
Lord Macartney was nominated to succeed him.
Great preparations were made to confer dignity on
this mission, and presents of every sort were collected
to serve as tokens of the friendly feeling of the third
George towards the aged Emperor.   On arriving off
the coast of the Celestial Empire, Lord Macartney
was met with every sign of consideration and good-
will, and pilots were waiting in readiness to steer
H.M.S. *Lion* through the straits of Formosa northward to the mouth of the Peiho.   There Lord
Macartney was received by a special Commissioner
of high rank, who bade him welcome in the name
of his Imperial master.   On the shores of the river,
where, in 1859, British soldiers and sailors were
treacherously fired on from the neighbouring forts,
were collected gifts and provisions for presentation
to "the great mandarin, who," as Ch'ienlung said,
"had come so far to testify the friendly feelings of
England towards China."   Twenty bullocks, a hundred and twenty sheep, a hundred and twenty pigs,
and countless other provender, were provided for the
food of the Englishmen.   A fleet of yacht-like vessels,
numbers of vehicles, and numerous horses were held

A CHINESE DINNER-PARTY.

in readiness to convey the Embassy to Tientsin. Preferring to go by water, a specially commodious vessel was prepared for Lord Macartney, while sixteen other boats provided accommodation for the members of the mission and the escort. At Tientsin the Embassy was royally entertained, and during their stay at that port dramas were continuously acted for their amusement in a temporary theatre erected on the shore opposite their vessels. After a further voyage Lord Macartney reached Tungchow, the port of Peking. Here preparations were made for the land journey to the capital, and here also discussions were renewed as to the etiquette to be observed on the Ambassador being presented to the Emperor. As has already been shown, the Chinese have persistently attempted to induce all foreign envoys to k'ot'ow when entering the presence of the " Son of Heaven." It was part of the duty of the Imperial Commissioner attached to the Embassy to induce Lord Macartney to perform this degrading ceremony, and he used his best endeavours to carry his point. But Lord Macartney, who had received positive instructions on the subject before leaving England, distinctly declined to yield, unless a Chinese official of equal rank with himself would k'ot'ow before the portrait of the English King. This condition was referred to Ch'ienlung, who, recognising the uselessness of continuing the discussion, had the wisdom to allow the matter to drop.

The transportation of the presents from Tungchow to Peking was a matter of some difficulty. They varied in size from carriages to watches, and some

idea of their number may be gauged from the fact
that ninety waggons, forty barrows, two hundred

A CHINESE COOLIE.

horses, and three thousand men were employed to
carry them. It speaks well for the manner in

which they were packed, that, though many were fragile, they all arrived safely at the house prepared for the Ambassador in the neighbourhood of the Summer Palace of Yuan-ming-yuan.

As the members of the mission entered the gates of Peking, on their way to their destination, a salute of guns was fired in their honour, and every courtesy was extended to them. Ch'ienlung was at this time at Jehol, in Mongolia, and as it was plainly impossible to carry the presents thither, it was agreed that they should be arranged in the throne-room of the palace at Peking to await the inspection of His Imperial Majesty on his return to the capital. The presence of Lord Macartney in this room of State suggested a recurrence of the vexed question of the k'ot'ow, and the Minister Ho, who was especially appointed to entertain the English Ambassador, was persistent in his endeavours to reopen the question. Lord Macartney, however, was firm, and explained that a derogatory action on the part of an Ambassador was in Europe regarded as a derogatory action on the part of the Ambassador's Sovereign, and emphasised the point by describing how Timagoras, a Greek ambassador to the Court of Persia, was executed on his return to Athens for having submitted to discourtesy at the Court of Teheran. Lord Macartney further took this opportunity of expostulating with Ho about the impertinent legend which had been inscribed on the flag of the vessel on which he had voyaged up the Peiho, and which had described him as a " Tribute-Bearer from the country of England."

So soon as was practicable, that is to say, on the 2nd of September, 1793, the Embassy started for Jehol, Lord Macartney travelling in an English postchaise. On the fourth day they reached the Great Wall, where a strong guard of soldiers was drawn up to do them honour. Three days later they reached Jehol, where they were accommodated in one of the most spacious houses in the town. After many discussions with Ho an audience was arranged for the fourteenth of the month. The Chinese have a most uncomfortable habit of holding their State ceremonies at daybreak, and it is part of the etiquette that those attending such functions should be in waiting some hours before the appointed time. Fortunately on this occasion the temperature was mild, and therefore no serious inconvenience was suffered ; but in the winter season not the least arduous part of a Minister's duty is to wait at the early hours of the morning in cold, fireless rooms for the honour of a momentary conversation with the " Son of Heaven." A tent set in the garden of the palace formed the Court of Audience, and so soon as Ch'ienlung had mounted the throne, Lord Macartney, with a number of envoys from tributary states, was admitted into the presence. It had been arranged that he should offer precisely the same homage to the Emperor as he was accustomed to offer to his own Sovereign. As he advanced, therefore, to the throne, he knelt on one knee, and, raising the gold box which contained the King's letter with both hands above his head, he presented it to Ch'ienlung, who, taking it from his hands, in-

quired as to the health of the English Sovereign,
at the same time expressing gratification that he
should have sent his Ambassador to so distant a
Court. In the course of the conversation which
followed there occurred a difficulty in interpreting,
and in reply to a question put from the throne,
Ch'ienlung was informed that the only member of
the Embassy who spoke Chinese was George
Staunton, the Ambassador's page, aged thirteen.
Ch'ienlung ordered the lad to be presented to him,
and, being pleased with the boy's manner and appearance, took his purse from his belt and presented it
to him.

Subsequently a feast was spread, when the seat of
honour was given to Lord Macartney with whom the
Emperor exchanged civilities, and to whom he sent
dainty morsels of food and wine from his own table.
So far, however, the object of the mission had not
been advanced one iota. The audience had been
merely formal, and in his conversations with the
Minister Ho, Lord Macartney had found it impossible to discuss at length the main issues between
them. Ho was a typical Oriental courtier, subtle,
polite, and apparently ingenuous. He possessed, also,
a full share of that Oriental diplomacy which enables
Chinese negotiators to avoid disagreeable topics. In
other respects, too, he was a typical Eastern statesman. "Born in the garret, in the kitchen bred," he
happened on one occasion to attract the Emperor's
attention by his courtly bearing and handsome
presence. With unusual rapidity, he was advanced
from office to office until he reached the highest rung

of the ladder. So long as Ch'ienlung lived, he maintained his position, but evil days fell upon him when Chiach'ing succeeded to the throne. The new Emperor had long disapproved of the unlimited power which Ho had exercised. He knew, also, that he had acquired immense wealth in other ways than by the lawful rewards of his official position, and Ch'ienlung was therefore, no sooner gathered to his fathers than Ho was arrested on a long series of charges embracing malpractices in every relation of life. The amount of wealth discovered in his palace must have been a surprise even to his judges. Gold, silver, and jewels to the value of £23,330,000 were discovered in his treasury. This alone was enough to convict him of the gravest crimes, and from a Chinese point of view, to justify the sentence passed upon him, of being cut to pieces. In consideration however of his long service the Emperor was graciously pleased to commute this cruel fate for the present of a silken cord, which brought the nefarious career of this illustrious culprit to a close.

But though corrupt and officially dishonest Ho was an agreeable companion, and made an exceptionally good cicerone on the occasion when, at the Emperor's invitation, Lord Macartney visited the Palace Gardens at Jehol. Indeed on this day he, in the exercise of friendship, exerted himself unduly, and was indebted for the recovery from his fatigues to the kindly attention of the doctor of the English Embassy. One other entertainment, which again took place at the very uncomfortable hour of sunrise, brought the Imperial hospitalities to an end, and, on the 21st of

September, Lord Macartney left Jehol for Peking.
After some weeks' stay in that capital it was arranged
that he should leave for the south, and the exigences
of his position obliged him to accept the route laid
down by the Chinese. This entailed a long land
journey through the provinces of Shantung, Kiangsu,
Chehkiang, and Fuhkien to Canton, where he arrived
on the 19th of December. He eventually reached
England on September 5, 1794.

It is impossible to study the history of Lord
Macartney's mission without observing the consistent political hostility towards foreign nations
which was shown by the Chinese Government, at
the same time that much good-will towards the
Ambassador personally was displayed by the Emperor
and some of the officials. No commercial privileges
resulted from Lord Macartney's negotiations, and
the ill-concealed contempt of most of those with
whom he was brought into contact marks but
too clearly the spirit of exclusive jealousy which
has guided, and is still guiding, the policy of the
Peking Cabinet. The impertinent inscription on the
Ambassador's flag, the facts that though treated with
personal respect he was guarded as a prisoner ; that
those of the mission who remained at Peking during
his absence at Jehol were practically confined to the
house, and were not allowed even to receive visits
from the European missionaries in the capital ; that
the tedious land journey from the north to the south
of the Empire was unnecessarily inflicted upon him,
all point to the same supercilious regard which it
is the habit of the Celestials to entertain towards

foreigners. The Chinese have habitually assumed such a distant and lofty attitude towards Europeans that they have by force of insistence succeeded to some extent in inducing these to accept them at their own valuation. In this attitude they have been strengthened by the fact that unfortunately the " Outer Barbarians " have invariably appeared as suppliants for favours to come, and that they have been always the dispensers of privileges for which they have not asked anything in return. Lord Macartney was doubtless pleased and surprised at the reception which he met with at the hands of the " Son of Heaven," and he was not inclined to observe too closely the political conduct of his enter-tainers. He was received as an envoy from a superior Tributary State, and he was treated as such ; and all that he succeeded in exacting from the Government was a permission that his country-men might trade at Canton on sufferance, so long as they obeyed the orders of the authorities. Under the circumstances it was quite impossible that he should have gained any diplomatic success. Con-cessions are only to be obtained from the Chinese by successes in the field, or by such a display of power as would command success ; Lord Macartney had neither of these sources of authority at his back, and the result which followed was inevitable.

In 1796 Ch'ienlung abdicated in favour of his son Chiach'ing, and three years later (February 8, 1799) be became a "guest in heaven." The native historians state with justice that during the sixty years of his reign the Empire reached its acme of greatness. From the northern steppes of Mongolia to Cochin China, and from Formosa to Nepal, the Chinese armies had fought and conquered. Upwards of four hundred million of the human race had obeyed the commands of the great Emperor, and in no instance had his foes been able to inflict more than a temporary defeat upon his troops.

VII

THE REIGN OF CHIACH'ING, AND THE FIRST YEARS OF HIS SUCCESSOR

To the splendid heritage bequeathed by Ch'ienlung his son Chiach'ing succeeded, and this change at once produced unfortunate results. The late sovereign was to his successor as Hyperion to a satyr ; the gracious presence, courteous manner, and marked ability which belonged to Ch'ienlung were exchanged for churlish conduct, a sordid disposition, and an uncouth bearing in the case of Chiach'ing. The reins of Empire, which for sixty years had been guided by the judicious hands of the father, were no sooner seized upon by his degenerate son than the forces of disorder and riot began to make themselves felt.

It is a current belief in China, as in many other lands, that the appearance of a comet forebodes ill to the ruling house, and history tells us that, during the year in which Chiach'ing ascended the throne, a "broom-tailed star" appeared in the west, and, if we are to believe their records, remained visible for twelve months. Such beliefs as this, have a way of bringing about their own fulfilment, and it is possible that the leaders of the "White Lily" Sect took advantage of this sign in the sky to raise the standard of revolt. This society like all similar associations in China, began as a purely philanthropic institution, intended for the benefit of the sick and the distressed. By degrees more ambitious designs attracted the energies of the leaders, and, on the ready excuse of friction with the local authorities, a general revolt broke out almost simultaneously in the provinces of Honan, Shensi, Kansu, and Szech'uan, in which last territory the ranks of the society were largely recruited from the disbanded soldiers of the Nepal campaign. The struggle was long and fierce, and it is said that, in one province alone, between twenty and thirty thousand members of the incriminated society were put to death, while the Imperial Treasury was the poorer by 100,000,000 taels at the close of the civil war.

A notable feature of this uprising and a marked evidence of the unpopularity of Chiach'ing was the fact that as part of the movement two attempts were publicly made to assassinate the Emperor, one in the streets of Peking, and the other in the private apartments of the Imperial Palace. In both cases Chiach'ing was saved by the courage of others rather than by his own valour. In the first instance the guards attached to his person, with the help of the people in the street, prevented the assassins from carrying out their fell intent, and on the other occasion his preservation was entirely due to the presence of mind and courage of Prince Mienning his second son, who subsequently succeeded him as the Emperor Taokwang. In this latter instance the assassins forced their way into the Imperial precincts, intent on finding their victim, who, according to some accounts, was not at the moment in the palace. But however that may be, Prince Mienning shot two of the would-be assassins, while a relative, who happened to be with him, accounted for a third. Chiach'ing's own description of the occurrence is as follows: "Suddenly on the 15th of the 9th moon, rebellion arose under my own arm. . . . A banditti of upwards of seventy men of the Sect Tienli violated the prohibited gate [of the palace]; they wounded the guard and rushed into the inner palace. Four were seized and bound; three others ascended the wall with a flag. My Imperial second son seized a matchlock and shot two of them; my nephew killed the third. For this deliverance I am indebted to the energies of my second son."

It might have been thought that as Chiach'ing had so signally failed in securing the regard of his own countrymen he might have sought the alliance of foreigners. But he was even less in sympathy with these than with the Changs and Lis of the Middle Kingdom. The missionaries to whom his father had shown respect and kindliness, were dismissed from the Imperial presence; Father Amiot, who had resided in Peking for thirty years, was expelled from the capital, and the traders of Canton were made pointedly conscious that the central power was against them. An overbearing attitude was adopted towards Europeans generally, and no velvet glove concealed the mailed fist of the Emperor,

except on occasions when, with that curious mixture
of arrogance and suppliancy, his representatives
besought the help of English seamen against their
domestic enemies.   The southern coasts of China
have always been the congenial haunts of pirates.
The numberless inlets and countless islands which
line the coast provide convenient and safe posts from
which to watch for prey or to escape from pursuers.
It will be remembered that Koxinga and his son
practically held possession of the southern seaboard
of the Empire for a considerable period of years,
and under the unsympathetic rule of Chiach'ing a
successor to these leaders appeared in the person of
one Ch'ai who harassed the native shipping and even
ventured to try conclusions with English vessels.
Occasionally he attacked, by mistake, boats of British
men-of-war, and in one case actually threw a large
fishing net over the crew and boat of H.M.S. *Dover.*
The boat was at anchor at the time and the crew
were asleep, but aroused by the onslaught they drew
their cutlasses, disentangled themselves from the
meshes of the net, and promptly put the pirates
to flight.   Such outrages did not disturb the official
conscience of his mandarins, but an event happened
shortly afterwards which as an insult to the Empire
roused even the dull sense of honour possessed by
the authorities.   The time had arrived for the payment of the Siamese tribute, and, as the cargo represented by this act of fealty was known to be a rich
one, the pirates prepared to attack the vessels, and to
lay violent hands on the presents intended for the
Imperial use.   The prospect of this robbery touched

the Imperial dignity, and a request was made to the English at Canton that they would fit out a vessel to save the Siamese fleet from the fate intended for it. The English consented, and a small though fit crew manned the *Mercury* for the venture. The result was eminently successful. The pirate fleet was scattered to the four winds of heaven, and the Siamese tribute was carried safely to Peking.

This is the first but by no means the only instance in which English courage has saved Chinese hoonur. The process has since been constantly repeated, notably in the case of the T'aip'ing Rebellion, the suppression of which was entirely due to the help afforded by England to the Imperial forces. The Chinese plume themselves on being a proud nation, but when danger threatens they descend with agility from their pedestal, and show an apt facility of falling on their knees. One remarkable instance of this curious want of self-respect was furnished during the war of 1857, when Yeh, while defending Canton against the English, had the craven impertinence to ask help from his foes to suppress a native rising against his rule.

But though glad of help from English ships, the increase in the number of men-of-war visiting Canton produced a disturbing influence on the minds of Chiach'ing and his followers. The war in Europe made it increasingly necessary that the English men-of-war should be available for the protection of British trade, and the seizure of Macao in 1802, and again in 1813, to prevent the settlement from falling into the hands of the French, produced violent

14

remonstrances from the mandarins accompanied by threats that the trade of Canton should be stopped if the port were not evacuated. The same hostile spirit marked the few communications which passed between Peking and London during this period. A present which was sent to an official who had been civil in his dealings with Lord Macartney was returned with scant courtesy, and a letter, addressed by Chiach'ing to George III., was marked by all the stilted arrogance common to the Chinese. "Your Majesty's Kingdom," wrote the Emperor, "is at a remote distance beyond the seas, but is observant of its duties and obedient to our laws, beholding from afar the glory of our Empire, and respectfully admiring the perfection of our government. Your Majesty has despatched messengers with letters for our perusal; we find that they are dictated by appropriate sentiments of esteem and veneration; and being therefore inclined to fulfil the wishes of Your Majesty, we have determined to accept the whole of the accompanying offering. With regard to those of Your Majesty's subjects who for a long course of years have been in the habit of trading with our Empire, we must observe to you that our Celestial Government regards all persons and nations with eyes of charity and benevolence, and always treats and considers your subjects with the utmost indulgence and affection; on their account, therefore, there can be no place or occasion for the exertions of Your Majesty's Government."

Being of very inferior ability to his father Chiach'ing had none of the breadth of mind which

suggested to Ch'ienlung the toleration which distinguished that Emperor's reign.   Being uncertain of
the respect of those about him, he was more punctilious as to outward forms and ceremonies.   A lack of
the spirit of veneration is often supplied by additional
scrupulousness about the minutiæ of ritual.   Ch'ienlung had looked upon the k'ot'ow as an obeisance
commonly due to him, but in receiving Lord
Macartney's mission he was wise enough to recognise that it might be given up without any loss of
dignity on his part.   His son had no such width of
view and insisted that any one entering his presence,
whether a native or a foreigner, should perform that
particular sort of debasement before his throne.   His
persistence in this matter wrecked two embassies to
his Court.   In 1805 a Russian Embassy, under Count
Goloyken, travelled overland on the way to Peking,
and reached the Great Wall in due course. · Here the
Count was met by emissaries from Chiach'ing who
informed him that unless he would consent to
perform the k'ot'ow when admitted to Imperial
audiences he might save himself the trouble of
coming any further.   The Ambassador firmly refused
so to degrade himself, and as the only way out of the
deadlock was to return from whence he came, he
turned his camels' heads round, and disappeared
across the desert.   Eleven years later George III., of
pious memory, determined to send a second envoy
to renew the negotiations opened by Lord Macartney.   For this important mission Lord Amherst, who
had distinguished himself at many courts, was chosen
as the King's representative.   Without adventure he

arrived at Tientsin, where he was met by Commissioners who, while preserving a semblance of courtesy,
began at once to raise the question of the k'ot'ow.
Day after day with wearisome reiteration they
brought forward the same demands, supported by
what they were good enough to call arguments, and
were answered in the same words based on the same
reasons. At one time it looked as though Lord
Amherst's fate was to have been that of Count
Goloyken. But for some reason, possibly the prospect of receiving presents similar to those brought by
Lord Macartney, Chiach'ing was evidently desirous
that the Ambassador should be admitted into his
presence, and hence, though Lord Amherst was firm
on the point in dispute, he was allowed to proceed to
Tungchow, within twelve miles of the capital. Here
two men of superior rank and condition met him and
at once urged him to consent to what they called the
national custom. Lord Amherst repeated the proposition made by Lord Macartney, that if a mandarin of equal rank with himself would k'ot'ow to a
portrait of George III. he would do likewise in the
presence of Chiach'ing. This concession was declined, and Lord Amherst next proposed that he
should bow low nine times before the Emperor, while
the courtiers performed the nine prostrations of the
k'ot'ow. This also was declared to be inadmissible,
and the prospect before the mission became black
indeed. To Lord Amherst's surprise, however, Duke
Ho, the Chief Commissioner, informed him that the
Emperor had given orders for the mission to be
brought to Yuan-ming-yuan on the following day.

The journey, barely more than twenty miles, might well have been made within the hours of daylight, even at a foot's pace. But as if to aggravate the discomfort of the Ambassador, Ho arranged that the cavalcade should start at five o'clock in the evening, with the result that it did not arrive at Yuan-ming-yuan until daylight on the next morning. While weary and worn with this tedious and untimely journey, the Ambassador and his suite were hustled into a small room where they were subjected to the inquisitive scrutiny of people of all ranks, who treated them, in the words of Mr. Ellis, the historian of the Mission, with "brutal rudeness and an insulting demeanour." While annoyed by these insults Lord Amherst was still further disturbed by the arrival of Duke Ho, who brought a message from the Emperor to say that he desired to see the Ambassador at once. Lord Amherst expostulated against this discourteous demand, and pleaded his fatigue and the non-arrival of his Court attire. Ho, however, was doubly and anxiously persistent, and even attempted, on one occasion, to force the Ambassador into the Emperor's presence. This impertinence was resented by Lord Amherst who sent a respectful message to Chiach'ing, informing him of the circumstances of the case, and begging to be allowed time to recover from his fatigue before presenting himself in the august presence. A peremptory answer was returned to this very reasonable request, ordering the Ambassador at once to set out for Tungchow, *en route* to Canton. No option was allowed him, and he, therefore, shook the dust of Peking off his feet, and turned his face southward.

The story is a disgraceful one, and it is only due to Chiach'ing to say that his natural discourtesy towards foreigners was aggravated in this case by the deceptions practised upon him by his Ministers. According to an Imperial Edict, published after Lord Amherst's departure, it appears that Duke Ho had reported to his master from Tungchow that "the English tribute bearer was daily practising the ceremony [of k'ot'ow], and was manifesting the highest possible respect and veneration." It is also stated on the Imperial word that Ho had concealed the fact that Lord Amherst declined the audience owing to fatigue after his journey, and represented him as being contumacious. For these offences Duke Ho was fined five years' salary, and was stripped of his yellow jacket. The further sentence that he should be deprived of all his offices, the Emperor was graciously pleased to remit in consideration of his many services. According to the Emperor, Ho, with his companion Mu, were overcome with remorse at the part they had played, and when introduced into the Imperial presence they made full confession, "pulling off their caps and dashing their heads against the ground." It is possible that this demonstrative contrition may have had the effect of mitigating the Imperial wrath.

Another and a remarkable Englishman suffered at about the same time a somewhat similar rebuff on the part of the Celestials. Manning, who was a considerable Chinese scholar, arrived at Canton in 1814 inspired by the vain hope that his knowledge of the language, and sympathy with the people, would gain him favour in their eyes. He was soon undeceived, and, disheartened with his failure, left Canton for India whence he travelled into Tibet. Here better fortune attended him. He gained admission into Lhasa, and thus secured the distinction of being the only Englishman who has ever entered the portals of that sacred city.

The remaining years of Chiach'ing were few and evil, and in 1820 at the age of sixty-one death overtook him. When quite a lad he showed some literary talent and we are told that when thirteen years of age on the occasion of his father, Ch'ienlung, examining him in the hall of Confucius, "the verses that might be expected from a boy of such an age were duly composed." But in after life all taste for literature disappeared and he found his principal amusement in the society of actors. Immediately after the morning Audience it was his wont to retire to his private apartments where, in the company of comedians, he sang and played. It is even said that when he went to offer the sacred sacrifices to Heaven and Earth it was his practice to take some of his favourites with him. With the courage which either makes or mars a Chinese statesman the Minister Sung took upon himself the invidious task of remonstrating with his liege lord on the impropriety of these habits. This reproval instead of producing the desired result only irritated Chiach'ing, who, however, was quite unable to deny the allegations contained in the accusing memorial. In answer to a summons calling on him to appear before his angry master, Sung presented himself on his knees, trembling. After some words of reproof Chiach'ing asked the Minister what he deserved for the crime of inculpating the Son of Heaven. "Quartering," was the answer. After an interval which must have contained anxious moments for Sung the same question was repeated and the Minister regarding the repetition as a sign of mitigating wrath replied, "Let me be beheaded." Yet a third time the question was put, "Let me be strangled," was the answer. At these words Sung was dismissed from the audience chamber, and the next day received the appointment of Governor of the Province of Ili, where, in the opinion of his Imperial master, he would be unable to pry into the amusements of the palace, and would at the same time be powerless to plead that the Emperor had trampled on the traditional rights of Ministers to expostulate with erring sovereigns.

Chiach'ing was of an indolent disposition, and was incapable of opposing the more violent spirits who disturbed the peace of the Empire during the quarter of a century that he sat on the throne. The faults of his father were exaggerated in him, and he had none of those virtues which added lustre to the long reign of Ch'ienlung. It is customary for an Emperor on ascending the throne to publish an Edict containing an obituary notice of his predecessor. The statements contained in such documents are probably no truer than epitaphs generally are, but it is only fair to Chiach'ing that we should glance at the other side of the shield and should listen to what his son, Taokwang, who saved his life on the occasion of the attack of his sacred person in the palace, has to say on the behalf of his august father. " His late Majesty," wrote Taokwang, "who has now gone the great journey, governed all under Heaven's canopy during twenty-five years, exercising the utmost caution and industry. Nor evening nor morning was he ever idle. He assiduously aimed at the best possible rule, and hence his government was excellent and illustrious ; the Court and the country felt the deepest reverence for him, and the stillness of profound awe. A benevolent heart, and a benevolent administration were universally diffused ; in China proper, as well as beyond it, order and tranquillity prevailed, and the tens of thousands of common people were all happy. But in the midst of the hope that this glorious reign would be long protracted, and the help of Heaven would be received many days, unexpectedly, on descending to bless by his Majesty's presence Lwanyang [in Tartary], the Dragon Charioteer (the holy Emperor) became a guest on high "!

In 1820 the Emperor Taokwang ascended the Throne in pursuance of the will of his father, who to his dying day never forgot that he owed the seven last years of his life to Mienning's courage and skill. That prince, who adopted the title of Taokwang, was born in 1781, and was therefore thirty-nine years of age when he was proclaimed Emperor. Though a favourite of his father he was not a *persona grata* with the ladies of the harem, more especially with the concubine who had succeeded his mother in the Imperial dignity. During the lifetime of his mother there had been much ill-blood between these two ladies, and the first Empress is said to have died in a paroxysm of rage, caused by the aggressive conduct of her successor, who revenged herself on Prince Mienning for the many slights which she had endured, by imposing on him all the indignities which it was in her power to inflict.

In early life Taokwang had been passionately devoted to martial exercises, in pursuit of which he is said to have fortified his muscles by taking certain strengthening medicines, which were reputed to have destroyed his teeth and so to have given to his jaw the peculiar character which it possessed. In figure he was tall, lank, and hollow-cheeked, and of a dark complexion. His habits were quiet and retired, and he was not credited with any great talent for business. In after life, however, he proved himself quite capable of holding his own with his Ministers. One of his first acts showed his disapproval of the policy of his father, of whose wisdom he had proclaimed himself such an ardent admirer in his Edicts. He recalled Sung from his banishment in Ili, and gave notice to quit to the comedians and others to whom Chiach'ing had given such a hospitable welcome in the palace. The members of his father's harem were also sent home to their relatives, and his wife was proclaimed Empress.

Unfortunately "the evil that men do lives after them," and the result of Chiach'ing's lax and discreditable rule was to leave a heritage of woe to his successor. Pestilence, famine, and war dogged Taokwang's footsteps, and no more uneasy head ever wore a crown than his. The feeble hand of his predecessor had so weakened the authority of the law that stringent measures had to be adopted for the preservation of peace and order. The same spirit of misrule which he found prevailing in the provinces had extended beyond the frontier into those regions of Mongolia where K'anghsi had fought and conquered. Here the standard of revolt was raised by a chieftain named Jehangir, in the neighbourhood of Kashgar, where recruits, tempted by the reported weakness of the Chinese power, flocked readily to his ranks. At first all went well with the rebel, who took and occupied Kashgar, putting the Chinese garrison to the sword. But, as so often had happened in Chinese campaigns in Central Asia, the weight of men and steady perseverance of the Celestials ultimately carried the day, and Jehangir was taken prisoner and sent to Peking. There the traditional fate of all such rebels overtook him, and he was hanged, drawn, and quartered.

It will be remembered that during the reign of K'anghsi the Russian garrison of Albazin had been brought to Peking as prisoners, and had there remained living among the natives of the capital as fellow-citizens. At stated intervals the Czar's Government had been in the habit of sending unofficial envoys with sums of money for the maintenance of these colonists. A communication was in this way periodically kept up between these two Empires, and was still further fostered by the establishment by Treaty (1728) of a Russian college at Peking, where students studied for ten years the Chinese and Manchu languages. In the first year of Taokwang's

accession a certain Timkowski arrived at Peking on
this eleemosynary mission, and though the name of
foreigner stank in the nostrils of Taokwang, he was
allowed to remain until he had fulfilled his charitable
duties. The same tolerance, however, was not extended to the Portuguese officials employed in the
Astronomical Department at Peking, who, though
they had been allowed to remain by Chiach'ing, were
summarily dismissed by his successor.

Meanwhile, in that hotbed of rebellion, the island
of Formosa, disorders broke out and were quelled,
though with difficulty, partly by crushing cruelty and
partly by the seductive lure of official bribery. By
Chinese statesmen the islands and outlying districts
of the Empire are comparatively lightly esteemed,
and it is only when the soil of the Eighteen Provinces
of China Proper is tampered with that their patriotism is aroused. It required no great effort to hand
over Formosa and the Pescadores to Japan after the
recent war, but it might fairly be questioned whether
they would not have fought to the death for a single
province of the sacred eighteen. So it was on this
occasion, and both in Formosa and Hainan, where
there were simultaneous outbreaks, the Imperial
commanders patched up a peace without troubling
themselves to attempt to lay the foundations of any
lasting tranquillity. But a rising among the Miaotzŭ
tribes which occurred about the same time was a
very different matter. The Viceroy of the province
of Kwangtung was sent against them, and when he
failed through incompetence and cowardice, Hsi An,
Taokwang's father-in-law, was ordered to take the

field.   Fortunately for this chieftain, who neither in
a public nor private capacity bore a good character,
he was given the immediate command of Hunan
troops, the best fighting material in China.   With
these soldiers he was successful.   He harried the
Miaotzŭ, burnt their villages, and drove the survivors
to the mountain tops.   The tribes resisted for a time,
but at last made their submission, and received from
the hands of the conquerors the bitter terms which
are commonly meted out to defeated rebels in
Oriental lands.

Taokwang was no more fortunate in his private
life than he was in his public career.   The news of
the outbreaks above mentioned reached him at a
time when he was suffering from severe domestic
bereavement.   In 1831 he had to mourn the loss of
both his Empress and his only son.   Accounts differ
as to how the latter met his end.   That he was a
debauched and vicious youth all authorities agree in
affirming, and while by some it is said that his death
was due to opium smoking, it is also commonly
reported that he received his deathblow at the hand
of his father who, enraged at his misconduct, raised
his fist against him.

During these and other absorbing anxieties Taokwang had little time to pay any attention to the
English residents at Canton.   They were allowed to
pursue the somewhat uneven tenor of their way
without incurring any additional penalties from
Peking.   All their communications with the authorities passed through the hands of a committee of
native merchants, known as the Cohong, and any

written statement was on compulsion made in the form of a petition. Ladies were forbidden to reside in the settlement, and a permit, which cost from seventy to a hundred pounds, was necessary to enable a merchant to visit his family at Macao, the nearest place where it was possible for ladies and children to live. Notwithstanding these and countless other disabilities, the number of resident merchants steadily increased, and the shipping returns went up with corresponding certainty. It was plain, therefore, that the growing importance of the port would soon render it impossible that the existing state of things could be endured much longer, and an opportunity shortly presented itself of putting matters on a more satisfactory footing.

VIII

FOREIGN RELATIONS WITH CHINA

THE Charter of the East India Company, which had been granted by Charles I., was about to expire in April, 1834. The importance of the trade made it impolitic to renew the charter, and the Government therefore determined to take over the administration of affairs at Canton. The old order of things must, they felt, pass away, and they decided to emphasise this change by appointing a representative who, it was hoped, would be able to deal directly with the highest provincial authorities. Lord Napier was chosen for this very difficult post, and received a commission from the King dated Brighton, December 10, 1833, in which his "loyalty, integrity, and skill" were justly lauded. With Lord Napier were associated two officials as sub-commissioners. Lord Napier's instructions, which were drafted by Lord Palmerston, were precise. "Your lordship," so they ran, "will announce your arrival at Canton by letters to the Viceroy. In addition to the duty of protecting and fostering trade at Canton, it will be one of your principal objects to ascertain whether it may not be practicable to extend that trade to other parts of the Chinese dominions. It is obvious that with a view to the attainment of this object the establishment of direct communication with the Court of Peking would be most desirable."

Lord Napier's course was therefore laid plainly before him, and on arriving on the China coast he proceeded at once direct to Canton. At this act of presumption, as it was described, the mandarins were furious, and so serious a view did the Superintendent of Customs take of it, that he proposed to the Viceroy that the foreign trade of the port should be suspended in consequence. The Viceroy on his part refused to receive Lord Napier's letter announcing his arrival, and justified his conduct by stating that the great Ministers of the Empire were forbidden to hold communication with barbarians except on certain specified subjects. Hitherto, so argued the officials, the leading Englishman had been a Taipan, or head merchant, and there never had been such a thing as a correspondence to and fro with a " Barbarian Eye " (Minister). The attitude thus assumed by the local authorities was highly commended by the Viceroy, who considered that it manifested " a profound knowledge of the great principles of dignity."

The juncture at which Lord Napier arrived was an unfortunate one. The Government had been much alarmed at the drain of silver consequent on the foreign trade, more especially in opium, and a report had lately been made to the throne that 60,000,000 taels were annually lost to the Empire by the foreign

connection. Already there had grown up a pronounced opposition to the opium trade on the part of

OPIUM SMOKERS.

some of the highest officials, and during the reign of
Chiach'ing more than one memorial had been presented to the throne proclaiming the evils which

15

were supposed to result from the use of the drug. But however strong the feelings of individuals on the subject might be, interests were at work which militated against any direct action towards prohibiting the traffic. The use of the pipe had spread to almost every yamên in the Empire, and already large areas of the country were devoted to the cultivation of the poppy. In the province of Yunnan several thousands of chests of opium were produced annually, and in other provinces vast tracts were sown with poppy seeds. The drug had thus taken a hold upon the nation, and it moderates our views as to the injurious nature of opium when we observe that after so many years the evils arising from it are so difficult to trace. But at the time when the Charter of the East India Company was abolished, there was another and a stronger reason why the local authorities at Canton and elsewhere were either openly or privately in favour of the continuance of the traffic. During the reign of Chiach'ing opium was recognised as an article of trade, and paid duty at the rate of three taels per hundred catties (one catty equals 1⅓ lb.).

Subsequently, however, the trade had been declared illegal, and as it was plainly impossible to prevent the importation of the drug, a wide door was opened for the energy and daring of smugglers. These men were tacitly recognised by the local mandarins, who drew large though irregular incomes in return for their benevolent inaction. The natural result followed. While occasional censors exposed possible and impossible evils of opium smoking, and while the Emperor fulminated Edicts against the practice, the officials throughout the country, from the highest to the lowest, countenanced the importation of the "foreign dirt"; and in inland districts, where it was difficult to obtain supplies from the coast, native farmers profitably supplied the officials and people with the means of indulging in the pipe.

But though these influences led, in the face of Imperial Edicts, to a continuance of the opium traffic, the supercilious conceit of the Government induced them to put a stop to the legitimate trade of the port as a protest against what they were good enough to call the highly improper conduct of Lord Napier in forcing his way to Canton without having given due notice of his approach. The Minister and his country-men were, in consequence, kept virtually prisoners within the limits of the foreign settlement. The native servants in their employ deserted them, and the boatmen refused to carry either them or their goods. In this way matters came to a deadlock, and the Viceroy had the further insolence to issue a notice containing a series of regulations designed for the management of the "Outer Barbarians." Among these ordinances was one forbidding ships of war to sail into the inner seas of the Empire; another pro-hibited foreigners from "stealthily transporting muskets and cannon, or clandestinely bringing up foreign women or foreign sailors"; and yet another proclaimed that idly rambling about beyond the limits of the settlement could not be allowed for a moment. To this and other such documents Lord Napier deemed it advisable to utter a counter blast, and in a public notice to the Chinese merchants he

wrote, " The Merchants of Great Britain wish to trade
with all China on principles of mutual benefit; they
will never relax in their exertions till they gain the
point of equal importance to both countries, and the
Viceroy will find it as easy to stop the current of the
Canton river as to carry into effect the insane deter-
minations of the Hong."

In this stress of circumstances and anxieties Lord
Napier's health most unfortunately gave way, and he
retired to Macao for rest and further medical advice.
His departure from Canton was regarded as a triumph
by the mandarins, who at once signalised the event
by removing the embargo on trade. Unfortunately
the change from Canton to Macao was too late to
save Lord Napier's life, and he died there on October
11, 1834. Meanwhile the British merchants at
Canton had presented a petition to the British
Government praying that steps might be taken
effectively to open the Chinese Empire to trade,
and to place the foreign communities on terms of
equality with the merchants of the country. This
document was firmly and judiciously worded. The
writers recognised as clearly as we do the preposterous pretensions of the Chinese Government,
and even more clearly than we always have done,
the folly of attempting to propitiate the officials by
yielding to their demands.

In response to this document Captain Elliot was
appointed in 1836 to take up the duties vacated by
the death of Lord Napier. On arriving at Macao he
communicated with the Governor of Canton announcing his arrival, and asking for the usual permit

for admission to the provincial capital. But though the mandarins readily gave this permission, as they fully recognised the advantage of having a representative of the merchants with whom they could negotiate, they were yet in no way disposed to recognise Captain Elliot as anything more than a superior supercargo, and chose to insist that all communications from him should be in the form of *Pin*, or petitions. This claim was clearly inadmissible, and as Captain Elliot insisted on his right to use the forms commonly employed among civilised nations, matters came once more to a deadlock. Seeing that nothing would be gained by remaining at Canton, Captain Elliot retired to Macao ; all trade was then stopped, and the merchants who chose to remain in the settlement were confined within its limits.

Meanwhile a brisk discussion was carried on in the pages of the *Peking Gazette* on the vexed question of the Opium Trade. It was strongly held that it was impossible to prevent the importation of the drug, and that an advantage would be derived on all sides by legalising the traffic. The evils of smuggling were further enlarged upon by these advocates, and, as was afterwards argued by Lord Elgin when making the treaty of 1858, it was put forward that it would be far better to place the trade under official control than that it should be carried on by illicit means amid scenes of violence and strife. The opponents of this statesmanlike suggestion broke out into wild oratory against the evils of the habit, and affirmed that the English had deliberately introduced the " foreign dirt " into the country for the purpose of so

ONS WITH CHINA*

debilitating the people as to leave them incapable of
resisting the demands of the "Outer Barbarians."
This line of argument was only another version of a
remark made by the Emperor K'anghsi long before
the question of opium had arisen, namely, that "there
was cause for apprehension lest, in the centuries or
millenniums to come, China may be endangered by
collisions with the various nations of the West who
come hither from beyond the seas."

The Opium Question was, as events fully demonstrated, only used by the officials as a convenient
weapon with which to attack the foreigner. The
refusal of the Governor to receive communications
from Captain Elliot except in the form of petitions ;
the ridiculous regulations which he laid down for the
management of the merchants at Canton ; and the
sumptuary laws which it was attempted to enact for
their guidance—all point to the real object of the
mandarins, which was to drive the obnoxious foreigner
out of the country. There was something particularly hypocritical in the horror professed by the mandarins at the continuance of the opium traffic, when
we call to mind that along the entire coast-line of
China from Canton to Tientsin the drug was smuggled
openly by the officials and others ; and that it was
only in Canton and the neighbourhood that any
attempt was ever made to check the practice. The
mandarins made much of the number of foreign
schooners which landed opium along the coast. But
these compared with the native customs cruisers and
other vessels, which performed the same service, were
in number as one to many thousands. While the

Governor at Canton was professing righteous indignation at the villany of the English opium traders it was an open secret that his own son was daily smuggling cargoes in official vessels within his father's jurisdiction. Our sympathy with the protestors is seriously diminished by this evident insincerity, and by the consideration that, though, according to them, the practice of opium smoking had become general throughout the Empire, the energy of the merchants, the scholarship of the *Literati*, and the industry of the people, remained unabated. As we have already seen Taokwang's son was a habitual opium smoker, and it would have been more to the purpose if, instead of emptying all the vials of his wrath on the heads of the foreigners, the Emperor had employed real and vigorous measures against the practice which he denounced, against the smuggling of the drug by natives, and against the cultivation of the poppy which was already largely engaging the attention of native farmers.

It is impossible under the circumstances to regard the professions of the anti-opium Chinese as being genuine, and there can be no doubt that the Government deliberately chose to make a stalking horse of the trade for the purpose of effectively exciting popular feeling against foreigners. In pursuance of this policy, Taokwang appointed Commissioner Lin to proceed to Canton with orders to legislate on all questions in dispute between the local officials and the "Outer Barbarians." Within a week of his arrival, Lin, with that impetuosity which distinguished him, issued a peremptory order to the foreign merchants,

over whom he had of course no control, charging
them to deliver up all the opium in their possession.
So powerless were the traders, and so long had they
been habituated to the dictatorial and violent methods
of the Chinese, that they were induced to surrender
over a thousand chests of the drug, in response to
the Emperor's demand. This quantity was promptly
declared to be insufficient by the Commissioner, who,
at the same time, sent a message to Mr. Dent, one of
the leading merchants, asking him to meet him for
consultation at one of the city gates. Former experience had shown that to yield to such an invitation
was simply to place the guest in the hands of the
mandarins as a prisoner and a hostage, and Mr.
Dent, therefore, naturally declined to venture into Lin's
clutches unless that official would give him a written
guarantee that he would be allowed to return at
pleasure to the settlement. Fortunately the Commissioner had sufficient honesty to decline to pledge
his word with the deliberate intention of breaking it,
and Mr. Dent refused to place himself in a position
of so much danger. Although it was now plainly
impossible that the relations between the two countries could be continued on peaceable lines, Captain
Elliot returned to Canton in the vain hope of being
able to arrange a *modus vivendi.* His re-appearance
on the scene caused much excitement among the
officials, and orders were instantly given to beleaguer
the foreign settlement. The narrow lanes and out-
lets leading into the city were walled up ; all communication with the outer world on the land side was
cut off ; and steps were taken to prevent foreign

vessels from leaving the anchorage. The position was one which might well have been brought to a head by a more determined and resourceful man than Captain Elliot, to whom the only remedy which presented itself was that of yielding to the Chinese demands. With unfortunate acquiescence he issued a proclamation ordering the English merchants to deliver up the supplies of opium in their possession. Recognising the weakness of the opponent with whom he had to deal, Lin had further the progressive assurance to publish a notification stating that so soon as one fourth of the opium was handed over, the servants who had been ordered to desert the settlement should be allowed to return to their foreign masters; that when half was given up the passage boats should again be made available; and that when three-quarters had been surrendered, trade should be resumed. He further had the insolence to threaten that if these conditions were not complied with within three days the supply of fresh water would be cut off, that in yet another three days all food would be denied to the merchants, and that the last degree of severity would attend a further delay.

In these circumstances and in obedience to Captain Elliot's circular 20,283 chests of the drug were handed over to the Chinese authorities by British merchants. As long experience has shown, to yield to Chinese bluster entails only the advance of still further demands, and the infliction of still greater indignities. In the present instance Lin rewarded Captain Elliot's complacency by claiming the right to punish Europeans for crimes committed on Chinese soil, and

expressed the greatest indignation when after a
sailors' riot in which one or two Chinese lost their
lives, his demand to have the English disturbers of
the peace handed over to him was refused. The
unwarrantable tone which he had taken up from
the first made it hopeless to attempt to carry on
relations with him, and he further provoked war by
calling on his countrymen to arm themselves against
the foreigners. The inevitable result was not long
delayed, and on November 3, 1839, a naval engagement was fought at Chuanpi, in which a number of
Chinese junks were sunk and destroyed.

This event in no way shook Lin's faith in himself
and his countrymen, and with hardened assurance he
issued a proclamation in which he claimed to possess
such an intimate knowledge of the divine intentions
that he was able to announce that the Imperial dynasty continued to repose under the direct protection
of Heaven, and that all those who should be presumptuous enough to oppose its will would inevitably be
overtaken by Celestial vengeance. Events which
were now hurrying on must have convinced him, if he
had been capable of reasoning, that at all events the
god of battles was on the side of the big ships of the
enemies of his master. But not only had Lin's
policy been unfortunate in bringing defeats on the
Chinese but his commercial strategy had had exactly
the opposite result to that which was intended.
The destruction of the foreign opium at Canton
led to a vigorous revival of the trade, smugglers
multiplied, and the traffic flourished as it had never
flourished before in spite of the fact that three

native victims were sacrificed on the altar of Lin's patriotism.

In the summer of 1841 Sir Gordon Bremer, the English Admiral, blockaded Canton, and then sailed northwards to attack Tinghai, the chief town on the island of Chusan. The result was an engagement such as those with which the late war has made us familiar. The defence of the fortifications was little more than momentary, and under cover of night the garrison took to their heels. From Ningpo the fleet sailed to Taku at the mouth of the Peiho, where Captain Elliot was met by Kishên, the Governor-General of Chihli. This mandarin was one of the leading officials in the Empire, and his career is so suggestive of the vicissitudes which attend Oriental administrators that it is worth relating. The son of an official who obeyed Ch'ienlung, he was given an appointment when barely twenty years of age. Seven years later he was made Secretary to a provincial Governor; and at the age of forty he was appointed Viceroy of Szech'uan, and in 1830 he was promoted to the viceroyalty of the Metropolitan province. So far his fortunes had been in the ascendant, but reverses quickly followed. When, as will be shortly seen, Lin was disgraced, Kishên was sent as Commissioner to Canton with the additional office of Viceroy of the two Kwang provinces. Foreign policy has in many cases been the rock upon which the careers of Chinese statesmen have been wrecked. And it was so with Kishên, who so deeply incurred the anger of his Imperial master that he was sent in chains to Peking there to answer for his crimes.

After a formal trial he was condemned to hard
labour in the province of Ili, and to the confiscation
of his property. This last penalty was a cruel
blow to the offender, for, like many mandarins who
have been long office-holders, he had great possessions. Years afterwards the Imperial wrath was so
far mitigated that a partial pardon was granted to
him, and he was later appointed to the office of
Assistant Resident at Yarkand.

His association with Captain Elliot at Taku was
the first step towards his fall, although at the moment
he unquestionably gained a temporary advantage
over his opponent. The arrival of the fleet at the
mouth of the Peiho had alarmed the Court, and
Kishên's first object was to induce Captain Elliot to
relieve the Imperial fears by returning to Canton.
With the same mistaken complacency which had
induced the English Minister to listen to Lin's commands, he complied on this occasion with Kishên's
wishes, and without having advanced matters in the
least degree he agreed to sail southward, and once
more to discuss negotiations on the familiar ground
at Canton. There matters had been going from bad
to worse. Lin had been devoting his energies to
raising troops and preparing to defend the city
against all comers. He had issued fiery proclamations offering liberal rewards for any Englishman
brought in dead or alive, and for any vessel which
the troops might chance to capture. A native army
which had been collected near Macao had been
attacked and dispersed with ease and rapidity by a
small British force, and a state of active warfare had

been brought about. Such were the results of the
impertinent bluster with which the now disappointed
Commissioner had attempted to influence the political
situation. The news of the existing unfortunate
state of affairs in the South no sooner reached Peking
that Taokwang ordered Lin to return to Peking
"with the speed of flames." As the Emperor wrote,
and with justice, "You," he said, addressing Lin,
"have but dissembled with empty words, and so far
from having been any help in the affair you have
caused the waves of confusion to arise, and a thousand interminable disorders are sprouting; in fact,
you have been as if your arms were tied, without
knowing what to do; it appears, then, that you are
no better than a wooden image."

The change of *venue* to Canton was at first unproductive of any good results in the negotiations. The
terror which had inclined the Emperor to sanction
discussions when the British fleet was at the mouth
of the Peiho changed into bluster and self-sufficiency
when the whole length of the Empire separated him
from his hated foes, and it was not until Sir Gordon
Bremer had taken several forts leading to Canton
that Kishên at last consented to treat for peace.
After the manner of all his tribe he yielded at once
and completely to pressure, and agreed, with protesta-
tions of sincerity, to accept Captain Elliot's proposals
for a convention. These were that the Island of
Hongkong should be ceded to the British crown, that
an indemnity of six million dollars should be paid in
consideration of the opium destroyed, that official
intercourse should be conducted between English and

Chinese officials on terms of international equality, and that the trade with the British at Canton should at once be resumed. It was further agreed that on the fulfilment of these conditions the Island of Chusan and the fort of Chuanpi should be restored to China, and that at the same time the English prisoners at Ningpo should be granted their liberty. Among these unfortunates was Captain Anstruther, R.A., who had been kidnapped at Chusan and carried off to Ningpo, where he had been imprisoned in a cage. Fortunately these captives were eventually released, though the treaty which had been agreed to by Kishên was torn up by the Emperor's orders. At this time the position of foreigners at Canton was well-nigh unendurable. All trade was stopped, the merchants were strictly confined to the foreign settlement, and any attempt to cross the boundaries of that narrow territory was accompanied by risk to life and limb. Even without this indiscretion their liberty was in jeopardy. The English chaplain, for instance, was seized in the settlement and carried off to the native city, where he was imprisoned in a loathsome cell for four months.

Meanwhile the Emperor was breathing out death and slaughter against the foreign devils. By a special edict he ordered troops to march upon Canton and Chusan, accompanying his commands with strict injunctions that they were to " destroy and wipe clean away, to exterminate and root out, the rebellious barbarians," and at the same time rewards of 50,000 dollars were offered for the capture of Captain Elliot, Sir Gordon Bremer, and Mr.

PRISONERS WEARING THE "CANGUE."

Morrison. In these circumstances Captain Elliot saw only one course open to him. Diplomacy had failed, and all that was left for him to do was to place the matter in Commodore Bremer's hands. That officer at once attacked the Bogue forts, which had already suffered capture at the hands of British sailors on several occasions. In this case the operation was repeated with ease, although three thousand Chinese soldiers stood for the defence of the position. With the same agility as that they displayed in the late war with Japan, the Chinese soldiers no sooner found their forts untenable than they took to their heels. On the following day the fleet proceeded up the river, and as they had done to the Bogue forts, so did they to the fortifications which lie in the higher reaches in the neighbourhood of the city.

These rapid successes disturbed the Chinese complacency, and as a symptom and a consequence of this perturbation, the Prefect of the city met the advancing hosts with a flag of truce, which covered a petition for a three days' suspension of hostilities. This was granted, and as no satisfactory arrangement resulted from it, the fleet moved up still nearer to Canton, capturing without the slightest difficulty every fort and camp on the way. This further advance again drew the Prefect, who appeared with the familiar white flag, and who again secured a truce, during which it was arranged that the trade of the port should be carried on as usual. The breathing time thus given to the Chinese was diligently utilised by them in collecting forces and materials in the vain hope of being able to overwhelm the barbarians. The most redoubtable troops of the Empire were hurried by forced marches to Canton, and the appetite of the men for foreign blood was sharpened by an Imperial Edict, in which the Emperor stated that it "behoved them to make a severe example of the foreign devils."

Kishên, who up to this time had shown a conciliatory spirit in his negotiations with Captain Elliot, adopted, probably from policy, the tone of his Imperial master, and memorialised the Throne in a paper in which he spoke of the " perverse craftiness of the presuming foreigners who have shown themselves to be obstinate and impracticable in every way." By his instigation there were collected by the middle of May, 1841, in the neighbourhood of Canton, fifty thousand troops, most of whom, however, were comparatively innocuous, being unarmed. The attitude of the people, however, now became so threatening, that Captain Elliot directed all foreigners to provide for their safety by leaving the settlement. This proceeding precipitated matters, and the Chinese, who had made ample preparations for an onslaught, immediately opened a night attack upon the British fleet. Sir Hugh Gough, who had taken command of the troops, and Sir Fleming Senhouse, the newly-arrived Admiral, at once took matters in hand, and promptly prepared to meet the emergency by investing the city. The Chinese made a show of resistance to the attacking force, but declined coming to close quarters, and eventually bargained to ransom the city on the following terms. They agreed to pay down 6,000,000 dollars, and they

16

undertook that the three Imperial Commissioners who had been sent to annihilate the foreign devils should march with their troops to a distance of sixty miles from the city; that they should pay compensation for the property which had been looted from the factories; and that the Chinese troops should evacuate the city.

The maintenance of a permanent peace had now become impossible, and the English Government, deeming it essential that the present very unsatisfactory condition of things should be finally put an end to, appointed Sir Henry Pottinger to succeed Captain Elliot as Minister, and Admiral Sir William Parker to take command of the fleet. Pottinger's instructions were precise. He was ordered to discard the existing system of dealing with the provincial authorities, and to open relations with the Imperial Government. The attitude, however, of the Emperor and his Ministers at this juncture was not such as to make it at all probable that they would be disposed to listen to reason, and it at once became apparent that it would be necessary to teach them wisdom by the hard hand of experience. Without wasting time with empty negotiations, therefore, Sir Henry placed matters in the hands of the Admiral, who, realising that to go northward was to approach the Court, set sail on August 21, 1842. The first point of attack was the city of Amoy, which yielded in the ready way in which towns garrisoned by Chinese troops are in the habit of submitting to superior forces.

After leaving a small garrison to hold the captured fort, the fleet sailed for the Island of Chusan, and proceeded at once to take the town of Tinghai. In two hours from the time when the first shot was fired the town was in our hands, and the Admiral and General were at liberty to sail across to the mainland to attack Chênhai (Chinhai). The British troops having landed from the ships, marched on this city in three columns, and the Chinese, having been unwise enough to venture out from the protection of their walls, were without any difficulty scattered to the four winds of heaven. The Chinese generals, in their ignorance, had deemed this place to be so strong that any attack made on it by the English barbarians would, in their opinion, be doomed to disaster. The result, therefore, came as such a surprise to Yukien, the Viceroy of the province, that in order to avoid the personal consequences of his Imperial master's displeasure, he committed suicide. The feeling of compassion with which we should otherwise be inclined to regard the end of Yukien's career is mitigated by the recollection of the extreme brutality with which he treated two English prisoners, one of whom was by his orders flayed alive and then burnt to death.

The possession of Chénhai was important as opening the way to the large and populous city of Ningpo, whither Sir Hugh Gough at once advanced. To his surprise he found the town practically undefended, and occupied its defences without being called upon to strike a blow. In the first instance the arrival of our troops alarmed. the people to such an extent that they carried off into the surrounding country their valuables and women concealed in baskets, and receptacles of all kinds, including coffins. When, however, it became evident that our ways were not as their ways, and that our rule was guided by justice and humanity, the remaining people gladly opened their shops, and eagerly competed for the privilege and advantage of supplying our troops with the necessaries of life. The news of these disasters—the fall of Amoy, Tinghai, Chênhai, and Ningpo—produced great alarm at Court, and two high officials, Ilipu (Elepoo) and Kiying were Imperially commissioned to provide for the defences of the rich and important city of Hangchow, near Ningpo. It so happened, however, that it did not enter into Sir Hugh Gough's plan of campaign to interfere with the Commissioners in their very comfortable quarters, and instead of marching on Hangchow he moved northwards, and, in passing, took the city of Tzuki on his way to Wusung, at the mouth of the Shanghai river. Here again the same condition of things that had prevailed at Chênhai and Ningpo were found to exist. Considering the defences of Wusung as impregnable, it had been deemed quite unnecessary to fortify Shanghai, and so soon, therefore, as the English troops had driven the Chinese from the ramparts of Wusung, Shanghai lay at their mercy.

But it was plain that though these successes had created alarm at Peking, it would be necessary to advance further inland in order to bring sufficient pressure to soften the hardened heart of the Emperor Taokwang. Sir Henry Pottinger, therefore, directed the Commanders to advance up the Yangtsze-kiang

A RIVER SCENE.

to Nanking, the ancient capital of the Empire. In course of this expedition it was considered indispensable to capture the important town of Chênkiang (Chinkiang), which stands on the southern shore of the Great River, at a distance of about seventy miles from Nanking. This town was strongly walled and fortified, and was further protected by entrenched camps outside the city. The garrison within the town consisted of twelve hundred Manchu soldiers, eight hundred Mongols, and about the same number of Chinese troops, while the encampments were held by three thousand men from the neighbouring provinces. The bombardment of the walls not effecting a breach as was anticipated, the soldiers placed scaling ladders against the walls and swarmed on to the top. At first the Chinese showed a certain amount of courage in defending the city, but, quite in accordance with their usual manner, they no sooner felt that they were overpowered than they scattered in all directions. On this occasion the loss of life was terrible. Not only were the soldiers mowed down by our troops, but in their despair thousands of them committed suicide, while whole families were ruthlessly murdered to prevent them falling into the hands of the English. The scenes witnessed were heartrending. The houses were full of the dead and dying, and the wells were choked with the bodies of women and children who had either thrown themselves in, or been thrown in to save them from capture.

On the opposite side of the river stands the town of Iching, which was visited in advance by one of the ships of the fleet. On becoming aware, in answer to inquiries, that the Commander had no intention of bombarding the town, the people vied with each other in showing attentions to the foreign devils, and actually, while the magistrate and magnates were entertaining the English captain and officers at dinner, the sound of the guns which were dealing out death and destruction at Chênkiang broke in on the feast, without in any way disturbing the revellers. So complete is the absence of all patriotic feeling among the strange people of " that jest and riddle of the world " China! With no undue delay before Chênkiang the fleet continued its voyage to Nanking, opposite which it arrived on the 9th day of August, and whither the Imperial Commissioners Ilipu and Kiying hastened to meet the English Plenipotentiary. Niu Kien, the Viceroy of the province, had already had some experience of English soldiers and sailors. He had saved his life by a rapid stragetic movement to the rear when Wusung had fallen, but even after this incident he was still disposed to regard with contempt the " rebel " troops of England, and professed himself determined to defend Nanking to the last gasp. The appearance of the fleet before the walls, however, had a modifying effect on his warlike ardour.

Fortunately, also, in the cause of peace Kiying and Ilipu quickly appeared on the scene, and in company with Niu Kien formed a triumvirate to whom the Emperor had entrusted the conduct of the negotiations. In reply to a preliminary report of these officials, the Emperor issued a decree full of lofty

platitudes and condescending phrases, but which to
all intents and purposes amounted to a full con-
currence in the views they had expressed on the
necessity of making peace.   Ilipu from the first had
worked in the cause of amity, and had on previous
occasions shown his goodwill by giving liberty to
English captives who had fallen into his hands.
With these plenipotentiaries Sir Henry Pottinger
immediately opened negotiations, and the weariness
of the discussions which followed were pleasantly
diversified by a series of entertainments, which were
given by the high-contracting parties.   Finally, after
some delay, a treaty was concluded by which it was
fairly hoped that a firm and durable peace might
be established between the two Empires.   By the
terms of this document it was agreed that the four
additional ports of Amoy, Foochow Foo, Ningpo, and
Shanghai should be open to trade, that Hongkong
should be ceded to the British Crown in perpetuity,
and that the sum of 21,000,000 dollars should be
paid to the victors in the war—6,000,000 as the
value of opium destroyed by Lin at Canton,
3,000,000 on account of debts due to British subjects, and 12,000,000 on account of the expenses
which had been incurred.   The treaty was signed
on the 29th of August, 1842, and though in the
negotiations the Chinese had displayed a conciliatory
spirit, they at the same time made no attempt to
conceal their desire to get rid of the Barbarians'
ships from the inner waters of the Empire.   Indeed,
in the edict already spoken of, the Emperor, in a
lordly manner, had issued an order " that the whole

of the Barbarian vessels were to leave the Great River by the 14th of September." To secure this end it was necessary that there should be no delay in ratifying the treaty at Peking, and with unexampled celerity the document was despatched to the capital, received the Imperial signature, and returned to Nanking. The date fixed by the Emperor for the departure of the ships was, however, somewhat exceeded, and it was not until the end of October that the fleet once more assembled off Tinghai in Chusan. This island was to be held as a security for the indemnity due, and a garrison of two thousand men was left for its defence. A further force of one thousand men was stationed at Amoy, and Hongkong was protected by seventeen hundred troops.

China is such an immense and dislocated country that events which occur in one portion of its domain in no way necessarily affect the remaining provinces. Thus it was that while the British forces had taken city after city in Central China, and a Treaty of Peace had been concluded between the two Empires, affairs in Canton remained unaffected by the war, and unpacified by the peace. Riots were, both before and after the treaty, of frequent occurrence, the city remained forbidden ground for foreigners, and large levies of militia were collected in the neighbourhood with the avowed intention of driving the foreigners into the sea. By a happy chance Ilipu, after the conclusion of the treaty at Nanking, was sent as Imperial Commissioner to this unruly district. The experience he had gained in the Central Pro-

vinces as to the superiority of foreign methods of
warfare led him to recognise the folly of the anti-
foreign efforts that were being made by the local
officials. Belonging to the Imperial kindred, and
having won laurels in his kinsman's service, he was
enabled to take a strong line on this occasion, and he
did not hesitate therefore to issue a proclamation in
which he announced that " it has now been arranged
by treaty with England that . . . as long as English
foreigners live quietly, and attend to their business,
our people may not disturb or molest them." Unhappily Ilipu did not live long enough to consolidate
the friendly *régime* which he had inaugurated. His
health was failing when he reached Canton, and on
the 4th of March, 1843, he died, in the seventy-
second year of his age.

In distant Formosa the anti-foreign feeling had
been conscious of no such check as that it had thus
received at Canton, and Sir Henry Pottinger was
met on his triumphant return to Hongkong with the
dispiriting news that upwards of a hundred British
sailors had been ruthlessly beheaded by the island
authorities. Inquiries confirmed the truth of the
report, and the few survivors who escaped the fate of
their comrades bore pathetic witness to a dismal tale
of intense cruelty on the one hand, and of courageous
endurance on the other. Sir Henry Pottinger at
once demanded reparation for this wrong, and Iliang,
the Governor of Chehkiang, was sent as Imperial
Commissioner to investigate the circumstances.
Iliang who, like Ilipu, was of the Imperial kindred,
took a reasonable view of the situation, and through

his instrumentality the Formosan officials who had authorised the massacre were degraded, and sent to Peking for punishment.

The treaty having been concluded, there remained only for Sir Henry Pottinger to arrange the regulations of trade. This was no easy task, as the Chinese in their usual manner, having agreed to the terms of treaty, devoted all their energies to whittling away its provisions. At length, after much discussion, and no little active diplomacy, the task was completed in July, 1843, and in the following June Sir Henry sailed for England, leaving to his successor, Sir John Davis, the management of affairs.

The new plenipotentiary soon found that in accepting the office of Superintendent of Trade he had entered upon a sea of troubles. At Canton the officials and people still gratified their hatred of foreigners by offering them continued and constant insults. They had been so long accustomed to tyrannise over the foreign devils, and to consider that their existence at Canton depended only on favour, and had no relation to right, that they were quite unable to accommodate themselves to the new order of things as laid down by the treaty. They declined to recognise the ex-territorial clauses, and on the occasion of a Chinese subject being accidentally killed by an Englishman they demanded that the slayer should be given up to the tender mercies of Chinese justice. This, of course, was refused, and the opportune arrival of Kiying served to suppress the popular ferment which was rapidly approaching the point of danger. The conclusion of the treaty at

Nanking having inspired other nations with a desire to follow in our footsteps, a French minister, and subsequently an American colleague appeared at Canton to negotiate with Kiying treaties for their respective countries. Under the sobering influence of Kiying's arrival and these negotiations, matters for a time proceeded more quietly at Canton, and the new ports were opened to trade without let or hindrance. It was once said to the writer by a Frenchman who was comparing the position of his countrymen with that of the English in China, "We come to China with our ideas, you with your merchandise." One form which French ideas have ever taken in China has been the furtherance of the Roman Catholic religion, and the first prominent step taken by Louis Philippe's representative was to urge on the Imperial Government the propriety of restoring churches and buildings which in preceding years had been destroyed by fanatical mobs. With a consideration which, so far as it went, was admirable, the Emperor granted this request, but accompanied his concession by peremptorily forbidding foreign missionaries from further propagating the doctrines of their faith.

The prostration which has always afflicted China after a foreign war has in most cases, as is natural, been instrumental in encouraging the turbulent and disaffected portions of the people to riot and rebellion. Thus the secret societies which had been crushed for the time being by the vigorous hand of Ch'ienlung began again to gather strength after the war of '42. The Triad Society, which was destined to be productive of the T'aip'ing Rebellion, became actively aggressive, and with its well-known motto, " Dethrone the Ch'ings and restore the Mings," led a rebellion which broke out in the southern and central provinces of the Empire. The example set by this Society was followed by the "White Lily" sect in Northern China, and at the same time, and probably from the same cause, the Mahommedans in distant Kashgaria broke out into revolt against the "Son of Heaven." With promptitude and vigour Tao-kwang despatched troops to meet these several emergencies, and we cannot but wonder at the inefficiency of the different rebel forces when we recollect that they were conquered and suppressed by troops armed only with bows and arrows, or with the scarcely more formidable gingalls and spears. However, the fact has to be acknowledged that the several victories were complete, and so comparatively potent became the commands of the Emperor, even in furthest Central Asia, that at his word twelve thousand families submitted to transportation from their native Kashgaria to the province of Ili.

" It is difficult work being a mandarin nowadays," once remarked a high Chinese official, and certainly in the 'forties it was no light task to hold office at the treaty ports. At Canton difficulties were constantly arising, and a brutal assault on a party of Englishmen when on a visit to the neighbouring town of Fatshan brought matters to a climax at this port. Sir John Davis, considering that a standing protest against such conduct should be made once and for all, requested the admiral and general commanding, to make reprisals at the source of the mischief. With

admirable promptitude the commanders led their
forces up the Canton river, and having once again
captured the Bogue forts and the other defences in
the way, took up a position opposite the city walls.
In his memorial to the throne on this occasion
Kiying expressed his supreme surprise at the appearance of the British force, and complained of the tone
and attitude adopted by the English plenipotentiary.
But though thus protesting, he considered it wise to
yield to Sir John Davis's demands, and definitely
agreed that the city of Canton should be opened to
foreigners in two years' time from that date (6th of
April, 1847); that Englishmen should be at liberty
to roam for exercise or amusement in the neighbourhood of the city; that a church should be erected;
and that a site should be granted for building premises on the opposite side of the river. At about
the same time a somewhat similar outrage occurred
at Shanghai. Three missionaries who had visited
a town in the vicinity were attacked by a number
of junkmen belonging to the vessels which were
anchored at the port. Mr. Consul Alcock (afterwards Sir Rutherford Alcock) at once demanded
reparation for the outrage, and not receiving it,
requested the captain of H.M.S. *Childers* to prevent
all or any of the fourteen hundred grain-junks and
fifty war-junks, which were about to sail for Peking,
from leaving the anchorage until the culprits should
be given up. Commander Pitman was equal to the
occasion, and with his single ship held this vast fleet
in check. Meanwhile Mr. Alcock despatched Mr.
Harry Parkes on board H.M.S. *Espiègle* to Nanking,

to lay before the Viceroy a formal complaint against the local authorities. The effect of these measures was excellent. The rioters were seized and punished, reparation was made, and the lesson was duly taken to heart by the natives, who for years afterwards showed a friendly attitude towards Europeans. The English Government of the day disapproved of Davis's action at Canton, fearing the outbreak of another war, but Alcock escaped, censure. It is unquestionable that Sir John Davis's action was precipitate, and might in other circumstances have been conducive to a breach of the peace. But it is to be remembered that he was dealing with old offenders, and with men of a turbulent and unruly spirit. The Shanghai people, on the contrary, are, as a rule, peaceable, and in this case, as the result showed, Alcock's more constitutional treatment of the affair was crowned with complete success. But similar action under like circumstances at Canton would have been as futile as diplomatic pressure without the mailed fist has always been.

The Governor of Canton at the time was the redoubtable Yeh, who, after acting in opposition to foreigners, and to ourselves especially, for ten or twelve years, was made prisoner by Sir Harry Parkes, and ended his days as an exile in Calcutta. Under the influence of this man things went from bad to worse within his jurisdiction. Like most Chinamen, he had no idea of administration in its truest sense. His one remedy for all political offences was the execution ground. Popular rights he ignored with even more than Chinese indifference, and thus aroused a spirit of antagonism among his subjects, which made itself felt in every part of the province. Pirates swept the coast, seizing on every merchant junk which they encountered, until from the coast of Tongking to the neighbourhood of Foochow merchants ventured on voyages at the risk of their lives and goods. In the interior of the province the Triad Society spread its noxious branches, and at the port of Macao the anti-foreign feeling of the people found vent in the murder of the Governor, Signor Amaral. The people within the city still showed a determined opposition to admitting foreigners within their gates, and unfortunately found support for their antagonism from the Emperor himself, who proclaimed in an edict that, "That to which the hearts of the people incline is that on which the decree of Heaven rests. Now the people of Kwangtung are unanimous and determined that they will not have foreigners enter the city, and how can I post up everywhere my Imperial order, and force an opposite course upon the people." These utterances were quite sufficient to stiffen the backs of the Cantonese, and encouraged the inhabitants of other towns to enforce the same exclusive policy. Near Canton stands the town of Hwangchukki, which has always borne an evil repute for violence. Supported by the Emperor's apparent approval, the natives of this place determined to emphasise their adherence to the policy of the provincial capital whenever occasion should arise. They had not long to wait. On an ill-fated day six Englishmen made an excursion to the smaller city.

17

The mob at once rose, and with brutal violence murdered them all.   This was an outrage which might well have led to a renewal of hostilities, and which probably would have done so had Yeh been in supreme command.   The Imperial Commissioner Kiying, however, was still on the spot, and with wise and immediate action ordered the capture of the offenders, who in due course were tried at Canton, and beheaded for their crime.

In a country such as China there is always a certain amount of discontent floating about which needs but the appearance of a leader to crystallise it into a body ready for action.   As we have seen already, there had long been a feeling of more than ordinary unrest among the Cantonese, and there now arose a man who was destined to give expression to the prevailing disloyalty, and in the course of his exploits to shake the Empire to its very base. In a village in the neighbourhood of Canton there was born of a Hakka, or emigrant family, a youth possessing the name of Hung Hsiuts'uan, who, being endowed with abilities, and with a considerable amount of ambition, desired to place his foot on the rungs of the official ladder.   With this object in view he studied the wayworn classics of his country, and presented himself at Canton as a candidate for examination.   But the fates were against him, and his failure is accounted for by some who attribute it to the fact of his parentage —the Hakkas being looked upon as a pariah class —and by others to his want of scholarship.   On the occasion of his first visit to the provincial capital in 1833 he chanced to meet an evangelist, who interested him for the time being, but whose doctrines soon lost all salutary effect upon him. Four years later, however, he again appeared as a candidate, and again met the Scripture reader, to whose teachings, as was subsequently proved, he listened attentively. Returning to his home for the second time unsuccessful, he fell ill with what appeared likely to prove a fatal malady. As he tossed upon his bed in his delirium he saw many strange and weird visions. He listened to the music of the spheres. He was visited by ominous beasts, and he had a vision of the Almighty, who entered his room and placed a sword in his hand, with which he commanded him to exterminate the ruling powers, at the same time foretelling that there lay a great future before him. For forty days he remained in this delirious condition, and at the end of that time he arose endowed with strength, and with a firm determination to execute the behests of his heavenly visitor.

It is more than probable that Hung really believed in his divine mission. It is no uncommon thing for hysterical youths, especially when under the influence of pseudo-religious fanaticism, to place faith in visions and prophetic utterances. In his case also it is plain that the illness which overtook him was of a purely nervous character. But notwithstanding their neurotic source his convictions were strong, and he was able to impress those about him with a belief in his views. By degrees, first of all in his own household, and afterwards in the neighbourhood, followers gathered

to him, and he and they attempted to spread the
doctrines of the Shangti Hui, or the " Association of
the Almighty," which he established.   The term *Hui*,
however, alarmed the authorities.   It is the common
title taken by the Secret Societies which so largely
infest the Empire, and which are so abhorrent in
the eyes of the mandarins.   They therefore declared
the association to be treasonable, and Hung found
it advisable to drop the epithet.   Though discarding
the obnoxious word, however, he proceeded at once
to associate himself with a far more treasonable
corporation than the Shangti Hui, viz., the " Triad
Society," and so active did his followers become in
this cause that the Government, in alarm, despatched
three Imperial Commissioners from Peking to stamp
out the movement.   Of these three men Tahungah,
who had ordered the massacre of the British sailors
in Formosa, was chief.   With him were associated
Saishangah, a notorious profligate and Prime
Minister, and Hsingte.   Though armed with plenipotentiary powers these three courtiers carefully
refrained from coming to close quarters with
Hung's troops, who, full of iconoclastic zeal,
destroyed the Buddhist temples in the country-
side, and threw down the idols.

But more serious matters than these anti-religious
ebullitions speedily demanded the attention of the
rebels.   Circumstances had driven them to take up
arms against the Empire, and having captured two
market towns in their neighbourhood, they ventured
to attack the city of Lienchow.   This place they took
without much difficulty, and in succession, Taitsun,

Yunganchow and Nanning Fu, the port which it is now proposed to open, fell into their hands. These successes created a panic at Canton, and Yeh made strenuous efforts to strengthen the defences of the city in anticipation of a siege. In a memorial presented to the throne at this time, a Canton official described the state of the province in these words, "the whole country swarms with the rebels. Our funds are nearly at an end, and our troops are few ; our officers disagree and the power is not concentrated. The commander of the forces wants to extinguish a burning waggon load of faggots with a cupful of water. . . . I fear we shall hereafter have some serious affair, that the great body of the people will rise against us, and that our own followers will leave us." After the above victories, Hung was gratified by experiencing the truth of the common saying that nothing succeeds like success. Following on each capture troops flocked to his standard, probably actuated more by the desire for plunder than from any political convictions. At all events they added to his strength, but the movement being rather of a destructive than constructive nature, it was necessary that he should constantly lead his new recruits forward, and having exhausted the resources of one district, seek fresh woods and pastures new, elsewhere. With this object he marched northwards instead of against the provincial capital, having first proclaimed his authority by issuing degrees purporting to have been communicated to him by the Heavenly Father. Crossing the northern frontier of Kwangtung he marched into Hunan, and striking the Hsiang river followed down its course taking all such cities as were not strong enough to resist him. Up to this point Hung had not met a single Chinese commander possessing any courage or a modicum of military ability. He was now to enter into conflict with a general of a very different stamp, and who was destined in the end to bring the rebellion to ruin.

On the approach of the rebels Tsêng Kwofan, the father of the Marquis Tsêng who lately represented China at the Court of St. James, threw himself into Changsha, the capital of the province, and with all speed set to work to fortify the town and to equip a defending force. The success of his tactics was complete. Thrice the T'aip'ings attacked the walls and thrice they were beaten back by the actively led garrison. This successful resistance having made it plain to the " Heavenly King " that the capture of the city was beyond his powers, he raised the siege, and leaving that and the important town of Hsiangtan in Imperial hands, continued his way to the Yangtsze-kiang. In quick succession Yochow, Wuchang and Kiukiang were taken by his troops, and at the last named place he successfully withstood a siege conducted by Tsêng Kwofan, who had followed close on his heels.

It is easy to believe that after these undoubtedly great successes Hung's belief in his divine mission became engrained in him, and in March, 1853, he published a book of Celestial Decrees, containing a series of revelations which to an unprejudiced observer have all the appearance of gross profanation. One of these documents contains the following passage : " The Heavenly Father addressed the multitude, saying, ' O my children ! do you know your Heavenly Father, and your Celestial Brother ? ' To which they all replied, ' We know our Heavenly Father and Celestial Elder Brother.' The Heavenly Father then said, ' Do you know your Lord, and truly ? ' To which they all replied, ' We know our Lord right well.' The Heavenly Father said, ' I have sent your Lord down into the world to become the Celestial King (T'ienwang, the title which Hung had adopted) ; every word he utters is a Celestial command to which you must be obedient ; you must truly assist your Lord and regard your King ; you must not dare to act disorderly, nor to be disrespectful. If you do not regard your Lord and King, every one of you will be involved in difficulty.'"

With such strange and unnatural incitements Hung secured the allegiance of his ignorant followers, and with full confidence of success led them to the attack on Nanking, the ancient capital of the Empire. Though the garrison was a large one, composed partly of Manchus and partly of Chinese soldiers, only a half-hearted defence was made. Without much difficulty a gate was blown up, and the T'aip'ings rushing into the breach secured possession of the walls. The miserable garrison, too cowardly to defend an exceptionally strong position, had the further baseness to plead—they pleaded in vain—for their lives at the hands of the conquerors. The T'aip'ings had not learned, and never did learn, the lesson that mercy blesses those who give, and without hesitation they made a clean sweep of their abject foes. It is said that out of twenty thousand Manchu citizens not a hundred were left to tell the tale of the slaughter. As a T'aip'ing said to Mr. Consul Meadows at the time, " We killed them all, to the infant in arms ; we left not a root to sprout from ; and the bodies of the slain we cast into the Yangtsze."

Having thus established himself in the second city of the Empire, the " Heavenly King " made some efforts towards introducing a system of administration among his followers. As self-assertion always exercises a powerful influence in the assumption of authority, he determined to adopt the Imperial purple and to proclaim himself Emperor of China, at the same time announcing that his Dynasty was to be known in the future as the T'aip'ing Dynasty. In support of this new dignity he severally appointed four of his principal supporters as Kings of the North, East, South, and West. These very incomplete efforts towards establishing a Government seem to have exhausted his exertions and ability, and he sank from this time into obscurity. He was never subsequently seen beyond the gates of his palace, where he was waited upon by women only, and where, in the midst of very questionable surroundings, he gave himself up to a life of indolence and self indulgence. In these circumstances the management of affairs naturally drifted into the hands of those who were able and willing to accept the responsibility of office, and practically the four kings exercised complete and irresponsible authority in all matters connected with the new dynasty. The Eastern King, who seems to have followed more closely than the others in the steps of his liege lord, was, or pretended to be, subject to trances, in one of which ecstatic conditions he received a " message from the Almighty " ordering him to rebuke and chastise the T'ienwang for his treatment of the women within the palace. Yang, who appeared to be by no means loth to exercise the delegated authority thus granted him, took his chief to task, and even induced him to prostrate himself to receive the chastisement decreed by the Most High. This humiliation was considered to be sufficient, and Yang, instead of inflicting the merited stripes, proceeded to remonstrate with him on the gross impropriety of kicking and otherwise ill using his concubines and female attendants. For a time the T'ienwang submitted to these rebukes, and even proclaimed Yang to be the personification of the Holy Ghost. But at last the yoke became unendurable, and on a charge of treachery which ill became his divine character, Yang was tried, condemned, and beheaded.

The position which the T'aip'ings had thus secured on the Yangtsze-kiang naturally induced foreigners, who had watched the progress of the movement with interest and some concern, to desire to gauge accurately the objects and power of the rebels. It was plain that if, as then appeared likely, they were destined to overthrow the ruling dynasty, it would be an advantage to be brought into contact with some of their leading men and to have some idea of the policy which they were likely to pursue.

Governor Bonham was among the first to visit
Nanking with this object in view, but beyond
satisfying his curiosity and exciting a superficial
interest among the rebels, the visit proved to be
singularly unproductive of results.

So far, however, fortune had smiled on the T'ienwang, but it was obvious that so long as Peking was
beyond his grasp he must be considered to have
failed of the goal which was his ultimate aim. At a
council of war held at Nanking this subject was
debated, and it was finally determined that the die
should be cast, and that an expedition should be
sent against the northern capital. In March, 1853,
a column started northwards on this adventurous
endeavour. So completely had the terror of the
T'aip'ing name influenced the garrisons of towns in
the neighbourhood of the great river that without let
or hindrance the column marched triumphantly as
far as K'aifung Fu, the capital city of Honan. Here
a bold front was shown to the invaders, who, finding
the capture of the city to be beyond their power,
raised the siege, as their manner was in all similar
cases, and continued their march northwards.
Without meeting with any serious opposition they
traversed the province of Shansi and captured the
town of Shênchow (Shinchow) in the Metropolitan
province. Thence they advanced to Tsinghai,
within twenty miles of Tientsin, and there entrenched themselves. The march had been daringly
and well executed, and it reflects infinite discredit
on the Imperial forces that so much had been
accomplished at so small a cost. In a six months'

raid the rebels had captured twenty-six cities, and
had finally established themselves within a hundred
miles of Peking. But the effort had been made in
defiance of the true principles of warfare. They had
no supports, and like all Oriental armies they were
absolutely without commissariat, being dependent
only on plunder for their daily bread. Movement
was therefore essential to their existence, and after
a short rest at Tsinghai, they marched to the attack
of the neighbouring city of Tientsin. Here they
found General Sankolinsin, who subsequently commanded the Imperial forces against the Allies, in
possession, and failed to make any impression on
the fortifications garrisoned by the troops of this
veteran. This check was fatal to the expedition.
To have marched on Peking with Tientsin untaken
in their rear would have been an act of full-moon
madness, and the general in command wisely determined rather to force his way back to Nanking than
to advance to certain ruin.

With some difficulty and considerable loss he man-
aged to cut his way through the intervening Imperial
host, and eventually succeeded in bringing a remnant
of his forces to the capital of his chief. Another
column which had started with the idea of supporting the first expedition, on hearing of the retreat
from Tsinghai, retired with alacrity and retraced its
steps to Nanking. It was in connection with these
expeditions that Li Hungchang, who has since
filled so prominent a place in Chinese politics, first
stepped on to the stage. Feeling that it was a time
when China might reasonably expect every man to

do his duty, Li, who was still residing under the parental roof at Hofei in Anhui, raised a regiment of militia to contest the progress of the northern column. Whether from a disinclination to meet the enemy face to face, or from the fact that he was too late in the field to do so, certain it is that his military tactics consisted in following in the track of the rebels and harassing their rear-guard so long as they remained within the frontier of Anhui. Though there was nothing striking in these military man-œuvres of the future Viceroy, his patriotic exertions were of sufficient value to attract the attention of Tsêng Kwofan, who from that time forth became his constant patron and friend.

The non-success of this attempt on Peking was a serious blow to the T'aip'ing cause. Not only had the rebels lost prestige by it, but it had deprived them of fresh districts from which they might recruit their ranks and plunder necessaries. In this dilemma they were driven to enlarge their borders on the banks of the great river, and from Ichang to Yang-chow they soon reigned supreme, if it is possible to speak of such banditti as reigning at all. Adminis-tration can hardly be said to have entered into their system, and the fiendish barbarity with which they desolated cities and villages has even to the present day left its mark on some of the fairest provinces of China. Nanking itself was at this time ruled without any regard for law and right, and presented a sordid scene of Oriental debauchery accompanied with all the intrigues and murders which usually belong to such a state. No man's life was safe for five minutes,

and a reign of terror took possession of the followers
of the Dynasty of Great Peace (T'aip'ing). As was
inevitable, this state of things at headquarters
affected by degrees the efficiency of the troops in the
provinces, and the Imperialists, taking heart of grace
at the disorder which prevailed, recovered a number
of cities with almost as much ease as that with which
the T'aip'ings a short time before had made themselves masters of them. Gradually the forces of the
T'ienwang were confined between the cities of Nanking and Anking on the Yangtsze-kiang, both of
which were closely beleaguered.

THE SECOND CHINA WAR

WHILE these things were going on in the central provinces of the Empire, movements unconnected with the T'aip'ings, but doubtless produced by the unrest occasioned by these truculent disturbers of the peace, broke out in various parts of the Empire. Canton, that hot-bed of disaffection, was in a state of ferment, and Yeh's energies were taxed to the utmost to preserve even the apparent supremacy of the Emperor. In Szech'uan and Kweichow bands of rebels appeared who desolated country districts, and held walled cities in defiance of the Imperial commanders. It was while the country was thus seething with discontent that Taokwang, whose health had for some time been failing, became seriously ill. The Chinese are firm believers in signs in the skies. To them a comet presages disturbance in the Empire and misfortunes to the ruling house, while an eclipse of the sun forebodes an equally ominous future. Curiously enough in nearly similar circumstances to those of the present year an eclipse of the sun was foretold for the Chinese New Year's day (A.D. 1850).

This combination of time added unnatural terrors to the portent, and in his superstitious terror Taokwang had the supreme imprudence to order that New Year's Day should be postponed for twenty-four hours. It is probable that the omen, as is so often the case, was the means of working its own fulfilment, and before many weeks were over Taokwang became, at the age of sixty-nine, a "Guest on high," leaving his distracted country to his fourth son, who adopted as his Imperial title the epithet of Hsienfêng, or "Complete Abundance."

Why Hsienfêng was chosen to succeed to the throne does not clearly appear. By the law of succession in China the dying Emperor has the right of nominating any one of his sons whom he may please as his successor, quite irrespective of the rule of primogeniture. Taokwang was blessed with eight sons, the next one to Hsienfêng being Prince Kung, whose name has long been prominently before the public as President of the Tsungli Yamên. A still younger brother was Prince Chun, the father of the present Emperor Kwanghsü. At the time of his assuming the Imperial crown Hsienfêng was nineteen years of age and with the blessing of youth combined the headstrong disposition which is commonly supposed to belong to it. The old councillors Kiying and Muchangah, who had served his father long and well, he incontinently dismissed from office, and appointed in their places men of far less ability, but who possessed in his eyes the qualification of being violently anti-foreign. The influence of these changes soon made itself felt in the provinces, and prompted the Foochow officials to imitate the example of the Canton mandarins and to refuse to admit foreigners within the walls of the city (1850). At the same time six Pailous or Gates of Honour were erected at Canton to the Viceroy Hsü for the part he had played in preserving the streets of the city from the polluting

ENTRANCE TO THE TSUNGLI YAMÊN, PEKING.

presence of foreigners. Altogether there were many signs that Hsienfêng's position would be by no means a bed of roses, and Nature combined with foreigners to disturb the peace of the Emperor. A famine occurred in the country round Peking which carried off many thousands of the people; a destructive earthquake swept over the province of Szech'uan;

while fires of unusual magnitude and ferocity destroyed whole districts.

It is part of the Imperial etiquette of China that the ruling Emperor should see in any convulsions of nature a reflection on his own conduct, and of that of the officials under him. And in this spirit Hsien-fêng, in face of the calamities which surrounded him, issued an edict in which, after belauding his "profoundly benevolent and exceedingly gracious" parent, he proceeded to depreciate himself and his officers in these words. "We, although not laying claim to the title of an intelligent ruler, will at the same time not lay the blame unnecessarily upon our Ministers and officers ; but we just ask them in the silent hour of the night to lay their hands upon their hearts, and see if they can allow themselves to rest satisfied with such a state of things ; if they do not now reproach themselves most bitterly for their remissness, they will, at some future period, be involved in evils which they will not be able to remedy. We, therefore, publicly announce to all our officers great and small, that if from henceforth you do not change your habits, and if you pay no regard to this our decree, we are determined severely to punish you according to the utmost rigour of the law, without allowing the least indulgence or permitting rigour to be tempered by clemency ; for the necessity of the present crisis demands it." Judging from appearances these admonitions fell on deaf ears, for no attempt was made to reform the glaring abuses which existed and still exist in the country.

At Canton the question of admittance into the

city was still straining the relations between Sir
George Bonham and Yeh. The promise that had
been given by Kiying that the gates should be
thrown open to foreigners in 1849 was not fulfilled by
his successor, who, as time went on, declared his
opinion that as the season had passed when the concession was to have taken effect, the promise must be
considered as abrogated. And he further protested
against yielding the privilege, on the ostensible
ground that the people were of so unruly a nature
that to grant it would be to incur serious danger
both to foreigners and to the Imperial authorities
themselves. This has always been a favourite excuse
with the Chinese when a request has been advanced
by foreigners with which they find it difficult to
comply. It was for many years the traditional
reason given for not allowing the establishment of
foreign Legations at Peking. But, as at Canton,
where on gaining possession of the city the people
proved to be perfectly friendly, so when in 1861 Sir
Frederick Bruce and his staff took up their residence
at the capital they were received with every civility
by the populace. It was, however, felt to be essential
that the point in dispute at Canton should be cleared
up once and for all, and when Sir John Bowring
succeeded Sir George Bonham in 1852 he took up the
question with energy. Writing to Lord Clarendon
he said, " I am still of opinion that, until the city
question of Canton is settled, there is little hope of
our relations being placed on anything like a satisfactory foundation ; and, moreover, that the settlement of the said city question might be brought

about without any risk or danger to our great
interests in China. In my matured judgment it has
been delayed too long."

Sir John Bowring's first step in the controversy
was to notify his appointment as Superintendent of
Trade to Yeh and to invite him to an interview.
Yeh's reply was characteristic of the man. He con-
gratulated Sir John on his appointment, and then
went on to decline the invitation on the ground that
his time was fully occupied in making dispositions
for the campaign against the rebels. Being further
pressed on the point he had the impertinence to propose that Sir John should meet him at a packhouse
outside the walls of the city. Sir John naturally
declined this proposal and it was while foreign
relations were in this condition that Yeh put forward
a request which could only have been made by a
Chinaman. While with one hand he dealt out scorn
and derision against foreigners, with the other he
asked their help to assist in the suppression of
the rebels who were troubling his peace. It is
needless to say that this also was declared to be
impossible.

It was while matters were in this condition that
Parkes (afterwards Sir Harry) was appointed Consul
at Canton (1856). His well-known ability, courage,
and perseverance peculiarly qualified him for the
post at this crisis, and throughout the whole quarrel
he ably supported Sir John Bowring in the line he
was adopting with regard to the great question in
dispute. Yeh had refused to receive Parkes, and,
though willing to keep up an official correspondence

with him, declined to change his main attitude in the
least degree. Led by their truculent governor, the
people of the city heaped constant insults on the
European merchants, and handbills were publicly
circulated throughout the city calling on the people
to expel the intruders. One of these documents
concluded with the following words : " Hereafter,
therefore, whenever any barbarian dogs come within
our limits, we ought, by calling together our families,
to maintain the dignity of our city (or province), and,
bravely rushing upon them, kill every one. Thus
may we, in the first place, appease the anger of
Heaven, in the second give evidence of our loyalty
and patriotism, and in the third restore peace and
quiet in our homes. How great would be the happiness we should thus secure !" Parkes remonstrated
vehemently with Yeh against the continued publication of this manifesto, but got no redress, though the
effect of it was presently illustrated by a violent and
most unprovoked attack which was made upon two
Englishmen in the neighbourhood of the city.

Affairs had now reached a point in which it was
impossible for Englishmen to preserve their dignity
and to maintain peace, and an outrage which occurred
almost immediately after the assault just referred to,
was of so flagrant a nature that it ended in a declaration of war. An English lorcha named the *Arrow*,
flying the British flag, was boarded when at anchor at
Whampoa by Chinese officials, who hauled down the
flag and threw it with contempt on the deck. So
soon as the news of this outrage reached the British
Consulate, Parkes wrote to Yeh remonstrating on the

action of his subordinates, who added to their guilt by carrying off the twelve men constituting the crew. Yeh's answer was, as might have been expected, evasive, but Parkes was persistent, and stated in good round terms that he would be satisfied with nothing less than an ample apology and the instant and public return of the captive crew. On this, in the true Chinese spirit, Yeh sent back nine of the men, and claimed two of the others as malefactors and one as a witness; after, however, boxing the compass of evasion, he was compelled eventually to deliver up the twelve sailors, but in so underhand a way did he effect the manumission that Parkes refused to receive them, and repeated his demand that they should be returned as openly as they had been carried off. Yeh still remaining recalcitrant, Sir John Bowring authorised the capture of a native vessel by way of reprisal. As this produced no beneficial effect, he recognised that matters had again reached that stage when, as had so often happened, it was necessary to place the affair in the hands of the Admiral. The British naval forces had become so accustomed by repeated experience to capturing the Bogue forts and the other defences of the city that Sir Michael Seymour moved almost automatically to the position which it was necessary to take up, and with no difficulty forced his way to Canton after having made himself master on his voyage up the river of the fortifications in which the Chinese so foolishly continued to trust. Towards the end of October (1856) the Admiral's ships appeared opposite the walls of Canton, and Sir Michael

Seymour, after having warned the inhabitants that he was about to inflict punishment on their obstinate governor, opened fire on the offender's yamên. Even this measure failed to bring Yeh to reason, who aggravated his offences by issuing the following ill-judged proclamation : " The English barbarians have attacked the provincial city, and wounded and injured our soldiers and people. Their crimes are indeed of the most heinous nature. Wherefore I hereby distinctly command you to join together to exterminate them, and I publicly proclaim to all the military and people, householders and others, that you should unite with all the means at your command to assist the soldiers and militia in exterminating these troublous English villains, killing them wherever you meet them, whether on shore or in their ships. For each of their lives that you may thus take you shall receive, as before, thirty dollars. All ought to respect and obey, and neither oppose nor disregard this special proclamation."

It was plain that with the issuer of this document there could be no exchange of compliments, and the Admiral, having shelled out Yeh's yamên, breached the walls of the city with his guns, and landed a party to accentuate the helpless condition of the town. Yeh's vaunted preparations to destroy the foreign devils proved, like all his boasts, to be of no value when brought to the supreme test. With little difficulty, and with only a small loss of men, the wall was gained, and the possession of a city gate was secured. Through this portal, which was now freely opened for the first time to foreigners, Sir

Michael Seymour entered with Parkes and visited the ruins of Yeh's yamên. Unfortunately the force at the admiral's command was quite insufficient to occupy the city effectively, and he therefore withdrew his men to the ships, and at the same time wrote home an urgent appeal for five thousand men to enable him to inflict the necessary punishment on the obstructive governor.

It was plain to Lord Clarendon, who was at this time Foreign Secretary, that the matter was of sufficient importance to make it necessary that a man with higher rank than that of Sir John Bowring should be on the spot to carry on the necessary negotiations. The choice of the Cabinet fell upon Lord Elgin, and though the natural kindliness of his disposition made him too often unwilling to inflict well-merited punishment, and inclined him to listen with too ready an ear to the excuses and apologies of the authorities, he yet proved himself an able ambassador and a skilful diplomatist. With as little delay as possible he sailed for China, taking with him the force for which Sir Michael Seymour had asked. In June, 1857, he arrived at Singapore, where his progress was stayed by an urgent letter from Lord Canning, the Governor-General of India, informing him of the outbreak of the Indian Mutiny, and begging him to divert his troops to help in the suppression of a revolt which threatened British sovereignty in the great peninsula. With rare unselfishness Lord Elgin at once acceded to the request, and, as events proved, he, by so doing, rendered eminent service to the Indian Government. Meanwhile the withdrawal of Sir Michael Seymour's troops from the city of Canton inspired the Chinese with fresh though deluded courage, and gave Yeh an opportunity of triumphantly announcing that the English, by a sudden and piratical attack, had succeeded in breaking into the city, but had been driven off by the indomitable courage of his men.

On Lord Elgin's arrival in Hongkong in July, he found that, though Canton had been evacuated, a series of minor engagements had been carried on during the winter, and that in May Sir Michael Seymour had conducted a number of attacks on the war junks which had collected in the creeks and rivers in the neighbourhood of the city. Happily at this time Commodore Keppel (now Sir Harry) was on the station, and after numerous junks had with his help been destroyed in the neighbourhood of Canton, it was determined to proceed to inflict an exemplary punishment on the war-ships collected at the town of Fatshan. Sir Michael Seymour himself headed the advance, while Captain Keppel had the command of the smaller boats, which were intended to deal more directly with the junks. Meanwhile a force of marines landed, and carried a battery above the town, the Chinese retiring sulkily, but without making any serious resistance. The fighting on the river was, however, of a more stirring kind. The fire from the junks was constant and fairly well directed, in spite of which the English boats, though hit time after time, went on. Keppel, at the head of a force of about five hundred men, took in the position at a glance, and, imitating the tactics of Nelson at

Trafalgar, charged into the middle of the fleet, and broke the centre. He himself, followed by the men of his boat, boarded the largest junk, out of which the Chinese sailors fled with alacrity as the Englishmen appeared upon deck. In this instance flight was, however, not altogether to be attributed to cowardice. They had, as it proved, lighted a slow match connected with the powder magazine, and Keppel's men had only just retired from the deserted ship when she blew up. So far a complete victory had been gained. A number of junks had been given to the flames, others had been taken as spoil, while a few only had escaped up the intricate waters which surround Fatshan. Though his loss of men had been considerable, and though a decisive victory had been achieved, Keppel, thirsting for fresh laurels, was minded to attack and take the town of Fatshan. Opposite that city a fleet of junks, whose fire was unusually well-directed, was formed in a serried line. Keppel's boat was sunk under him, and though he again succeeded in destroying the fleet, his hand was stayed, for the Admiral, deeming further operations to be dangerous, gave the signal to retire. These disasters to the Chinese arms made no impression upon the obdurate Yeh, who amused his Imperial master with a grotesque travesty of the engagements fought, and described with some approach to humour how "Elgin passes day after day at Hongkong, stamping his foot and sighing."

But it is ill jesting when the enemy is at your gates, and Yeh was soon to discover that Lord Elgin was not a foe at whom it was safe to laugh. The

English Ambassador, on arrival, had notified his presence to Yeh, and had set forth his demands, which were, roughly speaking, the complete fulfilment of all the treaty conditions so far as Canton was concerned, and the payment of an indemnity for the British losses sustained, owing to the action of the Canton authorities. This letter Yeh affected to treat with indifference, and had the coolness to suggest that the trade of the port should be revived on the old conditions, and that each party in the dispute should bear their own losses. There being no sign of a just appreciation of the position in the answer of this inveterate obstructionist, Lord Elgin presented an ultimatum on Christmas Day, 1857, giving him forty-eight hours for the evacuation of the city by his troops. To this communication Yeh vouchsafed no answer, and the forty-eight hours having elapsed, Sir Michael Seymour seized Honan, and prepared for an assault on the city. With a merciful consideration for the non-combatant citizens, Parkes issued, and personally distributed, proclamations warning the people that their city was about to be attacked, and explaining the circumstances which had led to this extreme measure. Captain Hall, R.N., assisted Parkes in this work of mercy, and happened " in one of his rapid descents to catch a mandarin in his chair not far from the outer gate. The captain pasted the mandarin up in his chair with the barbarian papers, pasted the chair all over with them and started the bearers to carry this new advertising van into the city. The Chinese crowd, always alive to a practical joke, roared."

On the morning of December 28th the ships opened
fire, and the next day an assault was made at three
different points of the walls. The result was the
repetition of the old story. The Chinese made no
serious defence, and in an hour and a half the city
walls were in our hands. Probably Yeh hoped that
Sir Michael Seymour would retire, as he had retired
before, but at all events he made no sign. For the
first few days it was not deemed advisable, for fear of
complications, for the troops to venture into the
narrow and crooked lanes of the city, but as the
Chinese showed no symptoms of surrender, detachments were subsequently moved into the town. No
resistance was offered, and Pikwei, the Governor, was
taken prisoner in his yamên, while the provincial
treasury was seized. A considerable amount of silver
was there found, and with the help of coolies, who
were picked up in the street, and who readily volun-
teered for the work, it was safely carried off to the
English camp. The capture of Pikwei was satisfactory, but the great object of the search was for the
offending Viceroy. Parkes, who had of late been his
great opponent, heading a search party commanded
by Captain Key, sought everywhere for him. At
length his hiding-place was discovered. He had
taken refuge in a small yamên in the south-west
portion of the city. Thither the search-party hurried,
and as they entered they found the rooms crowded
with mandarins, who were hastily packing up their
worldly goods preparatory to flight. In answer to
Parkes' inquiries for Yeh, a mandarin stepped
forward and declared himself to be the object of

their search. Parkes, however, who had seen a
portrait of the Viceroy, put this devoted follower
aside, and hastened with true instinct into the back
part of the yamên.   There he arrived just in time to
see a corpulent mandarin struggling to climb over
the wall at the rear of the yamên.   He at once
recognised his prey, and a sailor, catching the would-
be fugitive by the pigtail, made a captive of him.

An investigation of Yeh's boxes revealed many
things, and amongst others the ratified treaty with
Great Britain, which had evidently been considered
too insignificant to be deposited in the archives of
Peking—a strange commentary on the value attached
to treaties by the Chinese Government.   It was
plainly impossible that, after all that had passed, Yeh
should be allowed to remain at large, and he was
therefore placed on board ship, and carried off to
exile in Calcutta, where he eventually died.   A
characteristic incident occurred while he was being
taken to the wharf at Canton.   On his way through
the streets, escorted by his foreign captors, the coolies
laughed and jeered at the fallen condition of their
former oppressor.   It is probable that few men have
made themselves more detested than Yeh.   His
cruelty was excessive, and he is said to have executed
a hundred thousand rebels during his Viceroyalty of
four years.   A day or two before the assault on the
city, undeterred by the difficulty of his foreign policy,
he sent four hundred of these evildoers to the
execution ground, and, in the minds of the people,
his memory will long be associated with all that is
brutal and savage.   Yeh, having thus been disposed

of, it was necessary that arrangements should be made for the government of the city. Pikwei was re-established as governor, and a commission of three, consisting of Parkes, Colonel Holloway, of the Marines, and a French naval officer, was appointed to administer affairs. For three years, under the sway of these officers, a just and equitable rule was substituted for the tyranny which had up to that time disgraced the administration of justice in the city. The change was fully appreciated by the natives, who, for the first time in their existences, had their property guarded and their lives protected.

This important matter having been arranged, Lord Elgin was free to deal with the larger question of our relations with China, and, as a preliminary step forwarded a letter to the Chief Secretary of State at Peking, stating the course events had taken in the south, and declaring the concessions which he demanded before peace could be re-established. To this communication he received from his correspondent the following reply, which was addressed not to him but to the Viceroy of the Two Kiang Provinces. " I have perused the letter received, and have acquainted myself with its contents. In the ninth month of the year (1856) the English opened their guns on the provincial city (Canton), bombarding and burning buildings and dwellings, and attacked and stormed its forts. . . These are facts of which all foreigners are alike aware. The seizure of a Minister and the occupation of a Provincial City belonging to us, as on this occasion has been the case, are facts without parallel in the history of the past. His

Majesty the Emperor is magnanimous and considerate. He has been pleased by a decree, which we have had the honour to receive, to degrade Yeh from the Viceroyalty of the Two Kwang Provinces for his maladministration, and to despatch his Excellency Hwang to Kwangtung as Imperial Commissioner in his stead, to investigate and decide with impartiality; and it will of course behove the English Minister to wait in Kwangtung, and there make his arrangements. No Imperial Commissioner ever conducts business at Shanghai (Lord Elgin had proposed a meeting at this place). There being a particular sphere of duty allotted to every official on the establishment of the Celestial Empire, and the principle that between them and the foreigner there is no intercourse, being one ever religiously adhered to by the servants of our Government of China, it would not be proper for me to reply in person to the English Minister. Let Your Excellency therefore transmit to him all that I have said above, and thus his letter will not be left unanswered," &c.

This communication left little hope for the continuance of peaceful negotiations, and Lord Elgin determined to proceed to the Peiho, from which coign of vantage he, however, again wrote to the Chief Secretary, advising him that he was ready to receive any properly accredited plenipotentiary for the discussion of matters in dispute. With their usual discourtesy the Emperor's Government despatched three Commissioners of very inferior rank, and quite unendowed with the necessary powers to treat. Lord Elgin naturally declined to communicate

with such men, and, rightly considering their appointment an additional provocation, he requested Sir
Michael Seymour to assault and take the Taku forts.
This was no difficult task, and the way being now
effectively open, Lord Elgin proceeded up the river
to Tientsin.

The capture of the Taku forts, which had been
armed according to the most approved methods of
Chinese military science, disconcerted the Peking
Government not a little, and the necessity of
appointing commissioners with plenipotentiary powers
was forced on the stolid intelligence of the Emperor's
advisers. In an edict issued on June 1st the
summary dismissal of the former envoys was announced, and the appointment of Kweiliang and
Hwashana, both officials of high standing in the
capital, to confer with Lord Elgin at Tientsin was
made public. The approach of the British troops to
the neighbourhood of the capital influenced in a
marked degree the attitude of the Commissioners,
who at once assumed a friendly air, and discussed
the matters in dispute in a most conciliatory spirit.
While negotiations were in progress Kiying, who it
will be remembered took a prominent part in the
arrangement of the Nanking Treaty, suddenly
appeared upon the scene with secret orders to
induce Lord Elgin, by all the means in his power,
to sanction the withdrawal of the British troops from
the river. The proposal was too preposterously
Chinese to be listened to for a moment, and Kiying
returned to Peking to announce his failure, and to
meet his death. The unfortunate envoy was at once

thrown into prison, and as an act of grace was allowed to strangle himself in his cell, instead of being decapitated on the execution ground. After much discussion a treaty was signed by which it was agreed that the Queen might appoint a Resident Minister at Peking ; that in addition to the five ports already open to trade, the ports of Newchwang, Têngchow, Formosa, Swatow, and Kiungchow in the island of Hainan should be opened as Treaty Ports ; and that the traffic in opium should be legalised. This Treaty was signed on the 26th of June and received the Emperor's ratification on the 4th of July. But though the deed was thus signed, sealed, and delivered, the Commissioners, before the ink was dry that testified their agreement to the clause, used their best endeavours to postpone the condition which gave the Queen the right to appoint the Resident Minister at the Court. The old familiar arguments were once more furbished up to do duty on this occasion. Lord Elgin was assured that the people of Peking were turbulent and unruly, and that the advent of a Minister with his staff within the walls of Peking would give rise to outrages and riots, which the Government would be unable to prevent, and which would embitter the relations between the two countries. Lord Elgin so far yielded to the entreaties of the Commissioners as to agree that for the time being the right should be waived, and that it would be used only temporarily in the following year, when it would become necessary to exchange the ratifications.

But while the words of Kweiliang and Hwashana

were smoother than butter, war was in their hearts, and at the very moment when they were agreeing to the treaty with warm professions of friendliness, they were making every arrangement for renewing the campaign against the hated foreigners so soon as the occasion should offer. This compact having been ostensibly completed, and there being nothing further to detain Lord Elgin in the north, he returned to Hongkong, where he found that though the people of Canton were showing an amicable attitude towards the foreign garrison, the mandarins were doing their utmost to stir up strife, and were again offering rewards for Barbarian heads. In this savage barter a sliding scale was introduced, which varied from a small sum for the life of a soldier to as much as 30,000 dollars for Parkes, dead or alive. From a mistaken desire to keep the peace, the garrison had hitherto been confined within the city walls, and liberty was thus given to the neighbouring villagers to concentrate forces and establish camps, preparatory to an attack on the British. It was well known that a number of these associations were within the immediate neighbourhood of the city, and it was eventually thought desirable to employ expeditions to dissipate the forces of these would-be disturbers of the peace. A successful expedition of this kind was made against the "ninety-six" villages on the north of the city, and Shektsing, a place of considerable strength, was carried after some show of opposition on the part of the local troops. The effect of this sortie was most wholesome, and an armed visit to the formerly riotous town of Fayuan, not only did not meet with opposi-

tion, but was cordially received.   Even in those days
the importance of the West River, which has lately
been opened to trade, was appreciated by Parkes and
others, and at their instigation it was determined to
explore in force the waters of that important stream.
Again the expedition met with a ready reception, and
successfully explored the river as far as Wuchow Fu,
the highest town on its banks which has yet been
opened as a Treaty Port.   The effect of these military
parades surpassed expectation, and reacted so favourably on the streets of Canton that they became as
safe as the thoroughfares of London.

X

THE WAR OF 1860

IN the following year (1859) it became necessary to send to Peking an ambassador to exchange the ratifications of the treaty, and Lord Elgin's brother, Mr. Bruce, who was chosen for the office, arrived at Shanghai in due course. He had been warned by Lord Malmesbury, the Foreign Secretary, that the Chinese would probably use every endeavour to dissuade him from going to the capital, and he was instructed to insist at all costs on this clause of the treaty being fulfilled. He had no sooner landed on the wharf at Shanghai than the truth of Lord Malmesbury's words became apparent. Kweiliang and Hwashana were already waiting for him, in the vain hope of being able to persuade him to forego his purpose. At the same time reports reached him that warlike preparations were being made at Taku to prevent his passing up the Peiho. His duty, however, was plain, and by an arrangement with Admiral Hope, who commanded on the station, a considerable fleet accompanied the Ambassador to the mouth of the Peiho. On reaching the anchorage,

Mr. Bruce despatched an interpreter with a letter addressed to the commandant of the fort, announcing his arrival, when it at once became plain that the warlike rumours which had lately filled the air were well founded. The interpreter found the mouth of the river studded with heavy iron stakes, while huge chains were stretched across its waters from shore to shore. The guns of the forts were screened by mats, but it was plain that they were there in full complement and were well manned. The crowd that came down to the wharf to meet the boat, refused to allow the interpreter to land, but a man who appeared to be in authority, promised that by the morrow the stakes should be removed so as to admit the ships into the river. No dependence was placed on this man's word, more especially as it was abundantly obvious that the Chinese meant to fight.

On the following day Admiral Hope, with a force of eleven vessels including gunboats, steamed towards the river's mouth. Some of the stakes had already been removed by H.M.S. *Opossum*, but the booms remained, and the leading gunboats no sooner struck these obstacles than the guns from the forts poured a storm of shot and shell upon them. So terrible was the fire that two gunboats were quickly sunk, and all were more or less seriously damaged. The Admiral was wounded, and many of the officers and men were killed. It being plainly impossible to force the passage by water, a detachment consisting of marines and engineers was landed in the hope that they might be able to capture the forts by storm. With desperate gallantry they struggled to

make their way through the deep mud which lay on
the waterside of the forts. At every step they sunk
above their knees while the troops from the walls poured
a destructive fire upon them. The scaling ladders
were broken by the fire, the men's rifles were in many
cases choked with mud, and wide ditches half full of
water added a further difficulty in the way of their
enterprise. Darkness fell while they were in this
predicament, and reluctantly they were obliged to
retire to their boats. In this engagement three
gunboats were lost, and three hundred men were
killed and wounded. It being plain that to renew
the attack with a thus diminished force would be
inexcusable rashness, the fleet returned to Shanghai
to await re-enforcements. The news of the defeat of
the English was received with exultation at Peking,
and exercised an unfortunate influence on the natives
at the Treaty Ports. In England it produced fierce
indignation, and by all parties it was recognised that
it would be necessary to enforce on the Chinese the
lesson that treachery, in dealing with a friendly
power, is an act of barbarism, and must inevitably
meet with punishment. As the Minister of France
who had also a treaty in his pocket requiring ratification had equally with Mr. Bruce been refused
admission to the Peiho river, the two Governments
agreed to make a joint invasion of the "Middle
Kingdom." Shortly after this arrangement had been
come to, that is to say in March, 1860, Mr. Bruce
presented an ultimatum to the Chinese Government,
calling upon them within thirty days to make reparation for the treacherous attack at the Taku forts,

and further to fulfil both the letter and the spirit of the
treaty. The reply to his communication was made
in the same circuitous way in which the answer had
lately been made to a somewhat similar letter from
Lord Elgin. A Grand Secretary of State replied to
the Viceroy of the two Kiang provinces, and directed
that official to forward a copy of the despatch to Mr.
Bruce. The language of the reply was marked by
more than usual Chinese hauteur, and ignored altogether the obligations which Mr. Bruce attempted
to fasten on the Government.

Meanwhile, Sir Hope Grant, who had been
appointed to command the British force, arrived
at Hongkong, at the head of an army of thirteen
thousand men. The French contingent, consisting of
seven thousand rank and file, and commanded by
General Montauban, arrived about the same time.
So soon as the arrangements of the campaign had
been completed the allied forces sailed northwards
and rendezvoused at Talienwan, the port which has
lately been so much in discussion. Here the two
commanders discussed the plan of campaign, Sir
Hope Grant wishing to begin by attacking Pehtang
a fortified town about eight miles north of the Peiho
and to take the Taku forts by a circuitous route in
rear, while Montauban considered that to land in
the mud to the south of Taku would be the shortest
way to victory. The British plan of attack was so
plainly preferable that it was finally adopted, much
to the consternation and surprise of the Chinese
commanders, whose limited intelligences would have
laid it down that the Peiho being the recognised

road to Peking, the Allies were in duty bound to
begin the game by an attack on the Taku forts.
Fully possessed with this opinion they had made little
effort to fortify Pehtang, and the chief enemy that
the troops found on landing was the deep mud,
through which they were obliged to flounder in
order to reach the raised causeway, which connected
Pehtang with the neighbourhood of the Peiho river.
Sankolinsin, a cousin of the Emperor, was at the
time in command at Taku and in the neighbourhood,
and though fairly taken by surprise by the descent of
the Allies on the coast, had the assurance to report to
his Imperial kinsman that he had purposely allowed
the Barbarians to land. He explained his design by
saying that foreigners were acquatic creatures, and
though formidable on board ship, were helpless on
shore. His plan was, therefore, to entice them from
their ships, and to overwhelm them when thus
robbed of the support in which their great strength
lay.

The struggle at Taku was recognised as of vital
importance, and Hang Fu, the Viceroy of the
province, took up his quarters at the village of
Taku that he might the more readily superintend
the warlike operations. The disposition of Sankolinsin's troops was at first such as to appear that he
really had faith in the plan which he had unfolded
to his Imperial master. As the Allies advanced from
Pehtang, small detachments of Manchu cavalry
appeared on the scene on all sides, and as hastily
retired, as though to induce a further advance. If
such was their design they were not disappointed, for

with set purpose the Allies marched on steadily to the object of their attack, the Taku forts. So soon as the news of the landing at Pehtang reached Sankolinsin, he ordered the construction of a number of entrenchments to protect the rear of the forts, which like most Chinese fortifications were strong on the side from which attack was expected but weak elsewhere. These entrenchments with the neighbouring village of Sinho were flanked and protected by a huge body of cavalry, who owed their full equipment to one of those dishonest subterfuges which excite no astonishment in the Chinese army. Twenty thousand of these horsemen had been collected, on paper, in the neighbourhood of Peking, and for this number without deduction the general in command regularly drew full pay and rations. On the few occasions during the year when it was necessary to testify to the existence of the force, it was his habit to enlist men and hire horses for the time being. Being suddenly ordered on service he resorted to this time-honoured expedient, and when he had thus extemporised a full muster he marched his unsuspecting victims off, on pain of death, to face the Allies. Curiously enough these men fought well, and on one or two occasions charged up to the very guns. They further helped to defend the entrenchments with courage, but, in the congenial company of the infantry battalions, on the first reverse they melted away and left Sinho unprotected. The rapid advance of the Allies was not according to the methods of Chinese warfare, and when the Barbarians presented themselves before the further village of Tangku, the

Chinese troops were enjoying their breakfast. So quickly was the affair over and with such speed did the Chinese soldiers run, that the dishes on the tables were still warm when our hungry troops took the chairs vacated by the flying enemy.

There had been some differences of opinion between Sir Hope Grant and General Montauban as to the plan of attack on the forts, Sir Hope Grant being of the opinion that one of the forts on the north side of the river was the key of the position, while Montauban would have liked to have crossed the river and stormed the southern fort. Montauban was a gallant soldier but a bad strategist, as was constantly proved during the campaign, and in the present case the result fully justified Sir Hope Grant's view of the position.

From the Chinese standpoint the position was rapidly becoming critical, and Hang Fu resorted to the usual Chinese practice of attempting to gain time by drawing the British Minister into a correspondence. With childlike simplicity he wrote to ask the reason "of our hostile appearance at Pehtang, while the two nations were still at peace, and on terms of friendly relationship; if any questions did require settlement, he begged that Lord Elgin would appoint some time and place for a meeting, so that they might be amicably discussed and arranged." The only answer Lord Elgin vouchsafed to this communication, and to many others which followed on it, was that "the only terms on which he would consent to stay naval and military proceedings, were the un-qualified acceptance of the ultimatum sent to the

Court of Peking by Mr. Bruce, and the surrender of
the Peiho forts into our hands." As Hang Fu carefully ignored these conditions in all his letters, the
Allies continued their advance against the Taku forts.
These " were surrounded by a thick mud wall, pierced,
about ten feet from the top, for artillery ; gingals were
mounted on the upper parapet, which was also loop-
holed ; surrounding the walls on the inside were
covered buildings resembling in some degree case-
mates, but they were not shell proof ; a high cavalier
rose in the centre of the fort, mounting three or
four very heavy guns, the embrasures facing seaward,
but the guns could be slewed round in any direction ;
around the outer wall were two, in some cases three,
mud ditches, from twenty to thirty feet broad, full of
water, the ground between the ditches being protected
by sharp-pointed bamboo stakes driven deep into the
earth, and placed so close to each other as not to
admit of a person standing between them. The
south side of the northern forts rested on the Peiho,
which flowed at the base of the wall." The pieces
of ordnance which manned the embrasures were
mostly of native construction, though some few
proved to be English guns which had been recovered
from the sunken gunboats of the year before.

The attack began by an artillery fire against the
walls of the fort. This had not lasted long when an
alarming explosion occurred within the mud defences.
To onlookers this accident appeared to involve the
destruction of the fort. This was not the case, however, and when the dust and smoke cleared away,
the Chinese soldiers turned again to their guns in the

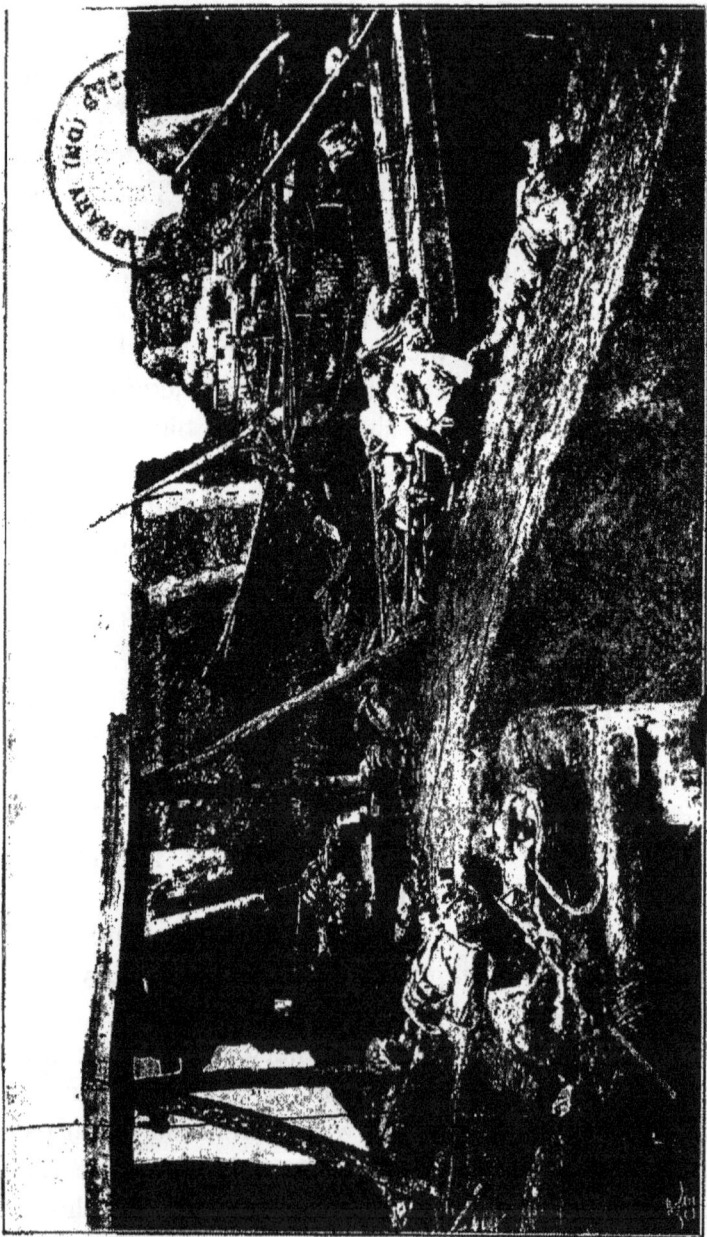

AFTER CAPTURE OF TAKU FORTS

vain hope of checking the advancing foes. When it
was considered that the fire had made storming
possible, orders were given for the assault. In preparation for the campaign, a native coolie corps,
several thousand strong, had been enlisted at
Canton, and had been carefully drilled in the duties
which were expected of them. Though the men
perfectly understood that they would be called upon
to assist in a hostile invasion of their native land, they
showed every alacrity in the service, and it was
evident that patriotism with them weighed nothing
in the scale against the regular pay and ample rations
which they received from their country's enemies.
During the artillery duel before the fort these men
had stood, with the scaling ladders, ready to advance
to the walls, and at the word of command ran readily
forward and planting their ladders against the fort
helped the storming party up. The result was "as
per before," and though the Chinese garrison fought
with some bravery they were speedily vanquished.
So soon as the garrison of the outer northern fort
(there were two large forts on the north bank of the
river and three on the south) saw that the Allies had
secured this first position, they hoisted white flags, and
allowed the Allied troops to march in without firing
a shot. A curious sight met the eyes of the victors
as they entered. Two thousand men were seated on
the ground who neither moved nor spoke. "They had
thrown away their arms and had divested themselves
of all uniform or distinctive badges that could distinguish them as being soldiers."

These men were made prisoners, but doubt was

still felt as to the attitude of the garrisons on the southern side of the river. It is true that white flags had been hoisted on the forts on that side, but so much uncertainty existed as to the meaning of these symbols in Chinese hands that it was thought advisable to communicate with the Viceroy and to receive the submission of the fortress from him before crossing the river in force. Parkes, Loch, and Major Anson were therefore sent across to Taku to find the redoubtable Hang Fu. This astute official received them hospitably, showing at the same time a suspicious inclination to detain them as long as possible. It subsequently transpired that his intentions were really the very opposite to his professions, and that while plying them with tea and sweetmeats his emissaries were engaged in searching for Sankolinsin, with a view to making his visitors prisoners. Fortunately for them Sankolinsin, after the fall of the northern forts, had mounted his horse and ridden to Peking. In a memorial which at this time he addressed to the throne, he admitted that the Barbarians had captured the forts, but besought the Emperor not to be the least alarmed, as his troops were still well able to protect the capital from the presence of the presumptuous foe. When Hang Fu's emissaries returned to their master and reported the flight of the defeated general, he allowed his foreign guests to depart, who on their way back discovered that a small force had already, during their absence, taken possession of the southern forts.

The road to Tientsin was now open, and the Admiral lost no time in clearing away the obstruc-

tions at the mouth of the river. These were of an
extremely formidable character. Huge pointed iron
stakes, each several tons in weight, were securely
fastened in the mud, while two huge booms, kept
afloat by immense earthen water-jars, made the
entrance to the river impossible. With much difficulty these were removed, and the smaller vessels of

A PEASANT WOMAN AND CHILDREN.

the fleet peaceably steamed by the embrasures which
had wrought such havoc in the preceding year.
Meanwhile Hang Fu had started for Tientsin, where
he met Hanki, the late Hoppo of Canton, and
Wangts'iian, who had been hastily despatched from
Peking to stay, if possible, the advance of the
foreigners. One great annoyance experienced by the

mandarins at this time was the attitude which the natives assumed towards the invaders. In 1858, when Lord Elgin first went up to Tientsin, the people in the villages through which he had passed had fallen on their knees before him, and had presented propitiatory offerings to mitigate his supposed wrath. Their experience had taught them, however, that so long as they maintained a peaceful demeanour they had nothing to fear from Englishmen, and on this occasion when he and his colleague, Baron Gros, advanced through the same hamlets the people had, without cringing or undue adulation, offered the produce of their fields and gardens readily for sale. A similar attitude adopted by the men of the Coolie corps was referred to in a memorial by Sankolinsin, which was discovered in the Archives of the Summer Palace, in which he stated that the Allied forces were for the most part composed of Cantonese, who had joined the invaders for the sake of profit; and he recommended that an offer of additional pay and perquisites should be made to bribe them to come over in a body to the Imperial side. Parkes, who was sent in advance to Tientsin, found the people there of the same mind with the villagers. They eagerly responded to his inquiries after provisions, and voluntarily formed a Committee of Supply to provide commissariat stores for the army.

At Tientsin Hang Fu was on the watch for Lord Elgin, and no sooner had the steamer carrying the Ambassador anchored off the Bund than the Viceroy appeared, and invited him to become his guest during his stay in the city. This was a piece of cool

impertinence of which only a Chinaman could have
been guilty, and Lord Elgin curtly informed him that
the Allied troops being now in occupation of Tientsin,
he should take up his residence in the building which
suited him best. The advance of the Barbarian
forces had produced some consternation at Peking,
and the Emperor despatched the Grand Secretary
Kweiliang, who had been one of the signatories of the
treaty of 1858, to join Hang Fu in arranging a peace
with the foreigners. Without any loss of time the
Commissioners sought to open negotiations with Lord
Elgin, who met their overtures by replying that the
conditions on which he was prepared to suspend
hostilities were as follows: "First, an apology for
the attack on the Allied forces at Peiho. Second,
the ratification and execution of the Treaty of
Tientsin. Third, the payment of an indemnity to
the Allies for the expenses of the naval and military
preparations."

With apparent readiness the Commissioners agreed
to these terms, but raised, as has always been their
wont, a number of objections on matters of detail.
It is a recognised practice among the Chinese in
similar cases to send in the first instance Commissioners who are ostensibly deputed to make
peace, but who are denied the necessary plenipotentiary powers. The object of this manœuvre is plain.
Should the Commissioners agree to any terms
distasteful to the Emperor, it is open to him to
ignore the agreement, on the plea that his envoys
had no power to pledge him to any terms. During
the late war with Japan two of these futile missions

were sent to negotiate peace before full powers were granted to Li Hungchang, and in the same way, when it became necessary to examine the credentials of Kweiliang and his colleague, it was found that they had no power whatever to conclude a convention. Lord Elgin, therefore, declined further negotiations with them, and continued his march northwards, at the same time giving them notice that he would listen to no further overtures of any kind, until he had arrived at Tungchow in the neighbourhood of Peking.

On the 9th of September Lord Elgin and Sir Hope Grant left Tientsin, and a day or two later reached Hosiwu, which stands about half way between Tientsin and the capital. Here they were met by a letter from Tsai, Prince of I, who with two colleagues announced his arrival to treat. At the same time he took occasion to add his supreme princely astonishment at the advance of the Allies beyond Tientsin, and strongly urged the British Minister to give the necessary orders for the troops to retreat. This proposal was typical of the native folly of the Chinese, and met with the answer which it deserved. The Prince was told that no negotiations would be entered upon before the arrival of the Allies at Tungchow. As time was precious, however, and as the autumn was already coming on apace, Lord Elgin determined to send Messrs. Wade and Parkes in advance to Tungchow, there to negotiate a preliminary convention with the Commissioners. The Commissioners received these envoys with cordiality, and the Prince of I, who was possessed of a fine presence and courtly.

bearing, treated them with especial civility. After a discussion of eight hours' duration, terms were agreed upon, and "it was arranged that the allied armies were to advance within ten or twelve miles of Tungchow, where they were to remain, while the ambassadors proceeded to Peking accompanied by a large escort. It was agreed also that Mr. Parkes was to return on Monday to Tungchow to make a few final arrangements."

On the day appointed Parkes, accompanied by Messrs. Loch, de Norman, an attaché, Bowlby, the *Times* correspondent, the Quartermaster-General of Cavalry, Colonel Walker, and Mr. Thompson of the Commissariat, with an escort of six troopers of the King's Dragoon Guards, and twenty Sowars of Fane's Horse, under the command of Lieutenant Anderson, started for Tungchow. On the road they met with some cavalry pickets which retired as they advanced, and their way was once stopped by a mandarin at the head of a small force of cavalry, who however let let them pass so soon as he became aware of their mission. Unexpectedly, however, the Commissioners, who before had been so genial, raised countless and vexatious objections to many of the points which had been agreed upon, and more especially to the reception of the Ambassador at Peking, and the delivery of the Letter of Credence to the Emperor. "The tone adopted by the Prince of I and other Commissioners was almost offensive, and they scarcely cared to conceal the repugnance with which they viewed us, and their disinclination to come to terms."

After a lengthy discussion, however, an arrange-

SIR THOMAS FRANCIS WADE, K.C.B.

ment was arrived at, and at twelve o'clock at night
Parkes returned to his rooms, with a draft agreement
in his pocket. Meanwhile Sankolinsin had been
busily employed. He was deeply concerned to
avenge his defeats at Taku, and he thought that
chance had now thrown the opportunity into his
hands. In conjunction with the Commissioners he
arranged that the camping-ground, which it was
proposed to allot to the Allied troops, should be so
situated as to enable him to surround it with his
warriors. The force under his command consisted of
eighty thousand men, and he felt confident that in a
surprise attack he would be able to overwhelm, once
and for all, the four or five thousand Barbarians who
were presumptuous enough to oppose themselves to
him. Being well aware that Parkes would be early
on the field, he moved his troops with secrecy and
despatch to their allotted posts. But not so secretly
as to conceal their movements entirely from the
observation of Parkes and Loch, who had ridden out
between five and six o'clock in the morning to
examine the camping ground. On the three sides of
the allotted space men were posted behind every
hillock, in every grove of trees, and in the deeper
water courses. Such unusual and secret preparations
at once induced Parkes to recognise that treachery
was intended, and he asked Loch to ride forward to
apprise Sir Hope Grant of the ambush which was
being laid for him, while he returned to Tungchow to
demand from the Commissioners an explanation of
the threatening aspect of affairs, and to warn those
who had been left behind of their danger.

The Prince of I, whom Parkes after some difficulty discovered, had now quite thrown off his disguise of the evening before, and curtly informed his unwelcome visitor that until the question of delivering the Letter of Credence was settled " there could be no peace, there must be war." Loch, with that rare loyalty which we are accustomed to regard as belonging to the Anglo-Saxon race, asked and obtained permission to return to Tungchow " to rejoin Parkes and the others, to urge on them the utmost expedition, and, if possible, to endeavour to find some other road by which we could extricate ourselves."

Captain Brabazon of the artillery and two Sikhs accompanied him, and after experiencing some difficulty in getting through the Chinese lines the party reached Tungchow. Having collected all their fellows, they returned·together in the direction of the British camp. By this time Sankolinsin had given up all pretensions to concealment, and the escape of the Englishmen was constantly impeded by the masses of troops which were marching southward. The camping ground itself was fully occupied, and Parkes and his friends at last found their way barred by a strong detachment of Chinese troops. The Chinese officer in command refused to yield them passage, and informed Parkes that his only chance of safety lay in his being able to get a pass through the lines from Sankolinsin. As this appeared to be the only hope of safety Parkes and Loch, taking a Sikh with them, followed the mandarin to Sankolinsin's tent.

That chieftain greeted them with triumphant jeers

and laughter, and his followers, taking their cue from their chief, dragged the foreigners off their horses and buffeted them on the head, while others rubbed their faces in the dirt. Sankolinsin shared the opinion of the Commissioners and others that Parkes was able, if he chose to exercise his powers, to stop the fighting at any moment, and he called upon him now to issue an order for the arrest of the Allied forces. Parkes naturally refused so absurd a request, and Sankolinsin, having lost his temper at meeting with this opposition, would probably have given vent to violence had not an officer hastily ridden up with the announcement that his presence was required at the front. Meanwhile the Chinese had made prisoners of the rest of the party with the exception of Colonel Walker, Mr. Thompson, and the men of the King's Dragoon Guards who had gradually become separated from their comrades. This detachment, finding that the Chinese soldiers were becoming aggressive and violent in their demeanour, charged through their ranks and escaped to the British lines. Immediately following on their flight the battle began, and the sound of the guns was a signal for Parkes and Loch to be carried off in search of the Prince of I. In a springless wooden cart and tightly bound they were driven to Tungchow, through the streets of which city they were carried in triumph, amid the jeers and insults of the people who the day before had offered them obsequious politeness. But the Prince of I was not to be found, and was reported to have started for Peking. The prisoners were, therefore, hurried on the road after him. It was said, however, that he had subsequently returned to Tungchow, and in this uncertainty the guard deemed it best to take the prisoners before General Juilin, who commanded another army on the Peking side of Tungchow. This man behaved to the captives with the utmost brutality, and, after subjecting them to the grossest insults, ordered their removal to a small temple in the neighbourhood, where they were searched, and everything valuable taken from them, including papers. After a short rest they were made to kneel in the courtyard before a posse of mandarins, several of whom they recognised as having been among the *entourage* of the Commissioners on the day before. But bad news from Changchiawan, the field of battle, was beginning to arrive, and their inquisitors suddenly rode off to effect their own escapes, leaving their victims to the tender mercies of the soldiers, who showed every disposition to behead them. Eventually, however, they were again thrown bound into a cart, and were driven off to Peking. Any one who has had the misfortune to travel in a Chinese cart, even when all the alleviations possible have been brought into requisition, will readily understand the intense agony which must have been endured by men bound as the prisoners were, and driven quickly over the terrible road which separates Tungchow from Peking. The miseries through which they had gone since their capture were terrible, but the acme of mental torture was reached when they were driven into the courtyard of the Hsing Pu, or Board of Punishments. " This is indeed worse than I expected," said Parkes.

" We are in the worst prison in China ; we are in the hands of the torturers ; this is the Board of Punishments."

This gloomy building has its foundation in the very earliest records of the Chinese race, and native historians find references to the precursors of the horrible prison which now disgraces the capital of China, in the reigns of sovereigns who ruled the Empire even before fable developed into history. The officials, doubtless acting under orders, assumed from the first a most uncompromising attitude towards their foreign captives. They bound them with chains, they subjected them to every kind of indignity, and added a further cruelty by separating them. Loch gives the following description of his first entrance into his dungeon : " My gaoler went up to the door, and gave three heavy blows, crying out at the same time. A most unearthly yell from the inside was the reply, the door was thrown open, and I found myself in the presence of, and surrounded by, as savage a lot of half-naked demons as I had ever beheld ; they were nearly all the lowest caste of criminals imprisoned for murder and the most serious offences. There were about fifty in all, of whom some eighteen or twenty were chained like myself, but with far lighter irons. A few of the prisoners were better dressed than the others." The capture and imprisonment of the captives had been a subject of congratulation and rejoicing to the Emperor and his advisers, who from their safe retreat in the hunting palace at Jehol in Mongolia, whither the " Son of Heaven " had fled on the

approach of the Allied armies, still directed the
affairs of State. At this time the war party was in
power, and being composed of men who were quite
ignorant of foreigners, and who were possessed with
an overwhelming idea of the power and prestige of
China, had with light hearts nailed their flag to
the mast of no compromise. It was still their belief
that Parkes could put an end to the march of the
troops if he pleased, and if he did not so please,
they were quite content to put him to death and to
allow the army to fight the matter out. Under the
inspiration of these men the President of the Board
of Punishments and his satellites indulged in every
insolence and cruelty towards their prisoners, and if
they stopped short of actual physical torture, it was
only with the idea that it might diminish the possible
usefulness of their victims. It is happily not often
that foreigners become acquainted with the insides
of Chinese prisons, and no apology is therefore
needed for dwelling for a moment on one of the
rooms in which Loch was examined on his knees
and which recalls the horrors of the Inquisition.
"On one side of this dungeon," Loch writes, " was
a table behind which three mandarins were seated.
There were various iron implements lying on the
table, and the walls were hung with chains and other
disagreeable instruments the use of which it was
unpleasant too closely to investigate. On one side
of the room was a low bench, at each end of which
was a small windlass, round which a rope was coiled ;
the use to which this machine might be applied
admitted of no doubt." For ten days the officials

kept their prisoners closely confined in their loathsome dens, and at the end of that time circumstances
arose which induced them to move Parkes and Loch
to a temple in the north-west quarter of the city,
where they were well treated and allowed their
liberty within the four walls of the building.

In order to make the story of this period clear, it
is necessary now to revert to the proceedings on the
day of the capture of the prisoners. It will be
remembered that the battle of Changchiawan was
opening when the supreme act of treachery was
perpetrated. Unfortunately for Sankolinsin's scheme,
events were precipitated before his arrangements
could be brought to perfection, and the unexpected
advance of the Allies somewhat disconcerted his
plans. The enormous force of Tartar cavalry under
his command, however, did their utmost to check
the onslaught of the Barbarians. They charged repeatedly and with considerable courage, while the
artillery served their guns with steadiness and effect.
But they were quite unable to resist the fire and
cavalry of the invaders, and after making a considerable stand, they tottered, turned, and fled,
leaving seventy - four guns in the hands of the
victors and countless dead upon the field. So soon
as the fate of the day was decided, Sankolinsin took
to flight, and only stayed to rally his fugitive forces
when he joined hands with Juilin on the Peking side
of Tungchow. A day or two later these combined
forces suffered another crushing defeat at Palichiao,
or "Eight-mile Bridge," a spot which is emphasised
in the French annals as having supplied the title of

PAGODA AT YUAN-MING-YUAN, NEAR PEKING

Count de Palichiao which was conferred on General
Montauban.

After the flight of the Emperor to Jehol, Prince
Kung, his brother, was practically left in command
on the spot. He took up his residence at Yuan-
ming-yuan, the Summer Palace, in company with the
dowager Empress, and there received from time to
time the dreary reports of his country's defeats.
The news of the disaster at Changchiawan no sooner
reached him than he recognised the wisdom of doing
his utmost to prevent, if possible, an attack on the
capital. He hurried, therefore, to meet the enemy,
and despatched in advance a letter to Lord Elgin
stating that he held plenipotentiary powers for the
negotiation of peace. At the same time, he had the
temerity to urge a request for a temporary suspension of hostilities. Lord Elgin's answer was short.
He gave his correspondent to understand that he
would not for an instant entertain any proposals for
peace until the prisoners were given up, and he
warned the Prince of the serious consequences that
would be entailed on the city of Peking, and even
on the fortunes of the dynasty itself, if in their blind
folly the Chinese compelled the Allies to attack the
capital. With this rebuff Kung returned to Yuan-
ming-yuan, and, resigning all hope of peace, gave
directions for strengthening and defending the walls
of Peking. Meanwhile the invaders marched un-
opposed along the east face of the city, the French
being on the right, in company with some of the
British cavalry. There had been some talk of
marching on Yuan-ming-yuan, and the French,

perhaps regarding the arrangement as more definite than it really was, crossed the rear of the
British unobserved, and marched straight on the
palace. This move was so sudden that Prince
Kung and the Dowager Empress were yet in the
palace when the French appeared before the gates.
With all haste the Imperial personages escaped out
of the back, leaving a party of eunuchs and one or
two mandarins to watch proceedings. One of these
officials, Wang by name, related to the writer his
experiences. He took possession of a pavilion at
the back of the premises and there waited on events.
The first visitors who intruded on his privacy were
two or three Sikhs who had followed the French to
the Imperial quarters. " These men," said Wang,
" looked round the room and took anything they
fancied, but left me unmolested. Presently there
entered some French soldiers, who took the pipe
out of my mouth, broke off the jade stone mouth-
piece and pocketed it. I then thought it was time
to go, and I followed Prince Kung to a temple on
the hills to the north of the palace."

Yuan-ming-yuan was the favourite palace of the
Emperor. It was there where he sought relief from
the cares of State, and it was there that some of the
prisoners had been taken and had been cruelly
tortured. The grounds covered an enormous extent,
and countless pavilions of all forms and shapes stood
on every spot where the natural lie of the land or
the skill of landscape gardeners yielded appropriate
sites. The gardens were bright with every kind of
flowering shrubs and plants. Quaint bridges crossed

the streams and lakes and led to buildings full of
rare and priceless objects. There were collected the
choicest specimens of porcelain from Kintêching,
bronzes from Soochow, and jade ornaments from the
quarries of Central Asia, while curiosities from
Europe — watches and clocks from France, and
objects of a more prosaic nature from England, as,
for instance, the carriage presented by George III.
to the Emperor Ch'ienlung — thronged the halls.
All these stores of wealth were now at the mercy
of the Allies, and for some days the palaces were
looted without check by the troops of both armies.
This last catastrophe disposed Prince Kung to listen
with a more willing ear to Lord Elgin's demand for
the surrender of one of the gates of the city, and
after some show of hesitation he found it wise to
yield to circumstances. It had been made clear to
him that there could be no peace so long as his
demand was refused, and though to submit to it
was as gall and wormwood to him, he finally gave
way, and handed over the Anting Gate, on the north
face of the city, to the Allied commanders.

Meanwhile the Council of State sitting at Jehol had
maintained a resolutely anti-foreign attitude. While
the troops were advancing from Tungchow on Peking,
the Emperor's advisers had been discussing the fate
which was to be meted out to Parkes and Loch. In
their headstrong folly they eventually determined,
against the advice of Prince Kung, that they should
die, and a messenger was despatched to Peking with
a warrant for their immediate execution. Happily
the peace party at Peking, consisting of Prince Kung,

Hang-ki, and others, had their spies at Jehol, and the instant that the death warrant was signed a swift courier was sent with all haste to the Prince to inform him of the fact. This fleet-footed envoy arrived at Peking early in the morning of the 8th, bringing news that the Imperial messenger was following closely at his heels. If the prisoners were to be saved, therefore, there was no time to be lost, and Hang-ki at once went to the temple to which they had been removed, and announced to them the glad tidings of their immediate release. Two days previously this same officer had solemnly stated to them that their execution was fixed, first of all, for that same evening, and then for the next morning. This further message of their proposed release was, therefore, received by them with some reserve, and Parkes, assuming an indifference which he was far from feeling, at once renewed a conversation on the motion of the moon, which had been cut short on the previous day. Hang-ki's manner and impatience, however, soon convinced him that his tidings were really true, and at two o'clock in the day this conviction was confirmed by the appearance in the courtyard of a covered cart, into which the prisoners, who were now to be free men, were hastily placed and sent out of the city. Being in ignorance as to the exact position of the Allied forces, they were uncertain which way to direct the driver, but going towards Yuan-ming-yuan they fell in with a British guard, and at once had the satisfaction of feeling that they were at last safe indeed. At the same time eight sowars of Fane's Horse and one French officer were restored to liberty. The

remaining prisoners had perished in the hands of their
torturers, and their remains, which were handed over
by the Chinese to the Allied Commanders, were buried
with all honours in the Russian Cemetery at Peking.
A quarter of an hour after the cart which carried
Parkes and Loch had passed out of the city gate, the
warrant arrived for their execution ; and as Hang-
ki afterwards said to Parkes, " If your deliverance
had been only delayed a quarter of an hour even
Prince Kung's influence could not have saved you."

The stories which the recovered prisoners had to
tell of their captivity, and the sight of the cruelly
mangled bodies of those who had died in their dun-
geons, aroused such deep and violent indignation at
the treachery and brutality of the Chinese, that Lord
Elgin felt that some signal punishment should be
inflicted on the Government. In this conviction he
wrote to Prince Kung to inform him that as a protest
against the infamous conduct of the ruling powers he
had determined to destroy the Summer Palace. In
meting out his punishment he was guided by the
principle that the penalty should be inflicted on the
Emperor and his personal belonging, rather than on
the people who were comparatively innocent of the
crime. Due notice having been given, a force was
marched into the palace, and fire was set to the
buildings, which were speedily laid level with the
ground. For several days the conflagration raged,
and, a north-west wind happening to blow at the
time, the smoke hung for days like a black pall
over the city of Peking.

Though the war party at Jehol were still breathing

out fire and slaughter against the foreigners, Prince Kung was quietly negotiating the terms of the treaty. By an act of poetical justice the Prince of I's house was appropriated as the temporary residence of Lord Elgin and Baron Gros, and on the 24th of October, when a complete agreement had been arrived at, these Ministers met Prince Kung at the Hall of Ceremonies, and there concluded the treaty which has guided the relation between China and the Western nations to the present day. With some reluctance the Emperor issued an edict authorising the publication of the treaty throughout the Empire, and after this final act the Ministers, accompanied by the troops, left Peking.

A time of great doubt and uncertainty followed on the conclusion of peace. It is in most cases difficult to determine the true motives of Chinese statesmen, but in the present instance there was no trace of ambiguity in the attitude of the anti-foreign party at Jehol. To Prince Kung, who had seen the Allied armies, who had recognised their strength, and who had felt their power, the idea of bringing about another war appeared downright madness. In this firm belief he used his utmost endeavours to induce the Emperor to move his Court to Peking, where he felt that he might have some chance of influencing the counsels of his brother. This proposal was vehemently and successfully resisted by the Prince of I, Shu Shun, and other evil counsellors who surrounded the inert and feeble "Son of Heaven." Throughout all these negotiations Prince Kung's hopes rested, and as it was ultimately proved, with good reason, on the

Empress, who was an able woman, and who had considerable influence over her husband. Hsienfêng himself was little more than a lay figure, and not unfrequently the members of his council flagrantly disobeyed with impunity his express commands. During the winter of 1860-61 Court intrigues, and more or less open contests, were continually in progress, and the only hope of continued peace rested on the wished-for triumph of Prince Kung over his truculent opponents. Associated with Prince Kung were Grand Secretary Wênhsiang and Hang-ki, who were all honestly desirous, in the circumstances, of maintaining peace. They probably had as little affection for foreigners as either the Prince of I or Shu Shun, and indeed in a moment of confidence Hang-ki said to Parkes, while he was yet in his bonds, " Do not mistake ; it is not for the sake of yourselves individually that I advocate your release ; far from it ; for, if I thought it would benefit our position, I would advocate your death ; but it is because I know your people. I am better acquainted with their powers of destruction than the other Commissioners are. I know they will carry out their threat and destroy Peking if harm falls on you two ; this will bring misery on the people and destruction upon us." This outspoken utterance is faithfully descriptive of the attitude of ninety-nine out of every hundred mandarins who are at the present date said to be amicably disposed towards foreigners.

But though peace with the foreigners was restored, *Væ victis* was the cry in the distracted Imperial Council, and the ratification of the treaties had no sooner been exchanged than the following edict appeared in the *Peking Gazette :* " Let Sankolinsin be deprived of his nobility ; let Juilin [who it will be remembered commanded in the neighbourhood of Tungchow] be immediately deprived of his office, as a warning. Respect this." This was the beginning of the fall of Sankolinsin, and though he was subsequently employed against the Nienfei rebels he remained under a cloud of official displeasure, and was eventually treacherously murdered by some of his own followers. In no country in the world is success regarded so emphatically as a sign of merit as in China, and the reverse—viz., that failure is synonymous with incompetence, holds good. Unsuccessful generals in the Flowery Land find their way, as a rule, to the execution ground, and it is probable that Sankolinsin's relationship with the Emperor alone saved his life on this occasion.

During the winter of 1860–61 the Emperor remained at Jehol much against the advice of Prince Kung and his colleagues, who felt, and rightly felt, that his absence from the capital at this crisis was a virtual abdication of his Imperial functions. But to all admonition from this quarter he turned a deaf ear, and at the inspiration of his *entourage* listened greedily to the false accounts of the disorders, which were said by his interested advisers to prevail in the capital. As the summer drew on his health began to fail. It was said that he caught a succession of bad chills, and it is possible that this may have been the case, for though quite a young man his strength was seriously undermined by the constant debaucheries and

acts of self-indulgence which made up his daily life.
At this time a comet appeared in the skies, an occurrence which is universally regarded in China an evil
omen. The alarm occasioned by this sign in the
heavens was excessive and prepared the people for
the reports which spread at the beginning of August
as to the alarming state of the Emperor's health. So
serious was the condition of things that Prince Kung
determined to go to Jehol, as he rightly considered
that his only chance of retaining power lay in his
being able to combine with the Empress against the
intrigues of the Prince of I and others, who still held
the Emperor's confidence. The political atmosphere
at Jehol was not a congenial one to the Prince, and
though he succeeded in forming a most useful alliance
with the Empress, which was destined to lead to great
consequences, he made no impression whatever on the
Emperor, who was evidently very near death. Prince
Kung had only just returned to Peking when the
well-known literary precursor of the end appeared in
the shape of the usual edict appointing a successor to
the throne. This document was as follows: " Let
Tsai Ch'un, the eldest son of the Emperor, be Crown
Prince. Our eldest son Tsai Ch'un being now constituted Crown Prince, let Ts'ai Yuan, Prince of I ;
Twan Hwa, Prince of Ching; Ching Shou ; Shu
Shun ; Mu Yin ; Kwan Yüan ; Tu Han ; Tsiang
Yuying, with all their might aid him as Counsellors
in all things pertaining to the administration of the
Government." On the 22nd of August the Emperor
died, and the Crown Prince was proclaimed Emperor
under the style of Chihsiang. As the new Emperor

was but four years old the conduct of affairs passed, even more definitely than had been the case before, into the hands of the anti-foreign Council appointed as above.

For a time things went smoothly ; the foreign relations were conducted by Prince Kung, Prince Ch'un, the father of the present Emperor, Grand Secretary Wênhsiang, and the veteran Kweiliang, while the general administration of the Empire was conducted from Jehol. This was plainly a state of things which could not continue to exist, and towards the end of October it was announced that the youthful " Son of Heaven " would return at once to Peking followed by the funeral cortège of his father. This decision brought matters to a crisis, and forced on a trial of strength between the two parties in the State. The ladies of the harem were the first to arrive at Peking. These were shortly followed by the boy Emperor, who entered his capital seated on his mother's knee, and attended by the Council of State, with the exception of Shu Shun whose duty it was to escort the remains of the late Emperor. Prince Kung's visit to Jehol was now to bear fruit, and the Peking world was thrown into a state of wild excitement by the appearance of an edict purporting by a pious fiction to proceed from the hand of the Emperor dismissing the Jehol courtiers from their offices, and ordering that the Princes of I and Ching with Shu Shun, should be put on their trial for having deceived their Imperial master, and for having grossly mismanaged the affairs of State. At the same time a

second decree appeared appointing the two Dowager
Empresses, the wife of Hsienfêng and the mother of
the Emperor, Regents of the Empire. With these
two State papers in his hand, Prince Kung presented
himself before the assembled council, and having
read in their astonished ears the sentence of their
degradation, he demanded to know whether they
were prepared to submit to the Imperial commands.
Kung had not been unmindful of the possibility of
opposition, and he had strengthened his position by
massing large bodies of troops under General Shêng
Pao, on whom he could implicitly rely, in the
neighbourhood of the capital. His enemies, recognising their impotence, at once declared their
submission to the decrees, and left the council
chamber in a body, but not before the Princes of
I and Ching had been taken into custody. So long,
however, as Shu Shun was at liberty Kung's triumph
was incomplete, and Prince Ch'un was therefore sent
with a body of Tartar cavalry to arrest the offender
on his way from Jehol in command of the funeral
procession. It so chanced that the Prince came upon
his prey late at night at one of the Imperial travelling
palaces on the road. Without the slightest compunction he broke in upon the peaceful slumbers of
Shu Shun, when it was proved to demonstration that
he had aggravated his offences by bringing the ladies
of his harem in his company, while on the sacred and
solemn duty of escorting the remains of his late
Imperial master to their last resting-place. With
stolid indifference Shu Shun yielded to *force majeur*,
and submitted to enter Peking as a prisoner. No

time was lost in putting the prisoners on their trial. In Eastern countries only one sentence is possible in such a case, and all three offenders were condemned to death. Shu Shun was declared worthy of *Lingch'ih*, or the Lingering Process, while the two Princes were sentenced to be beheaded. The severity of these verdicts was mercifully mitigated by the Dowager Empresses, who sent Shu Shun to decapitation on the execution ground, and as an act of grace allowed the two Princes to perform the happy despatch by strangling themselves in prison. Finally to disassociate the young Emperor once and for all from any association with his father's evil advisers, the title of Chihsiang, which had been chosen for his reign by the late council, was changed to that of T'ungchih.

XI

THE T'AIP'ING REBELLION

BEFORE the outbreak of the foreign war the T'aip'ing Rebellion, as we have seen, had been gradually dying out from want of vigour and initiative, and the two cities of Nanking and Anking were the only two places of importance remaining in the occupation of the rebels. But when it became necessary for the Government to defend the capital against the Allies, every available soldier was sent northward, and the local authorities were left to cope as best they might with the followers of the "Heavenly King." But though the rebels were thus relieved of a great strain, they would probably have been unable to avert an immediate collapse had it not been for the Chung Wang, or Faithful Prince, who throughout his whole career showed a staunch loyalty to the cause, and a marked capacity for military tactics. The Tien Wang was lost in a slough of debauchery within his palace at Nanking, and with the exception of Chung Wang none of the rebel leaders showed any considerable power of organisation or any love of fighting. At the time of which we speak (1859) Nanking was closely invested by the troops under Tsêng Kwofan, and it is beyond question that the city would before long have fallen into the hands of the Imperialists if Chung Wang had not come forward to its relief. He instinctively saw that, beleaguered as they were, it had become merely a question of time how long the provisions in the city would hold out, and he recognised that the only remedy left to the garrison was to raise the siege by an attack from outside. With the sanction of the "Heavenly King" he undertook this duty, and having made his way through the Imperial lines succeeded in collecting a rebel force at Wuhu. With these recruits he crossed the Yangtsze to the north bank, and laid siege to, and captured, the important city of Hochow in Anhui. This was the beginning of a series of successes. City after city fell into his hands, until the whole country on the north side of the river opposite Nanking passed into the possession of the rebels. Chung Wang's main effort, however, was directed to cutting off the base of supplies from which the Imperial army before Nanking drew its resources, and to harrying its supports. With these objects in view he crossed the river, and after a rapid march, during which he captured several positions, he suddenly appeared before the celebrated city of Hangchow. With comparative ease he made himself master of this important town, and was on the point of following up his successes by delivering an attack on Soochow when he received a positive command from the "Heavenly King" to march at once to the relief of the closely beleaguered garrison of Nanking. Without a moment's delay he started on his mission, and on arrival at the scene of action at once gave battle to the besieging force. Possessed with unbounded energy himself he succeeded on this, as on many other occasions, in imparting the same invaluable quality to his troops. With irresistible vigour they charged on the Imperial lines. The battle was hotly contested, and ended in a complete victory to the rebels, who dissipated the Imperial army and slew five thousand of its best troops.

Having achieved this signal success the Faithful Prince returned with the intention of completing his sinister designs against Soochow. But his way was not straight before him, for at some distance to the north of the doomed city was stationed an opposing army led by Tsêng's chief and ablest lieutenant, Chang Kwoliang. Here again the Imperialists were completely defeated with a loss of ten thousand men, but an even greater misfortune to their cause was the death of their able commander, who by some strange misadventure was drowned in the Grand Canal during the progress of the fighting. After another stubborn engagement with the remainder of the Imperial forces, led by Chang's brother, Chung Wang entered the city of Wusieh in triumph. It now seemed as though a vital, and, from their point of view, a most encouraging turn had been given to the affairs of the rebels. So fully was this realised that the Imperialist General

Ho, who had commanded at Wusieh, despairing of his master's cause, committed suicide.

The Imperialists were now in desperate straits, while in the north the dynasty was suffering a rude shock (May, 1860) at the immediate prospect of an invasion by the Allied armies. We have seen how Yeh, at Canton, while flouting the English one day, was ready to beseech their help against the local rebels on the next, and guided by the same instinct for self-preservation Ho, the Viceroy of the two Kiang Provinces, even went the length of begging for the help of some of the foreign troops, who were collecting at Shanghai preparatory to the campaign in the north, for the suppression of the advancing T'aip'ings. This strange request was of course refused, but at the same time the Viceroy was informed that the Allies would protect the city and settlement of Shanghai from any assault that the rebels might make upon them. Meanwhile the Faithful Prince pursued his victorious career. In rapid succession the cities of Soochow, Quinsan, Tsingpu, and Taitsan yielded to his arms, and thus it may be said that the whole of the rich peninsula formed by the river Yangtsze and the Bay of Hangchow had passed into the hands of the rebels. The news of these fresh disasters had no sooner reached Peking, than the Viceroy Ho received orders to present himself at Peking for judgment. It is difficult to know what more he could have done with the materials at his disposal. But his crime was failure to preserve the provinces entrusted to him, and after a short shrift he was executed.

The approach of the rebel legions to the neighbourhood of Shanghai gave rise to considerable consternation in the minds of native merchants, who, cut off as they now were from the districts which supplied them with silks, satins, and teas, felt that their occupations might be considered to be gone, unless they could by some means help the Government in its present and pressing difficulties. Like the late Viceroy they turned to Europeans for help, and established a Patriotic Association which they supported with large sums for the protection of their country's weal. At Li Hungchang's instigation they engaged the services of two Americans named Ward and Burgevine, who were instructed to collect as many stray Europeans as might be found on the spot available and willing to take up arms in the Emperor's cause. It was arranged between these adventurers and the Association that they should under any circumstances receive a certain fixed rate of pay, and that their stipends should be liberally supplemented by rewards in return for every city or stronghold they might take. To the south-west of Shanghai, at a distance of about twenty miles, stood the rebel stronghold of Sungkiang Fu. The proximity of this place and its strategic importance induced the Association to desire that it should be the first point of attack. To this Ward agreed, and at the head of about three hundred Europeans and natives of Manila, he led the assault, Burgevine acting as Quartermaster to the expedition. The first onslaught was repulsed with considerable loss, and Ward returned dis-

comfited to Shanghai to supply the deficiencies in
his ranks. Having thus succeeded in gaining fresh
recruits, he renewed the attack, and this time with
success. The amount of plunder secured in this
venture was very considerable, and the liberal
douceurs which were distributed among the troops
gained increased popularity for the force. In a sea-
port like Shanghai there is always a floating population of ne'er-do-weels, who are ready for " treasons,
stratagems, and spoils," and Ward found little
difficulty in filling the gaps made in his ranks
by wounds and death. The next object of attack
was Tsingpu, a strong city whose fortifications had
been designed and strengthened under the direction
and guidance of an Englishman named Savage, who
like many others had joined the rebel ranks.

As was the case before Sungkiang, Ward's first
assault upon Tsingpu was unsuccessful, and he was at
the same time still further discomfited by an attack
on his rear delivered by the ever-alert Chung Wang,
who not only utterly routed his force, but captured
his artillery and stores. At the close of the Peking
campaign the British authorities had leisure and
opportunity to consider the position of affairs in the
rebel districts, more especially in the neighbourhood
of Shanghai. That place had of late years become
such an important emporium of trade that it was
considered advisable to open negotiations with a view
of placing it beyond the possibility of warlike disturbance. Admiral Hope therefore steamed up the
river to Nanking, and in an interview with the
" Heavenly King" pointed out the advisability, in his

interest as well as in that of the British, of placing
the port beyond the sphere of hostile action. The
" Heavenly King " graciously accepted this view and
gave his word that no attack should be made on
Shanghai for at least one twelvemonth. The exac-
tion of this promise was the more necessary and
important as already the Faithful Prince had made
one attack upon the city. He afterwards stated that
he had been invited to this venture by the French,
but however that may have been, he found on approaching the walls that they were defended by a
garrison of English and French, before whose wither-
ing fire his men fled away dismayed. After some
desultory fighting in the neighbourhood of his defeat
the Faithful Prince returned to Soochow, whence he
was hastily summoned to Nanking to relieve that
city, which was being attacked for the sixth time by
the Imperialists. It is impossible to follow the
various manœuvres, assaults, and sacks undertaken
by that most energetic of commanders, the Faithful
Prince. These actions lose much of their interest
when we find that the T'aip'ing force was merely
destructive. The general proceedings on capturing a
city were to slaughter the inhabitants, and to loot
their homes, but in no sense to set up anything
approaching to a stable administration. On the
other hand the leisurely movements of the Imperialists incline one to lose sympathy with men who,
while engaged in a life-and-death struggle with the
promoters of disorder, were so strangely wanting in
energy and resource. But notwithstanding this
apparent apathy it was becoming plain to careful

observers that the Imperialists were gradually closing round the rebels. The capture of Nanking by Tsêng Kwofan was a serious blow to their cause, and after that catastrophe the action shortly to be taken at Shanghai placed the rebels between a double fire.

So long, however, as the Faithful Prince was in command of the rebel armies successes were always possible, and his rapid captures of Ningpo and Hangchow for a time revived the falling hopes of the T'aip'ings. The year during which the "Heavenly King" had promised that no attack should be made on Shanghai, had now expired, and Chung Wang, flushed by his temporary successes in the south, determined once more to lay siege to that city. In January, 1862, his troops arrived in the immediate vicinity of the town and settlement. Not wishing to repeat their former experience by making an actual attack on the walls, the rebels entrenched themselves in the neighbourhood, and devoted their leisure time to plundering the country side. In addition to the promise mentioned above, the "Heavenly King" had undertaken that his troops should not, under any circumstances, approach within a radius of thirty miles of the city. This undertaking was now plainly broken, and the Allied commanders, fresh from the victories achieved over the Imperialists at Peking, now undertook a campaign against the enemies of their former foes. Without much difficulty the foreign troops, although numerically infinitely inferior, drove back the invaders beyond the agreed-upon line, and recovered for the Emperor the town and cities within that district. Meanwhile Ward's force, which had adopted the grandiloquent title of the "Ever Victorious Army," was rapidly becoming an important factor in the situation. It numbered five thousand men and, by a constant and careful system of drill, was assuming somewhat the position of a regular force. It ably supported General Staveley in his campaign around Shanghai, and subsequently gained numerous victories single-handed over the rebels. But the necessity which compelled Ward, as it subsequently did Gordon, to place himself at the head of his men if he wished them to fight, at last proved fatal to him, and in an attack on the city of Tzŭki he received a wound which proved fatal. He was a brave man, and though quite uneducated, had learnt enough of military tactics to enable him to hold his own against the rebel leaders. It is illustrative of the amount of plunder obtainable under the Imperial banner, that although the deceased commander had only held the post for two years he left behind him a fortune of fifteen thousand pounds.

The man who was chosen to succeed him was his subordinate Burgevine, who was possessed of a more high-flying ambition than his predecessor, and who was loftily determined that if he commanded at all he would have his own way in everything. Li Hungchang, who had meanwhile become Governor of the province, was not a man to brook any such pretensions, and it was not long before a violent disagreement occurred between these two chiefs. The Patriotic Association, who were quite as distrustful of Burgevine as was the Governor, entirely took his view of the position, and as they held the purse strings they were a power which it was all important to consider. They, together with Li, had been in the habit of providing thirty thousand pounds per month for the support of the force, and they chose to make their authority felt by reducing this sum as soon as Burgevine came into power. The general was not likely to submit to such action, and he, thereupon, went to Shanghai with his body-guard, and after a personal altercation with the banker who represented the Association, in which even blows were struck, he impounded a considerable sum of money which he found on the premises, and carried it off to the camp. This made a breach which it was plainly impossible to bridge over, and Li dismissed Burgevine from his command. But it is ill swapping horses when in the midst of a stream, and the dismissal of Burgevine was followed by almost a mutiny amongst the troops, and by the appointment of a Captain Holland, under whose command only one expedition, and that an eminently unsuccessful one against T'aits'ang, was undertaken.

But a new turn was to be given to events by the appointment of Major Gordon to the command of the Ever Victorious Army *vice* Captain Holland. Gordon was a man who was known by his fellows as an officer of marked ability, great strength of character, and of unflinching courage. At the time of which we speak, he was engaged in making a survey of the country round Shanghai, a useful work which in other circumstances he would have been allowed to complete. But his help was immediately called for, and he no sooner received the appointment of

22

commander to the Force, than he exchanged the theodolite for the sword, and marched out of Sungkiang to meet the enemy. His first objective was a place called Fushan, which fell an easy prey into his hands. The fall of this place entailed the evacuation by the rebels of Changshu, a neighbouring stronghold, and thus Gordon's first engagement secured a double victory. Li Hungchang was delighted with the success thus easily won, and he reported to the throne in glowing terms on Gordon's generalship. In response to this effusion he received a Rescript which contained the following reference to the achievement: "Gordon, on succeeding to the command of the Ever Victorious Force, having displayed both valour and intelligence, and having now, with repeated energy, captured Fushan, we ordain that he at once receive rank and office as a Chinese Tsungping (General), and that we at the same time command Li to communicate to him the expressions of our approval. Let Gordon be further enjoined to use stringent efforts to maintain discipline in the Ever Victorious Force, which has fallen into a state of disorganisation, and thus to guard against the recurrence of former evils. Respect this."

Next to Nanking the most important place in the possession of the rebels was Soochow, and it was now Li's main object to recover this city. As a preliminary step, however, it was necessary to capture the city of Kunshan (Quinsan) before advancing to the walls of the great stronghold, and at Li's instigation Gordon marched to undertake this initial venture. The successes which he had already gained,

ANGLO-CHINESE CONTINGENT— ARTILLERY.

and the confidence which he had inspired, gave
courage to his men; and they marched willingly to
the attack, being not altogether unmindful, also, of
the spoils which a successful assault would give
them an opportunity of reaping. While yet, however,
on the way thither Gordon received a pressing
message from Li beseeching him to march on the
city of T'aits'ang to avenge the defeat which his troops
had suffered at that place. Li had been under the
impression that the rebels were prepared to negotiate
for the surrender of the town, and he was justified in
his belief by the results of several interviews which
his lieutenants had had with the rebel commanders.
But in Chinese warfare it is never safe to trust in
your adversary's professions, and when the rebels
opened the gates and admitted fifteen hundred
Imperialists within the walls, it was only that they
might the more easily cut them down to the last
man.

The city was so strongly fortified that Gordon's
first attack proved unsuccessful. A second assault,
directed by more matured counsels, however, ended
in a complete victory, and though Gordon had good
reason for congratulating himself on the capture, his
rejoicings were unhappily marred by one of those
inhuman acts of cruelty which are inseparable from
Oriental warfare. "Among the prisoners taken at
T'aits'ang were seven notorious rebel chiefs, who
were handed over by Gordon to the custody of the
Chinese General. It is not clear whether or not this
officer communicated with Li on the fate of these
captives, but it is clear that the inhuman punishment

inflicted on them met with his approval. Oriental
ideas on the subject of punishment differ so widely
from our own, that it is impossible to judge them
by the same rules. Following a practice not at all
uncommon, the Chinese general ordered the men to
be fastened to crosses, to have arrows thrust through
their flesh, to have strips of skin cut off from various
parts of their bodies, and in this state to be exposed
till sundown, and then beheaded."

Having avenged the defeat of Li's troops, Gordon
was free to order an advance upon Kunshan. But
he had forgotten that his men were mostly free-
booters and only partly soldiers, and that after the
capture of a city it was customary for them to carry
their spoils to headquarters, *i.e.,* Sungkiang. The
order, therefore, for an immediate advance aroused
anger among the troops, and produced open mutiny
among some of the regiments. To give in to these
predatory habits would have been fatal to the efficiency of the corps, and Gordon, therefore, marched
with those who fell into the ranks and warned the
remainder that any man who was not in his place by
the time the force had performed half its march,
would be struck off the rolls. The result of this
threat was most salutary. The mutineers submitted
at once, and marched with their comrades to the
attack. A General Ch'êng, in command of a Chinese
force, had been appointed to act in concert with the
Ever Victorious Army in the siege of Kunshan.
This redoubtable officer knew as much about military tactics as most Chinese generals, and, after much
reconnoitring he had come to the conclusion that

the assault should be made on the side of the eastern
gate. Gordon's knowledge of Chinese commanders
prepared him for the discovery that his colleague
had selected the strongest part of the defences for
the attack, and after a careful survey he was led to
the conclusion that the weakest point was on the
western side of the city. In front of this part of the
walls were a number of stockades which were taken,
not without some fighting, but with the result that
the garrison of Kunshan, losing heart at the defeat
of their comrades, evacuated the city and retreated
along the raised causeway which connects Kunshan
with Soochow. The exposed position of this roadway left the fugitives an easy prey to the guns of
Gordon's artillery, and of the steamer *Hyson*, which
enfiladed the causeway from the waters of the neighbouring canal. It is said that during the day
between three and four thousand of the rebels
were killed, while Gordon's death roll amounted
only to two who were killed in action and five
who were drowned. Thus the key of Soochow was
captured.

For several reasons, partly strategic and partly
disciplinary, Gordon determined to make Kunshan
the headquarters of the force. This move was bitterly
resented by the rank and file, who, under the lax
system of Ward and Burgevine, had been allowed
a latitude which had destroyed in them the habit
of implicit obedience. So strong was this want of
discipline that they broke out into open mutiny at
this supposed wrong. Gordon at once grappled
with the difficulty. He readily divined that the

non-commissioned officers were the centres of the dissatisfaction, and he took his measures accordingly. He announced to these sedition-mongers that unless within one hour the men fell in, every fifth man among them would be shot, and by way of pointing the moral of his threat, he ordered out the ringleader of the whole movement to instant execution. The sight of his exemplary punishment brought reason to the counsels of his former comrades, and within the appointed time the men gave in their loyal adhesion to their leader.

This was only one of the difficulties which Gordon had to encounter at this time. His colleague, General Ch'êng, had never forgiven the neglect of his advice which had led to the capture of Kunshan, and, on the excuse of a mistake, but really by malice prepense, he directed on one occasion the fire of his guns against a regiment of the Ever Victorious Army. Money difficulties with Li further added to his anxieties. The system of looting which had been encouraged by Ward and Burgevine was repugnant to Gordon's ideas of soldiering, and he proposed to Li that after the capture of each town a gratuity should be distributed amongst the men in place of the spoils which used to be their portion. Li objected to this plan as being less economical than allowing the troops to gather their own rewards, and, though agreeing with the proposal so far as Kunshan was concerned, gave notice to Gordon that such irregular payments were "very inconvenient." These and other money difficulties so strained the relations between Gordon and Li, that Gordon determined to resign his position, and he announced his intention in the following letter to the Governor :—

"YOUR EXCELLENCY,—In consequence of the monthly difficulties I experience in getting the payment of the force made, and the non-payment of legitimate bills for boat hire and munitions of war from Her Britannic Majesty's Government, who have done so much for the Imperial Chinese authorities, I have determined on throwing up the command of this force, as my retention of office in these circumstances is derogatory to my position as a British officer, who cannot be a suppliant for what Your Excellency knows to be necessities, and which you should be only too happy to give."

Having written this despatch, Gordon left Kunshan for Shanghai, and on arriving at that port was met with the news that Burgevine, who had been for some time at Shanghai, had joined the rebels, and had gone to Soochow to assist in the defence of that city. This deed of infamy completely changed, in Gordon's opinion, the aspect of affairs, for not only was Burgevine's help likely to strengthen the rebels' position at Soochow, but, as Gordon was well aware, a number of officers and men of the Ever Victorious Army had a strong affection for their late commander. "In these circumstances loyalty to the cause he had adopted made Gordon forget for the moment Li's parsimony and Ch'eng's treachery, and without the loss of an hour he turned his horse's head and rode back to Kunshan."

For some days Gordon remained at Kunshan, waiting to see what developments would arise from the presence of Burgevine in the rebel ranks. As nothing, however, occurred, he again took the field, and after some severe fighting captured an important outwork before Soochow. The turn which things had taken since Gordon had held command, and the capture of so many cities and fortified places had a depressing effect upon the T'aip'ings, and Gordon quickly learnt that within the walls of Soochow there was a strongly-supported movement in favour of making terms with the Imperialists. Several of these faint-hearted leaders opened negotiations personally with Gordon, and at several of the meetings which took place Burgevine was present. Disappointed with the want of spirit which he found to exist in the rebel camp, this versatile traitor proposed to come over to the Imperialists, on condition that he and his men should be declared free from any penalty for the part they had taken in supporting the rebel cause. While preparing for this tergiversation he had the folly to propose to Gordon, of all men in the world, that they should together raise a force and march on Peking, overthrow the dynasty, and on its ruins establish an empire for themselves. One can understand the difficulty which Gordon had to refrain from expressing his contempt and disgust at the folly and crime of such a proposition. Meanwhile negotiations went on, and matters were hastened by a violent incident which occurred within the city walls. The garrison was commanded by Mu Wang, one of the few

honourable men in the rebel ranks, and one who
had not joined the other chieftains in the negotiations with Gordon. He, however, was aware of what
was going on, and invited the commanders to dinner
to discuss the situation. Considerable heat was
shown in the course of the proceedings, and in the
midst of a vehement dispute one of the commanders
drew a dagger and stabbed Mu Wang to the heart.
The conspirators then agreed to give up one of the
gates to Gordon's force. Li, who was cognisant of
the course of events, moved to the neighbourhood
of the city in order to grace with his presence the
expected triumph. On the gate being surrendered,
the commanders went out in a body to Li's quarters
to complete their surrender. What exactly happened
on their entering the presence of the Governor has
never been clearly ascertained. Li subsequently
accused them of having been violent in their
behaviour, and exorbitant in their demands; but,
be that as it may, Li, in spite of his solemn
promise that Gordon's agreement should be observed, and that the lives of the commanders
should be spared, ordered them out to instant
execution. The news of this inhuman treachery
reached Gordon in Soochow, and he then for the
first time during the campaign took a weapon in
his hand. Arming himself with a rifle, he went in
search of the treacherous Li, and would unquestionably have shot him, if the Governor, having received
timely warning of his danger, had not taken to flight.
Outside Li's late headquarters Gordon found the
mangled remains of the men to whom he had

promised life, and the sight of their mutilated bodies added grief and anger to his mind. Only one course was, he felt, open to him in these circumstances, and he wrote to Li " an indignant letter, in which, while proclaiming the infamy of his conduct, he resigned the command of the force."

The capture of Soochow was a crushing blow to the T'aip'ings, and with a great flourish of trumpets Li announced the victory to his Imperial master, who, taking up his vermilion pencil, indicted an edict, in which he described how " the army, acting under orders from Li Hungchang, captured in succession the lines of rebel works outside the four gates of the city, and so struck terror into the enemy, that urgent offers of returning allegiance were made. . . . As a mark of his sincere approbation his majesty is pleased to confer upon him (Li) the honorary title of ' Guardian of the Heir-Apparent,' and to present him with a yellow jacket (which was temporarily taken from him at the close of the Japanese war). Gordon, especially appointed General in the army of Kiangsu, was in command of troops who assisted in these operations. His Majesty, in order to evince his approval of the profound skill and great zeal displayed by him, orders him to receive a military decoration of the first rank and a sum of 10,000 taels." In obedience to this edict, Li sent messengers bearing the 10,000 taels to the still indignant Gordon, and probably never in the history of the Empire have Imperial envoys *dona ferentes* met with such a reception as was accorded to these men. Gordon had been in the habit of leading his men into the

thickest of the fight, carrying in his hand only a stick
with which he directed their movements. On this
occasion he seized the same weapon, and applying
it vigorously to the backs of the astonished envoys,
drove them from his presence, carrying with them
the blood-stained money which had been sent for
his acceptance.

For two months Gordon remained inactive, but at
the end of that period, after much negotiation, he
was induced once again to take the field. Soochow
having fallen, Gordon's prime object was to join
hands with Tsêng Kwofan, who was at this time
closely besieging Nanking. With complete success
he captured the two cities which stood between
him and his objective, and was about to continue
his march towards the "Southern Capital," when
he received an urgent message from Li, begging
him to join him before Changchow Fu. Li's appeal
for help was the more pressing, as he had just lost
the services of General Ch'êng, who, with all his
faults and failings, and they were neither few nor
inconsiderable, was one of the best generals of which
the Imperialists could boast. In an attack on
Kashing Fu he had received a wound when leading
his men, which rapidly proved fatal. Gordon consequently hastened to the succour of his colleague,
and after some stiff fighting captured the city. With
the fall of this stronghold the province of Kiangsu
was restored in its entirety to the Imperialists, and
Hangchow having fallen to the prowess of Tso
Chungt'ang, there remained to the rebels only the
one city of Nanking. The defences of this citadel

were fast crumbling away. Tsêng Kwofan had completely surrounded it, and provisions and ammunition were falling short within the walls. By way of lightening the burden on the rebel commissariat the " Heavenly King" sent out the women and children, as being *bouches inutiles*, to the Imperialist lines. To the credit of Tsêng Kwofan it must be said that he treated these helpless refugees with all consideration. He provided for their wants, and sent them to a place of safety. This was the beginning of the end. A few days later a mine which had been laid by the besiegers was fired, and a wide breach was made in the city wall. Through this opening the Imperialists rushed in, and the fate of the city was at once decided. The " Heavenly King" poisoned himself with gold-leaf, and the Faithful Prince, who had defended the place with the greatest courage, carried off the youthful heir to the T'aip'ing throne, in the vain hope that he might be able to establish an empire in some other part of the country. With characteristic unselfishness he placed the boy on his own horse, and mounted himself on a less well-favoured animal. But the pursuit was too quick for them, and they were both captured. The boy was beheaded on the spot, and Chung Wang was allowed a week's respite for the strange purpose of thus having time to write his own memoir. So soon as he had finished the last line of this curious production he was carried out to the execution ground. The pages which he composed when about to die have since been printed, and are full of interesting matter, though, as might be imagined, strict historical accuracy is not always to be found in them. It is impossible to deny to this man the credit of having fought bravely and well for the cause which he had adopted, and it is not too much to say that if all the other T'aip'ing leaders had been animated with the same spirit of devotion and energy as that by which he was actuated, the T'aip'ing cause might have had a very different issue.

The Ever Victorious Army having now served its end, Li Hungchang, who had always been jealous of it, at once proposed its disbandment. Like all Chinamen, Li is a thorough opportunist. When difficulties present themselves he does his best to grapple with them, but when once they disappear he regards it as quite unnecessary to prepare defences against future evils, or to take to heart any lessons from defeat and failure. We have had abundant evidence of this spirit of late years. The wars of 1858 and 1860, the T'aip'ing Rebellion, the Russian scare, the French war, and the Japanese invasion, have all furnished examples of the inability of Chinamen to do more than struggle, and generally ineffectually, with immediate events. In this respect they are like children in whose eyes the present difficulty is the all-absorbing subject, and who do not understand the possibility that the crisis may occur again. One would have expected that after the experience of the T'aip'ing Rebellion and the very material aid given to the Imperial cause by Gordon's force, Li would have attempted to raise a corps which should be drilled and armed on the same lines. But the instant that Nanking had fallen he was only

too ready to pay off the Ever Victorious Army,
and to rid himself of the hateful intermeddling of
foreign officers in native concerns. Gordon had
proposed that in order to maintain a disciplined
force, a camp should be formed in the neighbourhood
of Shanghai, where a native army could be drilled by
European officers on the English model. But Li
would have none of it, and was quite prepared to
allow his province to revert to its original condition
of corruption and inefficiency until such time as some
new emergency might arise to call for fresh exertions.
But the most signal example of this *laissez-faire*
policy has been displayed since the Japanese war.
Such a crushing defeat by a neighbouring, hitherto
despised, State, would, one would have thought, have
shamed the mandarins into taking measures to make
another such disaster impossible. But they have
done next to nothing to strengthen their position,
and the little that has been effected has been entirely
due to the pressure which has been brought to bear
upon them by Russia and Germany. Another war
would practically find them in as hopeless a condition
as that in which they were in 1894, and the position
is the more hopeless since they feel no shame at
their defeat. Their national pride covers them as
with a garment, and they affect to regard the
invasion of Korea and Manchuria as burglarious
attempts on the part of Japanese pirates to rob them,
by a raid, of their rightful possessions. They are
content to declare that such conduct is contrary to
the rules of propriety, and with this soothing consideration they try to dismiss the subject from their
minds. Shortly before the fall of Nanking some gun-

boats, which in the hour of their emergency the Government had ordered from England, arrived at Shanghai, commanded by Captain Sherard Osborn of the Royal Navy. As their active services were no longer required, Li set to work to destroy their efficiency. His emissaries attempted to bribe the sailors to come over to the native gunboats by offers of large increases of pay, and he proposed such impossible conditions on Sherard Osborn in the case of his fleet being employed, that that officer left the port and steamed to the Peiho to lay his case before the Central Government. But referring from Li Hungchang to the Tsungli Yamén was like asking Mr. Spenlow to decide a question in opposition to Mr. Jorkins. Prince Kung and his colleagues were in full sympathy with Li Hungchang in this matter, and having no immediate use for the gunboats, they were only too glad to have the excuse of Captain Osborn's demands for declining altogether to receive them. In the same spirit Li Hungchang, shortly before the outbreak of the Japanese war, got rid of Captain Lang, who had been for years in command of the northern fleet, and whose continued presence might have put a different complexion on the battle of the Yalu. This curious failure to understand the necessity of preparing for emergencies has brought disaster after disaster upon the country, and at the present moment there is no sign that the authorities are at all alive to the obligations which rest on them if they would preserve the existence of the Empire. Many regiments of their troops are still armed with bows and arrows; immense stores of ammunition are absolutely useless, and their best weapons are obsolete.

XII

THE NIENFEI AND MOHAMMEDAN REBELLIONS

LI HUNGCHANG was called upon to meet, sooner
than might have been expected, an emergency in
which he had again to appeal to foreigners for help.
The suppression of the T'aip'ing Rebellion had not
altogether restored peace to the country. The storm
was over, but the ground-swell still remained, and
from the disturbing elements which had been evoked
another movement, hostile to the Imperial Government, rose in arms. The rebels had been so long
accustomed to live by plunder rather than by honest
work, that when as T'aip'ings their occupation was
gone, they combined together again to raise the
standard of revolt in the provinces of Shantung and
Honan. Under the title of Nienfei these restless
marauders wandered over the country looting and
murdering. With some success they captured open
towns and villages, and so serious was at one time
the aspect of affairs that Li, whose experiences at
Kiangsu were considered to have peculiarly fitted
him for the task, was appointed Commissioner to
suppress the rising.

23

On receiving his nomination Li at once enlisted the services of as many of his old European officers as still were to be found in Shanghai, and with these as the backbone of his force he took the field against the rebels. The province of Shantung, where the rebels were strongest, so far resembles in outline the province of Kiangsu that three sides of it, the north, east, and south, are washed by the ocean. It had been Li's aim in the previous campaign to drive the T'aip'ings into the promontory of Kiangsu, and now, imitating the same tactics, he attempted to urge the Neinfei against the seaboard in Shantung, and there to overwhelm them. He was so far successful that he succeeded in driving the enemy into the desired position. But he had forgotten that troops could be transported by sea as well as moved on land, and to his extreme mortification, after having built a wall across the neck of the promontory, he found that the rebels had taken ship, had outflanked his position, and were pursuing their predatory career in the districts in his rear. For this and other failures he was robbed of the Yellow Jacket which he had won against the T'aip'ings and was ordered back to his Viceroyalty—he had in the meantime become Viceroy of the Liang Hu Provinces. By the skilful use of his Court influence, however, he retained his position, and by a fortunate series of victories, finally achieved the success which at first was denied him. At the conclusion of the campaign he was granted an Imperial audience, when he had the gratification of once more finding the Yellow Jacket placed upon his shoulders.

By a merciful dispensation of Providence, so far as the Manchu Dynasty of China is concerned, the rebellions which have disturbed the peace of the Empire during the present century have been guided by men who have proved themselves quite incapable of establishing a settled government in the districts over which they have established their power. While the Imperial forces were engaged in a death struggle with the T'aip'ings, a rebellion, which at one time seemed likely to assume very serious proportions, broke out in the province of Yunnan. That district has always contained a large Mohammedan population. Accounts differ as to whence these followers of the Prophet originally came. They themselves have a legend that during a rebellion which broke out in the eighth century, a mission was sent by the reigning Emperor to Bagdad asking the Khalif for succour against his revolting subjects. In answer to this appeal three thousand Turkish soldiers were lent to the hardly pressed "Son of Heaven." Having successfully accomplished their errand they were naturally inclined to return to their native lands, but were refused admission among their countrymen on the ground that they had been defiled by a residence among pork-eating infidels. They, therefore, made up their minds to settle in Yunnan, where some few remnants of these first immigrants remain at the present day. Some colour is given to this account by the fact that the people in their appearance more nearly resemble natives of Arabia than sons of Han. By the constant inter-marriage with the Chinese their features have become

to a great extent sinicised, though they can be still
readily distinguished by their superior stature, greater
physical strength, and more energetic physiognomies.
But whatever may be the semblance of truth in this
story, it is a well-known fact that in the early part of
the fourteenth century the province of Yunnan was
largely populated by Mohammedans, and we know
from the records that a century earlier the faith
of Islam was carried into China by Mussulman
emigrants from Central Asia.

Up to the middle of the present century these
strangers and pilgrims seem to have lived at peace
with their Confucianist and Buddhist neighbours.
At times no doubt they felt the heavy hand of
oppression, at the instance of narrow-minded officials,
and in 1851 so fierce a persecution arose that an
urgent petition was presented to the Throne accusing
the Emperor's officials of gross oppression and
wrong, and praying that a just and honest man
might be sent to rule in Yunnan. This memorial
was unproductive of any results, but for a time
nothing occurred to disturb the peace of the province.
In 1855, however, a riot broke out at one of the
copper mines for which Yunnan is famous. Unfortunately the mandarin in command of the district
combined cowardice with incompetency, and took to
flight, leaving the rioters to fight out their difficulty.
A general massacre is a very common Chinese
remedy for suppressing a revolt, and the Yunnan
officials deemed this a proper opportunity for
applying the exterminating cure. The Viceroy, to
his credit be it said, raised a protest against so

drastic a remedy, but finding himself unable to check his subordinates, committed suicide in order to emphasise his disapproval of their brutal proposal. Unfortunately this self-sacrifice was unavailing, and in spite of the Viceroyal incident a day was fixed for the slaughter. Although rumours had been rife that this wholesale murder was to be committed, the Mahommedans were, strangely enough, taken by surprise, and many fell victims to the relentless swords of the mandarins. But a remnant was left, and these men, driven desperate by the conduct of their oppressors, banded themselves together, vowing to oppose to the death the Imperial rule in Yunnan. Two leaders were at this time forced to the front by circumstances. One was a man named Ma, who exercised priestly functions, and who had accumulated religious sanctity by having made a pilgrimage to Mecca. After his visit to that sacred city he had travelled through Egypt and Turkey, and had returned to China with a high reputation for religious zeal and knowledge. The other chieftain was known as Tu. This man, who, as was afterwards seen, proved to be the staunchest commander of the two, took early possession of the important city of Talifu, and there organised some sort of local government. In choosing this city as his headquarters he showed a keen eye for military defence. Dr. Anderson in his "Mandalay to Momein," thus described this stronghold : "Although Talifu is a small town the population of which did not at that time (1857) exceed thirty-five thousand, the rich plain walled in by mountains, and with a lake teeming with fish, stretching forty miles in length and ten in breadth, maintained a population estimated before the war at four hundred thousand ; . . . the mountains to the north and south close in upon the lake, and the plain and city are accessible only by two strongly fortified passes. . . . Thus Tali has been from the earliest times a strong city ; it was the capital of a kingdom at the invasion of Kublai Khan, and is still regarded by the Tibetans, who make pilgrimages to its vicinity, as the ancient home of their forefathers."

Secure in the possession of this stronghold Tu declared himself independent of Ma, who was thus left to command such forces in the field as he was able to collect. At the head of his somewhat ragged regiments he attacked the city of Yunnan Fu, and was repulsed without much difficulty. In 1859, however, he reappeared before its walls at the head of fifty thousand fighting-men. This attack was seriously meant, and the Imperialist garrison was reduced to such a parlous state that they were on the point of surrendering, when to their infinite surprise and relief they received proposals from Ma of negotiations for peace, on the understanding that he and his men should be accepted as Imperialist recruits. This opportunity of escape from a dire and impending disaster was too convenient to be allowed to lapse, and the terms were not only promptly arranged between the leaders on the spot, but met with full and instant approval at Peking. Ma himself was promised high office in the State, and his kinsman of the same surname, and who enjoyed the personal name of Julung, was made a general in the

Imperial army. When sides are so easily exchanged
and prizes so easily won, the temptation to indulge
in personal ambitions is more than most men, and
especially Orientals, can resist, and on the occasion of
Ma Julung taking the field against the rebel force,
his lieutenant, whom he had left in command at
Yunnan Fu, raised the standard of revolt, murdered
the Viceroy, and took possession of the town in the
Mohammedan interest. This treacherous move was
short-lived. Ma hastened back to the city, effected
an entrance through the walls, and after five days'
hard fighting, restored all that was left of it to the
Imperial sway. During this time Tu was consolidating his power at Tali Fu, and being a man of
determination and vigour, whose authority it was
essential to check, it was deemed best and safest by
the Imperialists to attempt to subdue him by offers
of preferment rather than by attacks on his fortress.
The priestly Ma, being of a diplomatic turn, was
deputed to open relations with him, and by displaying the honours which had rewarded his own
treachery to persuade him to follow his example. But
the chieftain was made of sterner stuff than his inter-
viewer, and treated with disdain his dastardly proposals.

When so vast a province as Yunnan, covering as it
does an area of 107,969 square miles, is in the throes
of rebellion, it is impossible to suppose that the spirit
of unrest should not spread to the neighbouring
districts. In the adjoining province of Kweichow
existed, and still exists, a large population of Miaotzŭ
who have a distinct origin from the Chinese, and who
are survivors of one of the original races which occu-

pied the Empire before the advent of the Chinese.
As the primitive invaders advanced into the country
the Miaotzŭ, like the other aboriginal tribes, retreated
to the mountain fastnesses in Kweichow, Kwangsi,
and on the Tibetan frontier. In these places they
have persistently held themselves aloof from their
more powerful neighbours, and though ordinarily
peaceful, have on repeated occasions been goaded by
oppression into taking up arms against their tyrants.
At the time of which we are speaking (1863) they,
for some unexplained reason, broke out into revolt,
and thus placed the Imperial forces in Yunnan
between two fires. Another aspirant to leadership,
named Liang, at the same time raised the standard
of disaffection at a town called Linan Fu, and thus
further added to the difficulties of the Imperialists,
which were already sufficiently embarrassing. For
some three or four years this most unsatisfactory
condition of affairs remained practically unchanged.
There was fighting here and there, but no distinct
advantage was gained by either side. Later on an
attack (1867), made by Ma on the defenders of Tali
Fu, proved unsuccessful, and he in no way succeeded
in preventing Tu from keeping open his communications with Burma, from which convenient territory
he was able to procure an unfailing supply of arms
and ammunition for the support of his cause. But
after all he was constrained to feel that though
holding his own he was not making headway, and he
could not but recognise that support from the outside
was necessary to enable him to continue to maintain
a successful struggle. He had entertained in his

dominions, and had been civilly treated by, the members of an English mission sent from Burma to report upon the trading facilities which might be hoped for from Yunnan. His thoughts, therefore, naturally turned towards England, and he despatched a nephew to London with directions to open relations with the English Government, in the hope that they might be induced to lend their countenance to his cause. It is needless to say that these overtures were declined. But this was not all. They indirectly had a most diastrous effect on the fortunes of the rebels, for the Chinese Government, alarmed at the mere possibility of foreign interference, determined to crush once and for all the Mohammedan movement. Meanwhile Tu had attempted to turn the scales on his enemies, and had besieged Yunnan Fu. The venture, however, proved unsuccessful, and he had again to betake himself for shelter to the stout walls of Tali Fu. While the Imperial authorities were, in that leisurely way which belongs to them, gathering themselves up for the fatal spring upon the Mohammedans, matters dragged on and were diversified only by petty engagements, and by the treacherous murder of some rebel chiefs who had surrendered themselves on the usual understanding that their lives would be spared. Like most acts of treacherous cruelty, this one was both unwise and uncalled for. It embittered the feeling on the part of the Mohammedans against the Imperialists, and disinclined men who were disposed to go over to the Emperor's generals to trust themselves to their tender mercies.

A large importation of Hunan soldiers, commanded
by one of Tsêng Kwofan's lieutenants, added greatly
to the Imperial strength at this time, and a forced
contribution of 70,000 taels per month, which was
contributed by six of the other provinces, placed the
provincial exchequer in a comparatively flourishing
condition. With these auxiliary forces the Emperor's
cause began to make way, and gradually the whole
province was recovered with the exception of the one
city, Tali Fu. With an irresistible weight of numbers
the Imperialists closely besieged this doomed stronghold, and it soon became evident that it was destined
to fall into their hands. In so exhausted and starving a condition did the garrison become at last that
Tu opened negotiations for the surrender of the town.
One wonders at the folly of men who could trust their
lives in the hands of opponents who had in almost
every case falsified their treaty oaths, and had
slaughtered without mercy those to whom they had
promised life. But so it was. Tu surrendered himself knowingly to death, the Imperialists having
refused to spare his life. But the other chieftains
encouraged themselves to believe that in their cases
the compact would be kept. On the day appointed
for the delivery of the city, Tu was carried through
the streets and out to the Imperial camp in a sedan-
chair, accompanied with every insignia of Empire.
With impatient desire General Ma received this
equipage, which, when opened, however, revealed, to
his disappointment, that he was possessed with but
the corpse of the dreaded chief. Another version of
the surrender states that Tu, on presenting himself

before the Commander-in-chief, asked for a cup of cold water. This was given him, and he fell dead from the effects of a poison which the water had suddenly brought into action. Though robbed of his living victim, Ma decapitated the corpse, and sent the head, preserved in honey, to grace the palace of his Imperial master. The usual events followed on the surrender of the city. The Mohammedan leaders were invited to a grand feast, and while yet they sat at meat, a body of soldiers who had been concealed in the room rushed out on them and cut them down to the last man. This villainy having been effected, a further outrage was committed. At a given signal the soldiers were let loose on the inhabitants of the city. The scenes that were there witnessed are not to be surpassed in horror. The troops slaughtered their helpless victims until fatigue made it impossible for them to deal out further murders, and no fewer than thirty thousand men, women, and children perished in the massacre.

For seventeen years the province had been desolated by the relentless wars of which it had been the scene, while to add to the horrors of the situation the plague had swept over whole districts, carrying havoc into the ranks of both the rebels and their opponents alike. Up to this day Yunnan has not recovered from these fearful visitations. Whole neighbourhoods are still untenanted and the lands uncultivated. Though rich in minerals, the soil is not on the whole productive, and as the mandarins hold with a jealous care a monopoly over the mines, there is little to attract immigrants into the province. That as a mining district it has great possibilities there can be no doubt, and with the prospect of railway communication with Burma, it may be that a great future lies before the present unhappy district.

It is a curious coincidence that while there was no kind of connection or intercommunication between the Mohammedans of Yunnan and their co-religionists in North-western China, a wave of rebellion should have swept over the provinces of Shensi and Kansu at the same time that Ma and Tu were raising the standard of revolt in the south-west. At this time (1857) the Taip'ing Rebellion was so fully occupying the attention of the Chinese Government, that they were unable to do more than hold in check the revolting followers of the Prophet, and it was not until five years afterwards that an act of treachery on the part of the Chinese fanned the smouldering ashes of discontent into a flame. The position now required more stringent measures than had hitherto been taken, and two Chinese Commissioners were despatched to restore order in the disturbed districts. In an ill-fated moment a plot was laid for the murder of these men, and while one escaped, the other suffered death at the hands of the assassins. The murderer, when taken, was done to death with the utmost refinement of cruelty, and a decree was issued by the young Emperor T'ungchih ordering a general massacre of all those who should persist in following the creed of Islam. With considerable and unwonted success the Emperor's forces suppressed the rebellion within the frontier of China proper. But beyond the great wall stretches a dreary waste as far as Aksu which is dotted at distant and lonely intervals by cities held in the name of the "Son of Heaven." These garrisons were mostly Mohammedan, and, infected with the desire of throwing off the Chinese yoke, they broke out into a simultaneous revolt. In these wild districts there are always elements of disorder lying dormant but ready to rise into action at a moment's notice, and on all sides the pretenders to lost thrones and aspirants to chieftainships took up arms against the paramount power in the hope that in the prevailing disorder they might be able to satisfy their ambitions. By the surviving loyal garrisons T'ungchih's truculent order was, however, faithfully obeyed, though in one instance at least the tables were turned on the would-be murderers. It had been arranged by the Chinese garrison in Yarkand that they should at a given hour put all their Mohammedan fellow-soldiers to the sword, and this would doubtless have been done, had not the followers of the Prophet taken time by the forelock and risen against the too dilatory Chinese. At Khokand the last surviving son of Jehangir, who had been Taokwang's restless opponent, attempted to wrest from the Chinese the city which he pretended to regard as his own. Had this man been left to fight his own battles his career would probably have been a still shorter one than it was. But with the assistance of Yakoob Khan, an able and energetic officer, he succeeded in establishing himself as ruler in Khokand. He had no sooner, however, reached the pinnacle of his ambition than he was deposed by Yakoob, who, having won the laurels of victory, thought himself entitled to wear the crown of Empire. In the East such acts of treachery receive no condemnation so long as they are successful, and Yakoob's sovereignty received the seal of general recognition by a solemn act by which the title of Athalik Ghazi, "The Champion Father," was conferred on him at the hands of the Amir of Bokhara. Unfortunately for the Chinese, the movement which had swept over the wide regions south of the T'ienshan mountains spread into the province of Ili, where occurred a repetition of all those unspeakable horrors which usually accompany Asiatic outbreaks. In this case, however, the rebels and their opponents came into contact with a power which has not on all occasions shown itself friendly to the cause of the "Son of Heaven." For some time Russia endured in silence the local disturbances which broke out across her frontier, and ignored the raids which were not unfrequently made into her territory by flying rebels or retreating Imperialists. At length the disorders reached a point, or the Russians were good enough to think that they had done so, when they could no longer be endured, and the Muscovite authorities gave formal notice to the Chinese Government that they were about at once to march in and take possession of the province until such time as the Chinese Government was able effectively to reoccupy the territory. Meanwhile, the Chinese Government was moving up troops preparatory to a regular campaign against the rebels further south. Tso Chungt'ang, who had served against the T'aip'ings with distinction and honour, was made Viceroy of Shensi and Kansu, with complete control over the military movements. Fortunately Tso was a man of

proved ability and of great steadfastness of purpose.
The task before him was one of supreme importance,
and practically meant the recovery to the Chinese
Crown of the whole of Central Asia, as well as the
pacification of the two provinces over which he was
directly called upon to preside. With indefatigable
energy he set about the gigantic undertaking, and
was fortunate in the choice of his subordinate, General
Kinshun, who throughout the campaign showed
marked military ability. By the end of 1872 Tso
had closely besieged the important city of Suchow,
which ultimately surrendered to his arms. Having
achieved this success it was arranged that he should
remain at the base to organise the expeditionary
forces, while Kinshun should march across the dreary
desert of Gobi which lies between the frontier of
China Proper and Barkul. Without meeting with
any serious resistance he captured that town, and
then, returning to Hami, succeeded in adding the
capture of that stronghold to his triumphs. With the
force at his command, however, he felt unable to
advance further into the rebel country, and in conjunction with Tso desired the establishment of communications over the three or four hundred miles
which separate Hami from Suchow. Then followed
one of those strange episodes which could not occur
in any other country in the world except China.
Chinese methods occasionally grind surely, but they
always grind slowly, and with the most leisurely
indifference the two chiefs arranged that on the
several oases in the desert crops should be grown
for the supply of the expedition which was to be

despatched into Central Asia. For the time being the soldiers were turned into farm labourers. They sowed their seed, they watered their fields, and when the autumn sun had ripened their crops they reaped their harvests. By this time (1876) Tso's legions were ready to advance. After a successful march Kinshun's troops appeared before Urumtsi, which to their surprise and relief surrendered without striking a blow. Manas was the next objective of the Imperial forces. Here the defence was ably conducted, and it was only by closely besieging the walls that at length the garrison was starved into the act of surrender. Experience had probably taught the rebels that a vanquished foe had no mercy to expect from Chinese soldiers, and when, therefore, the time came to surrender the city, the garrison marched out in fighting order, and with their women and children enclosed within solid phalanxes of men. Their object in adopting this order was obvious, and was put beyond doubt by a desperate charge which they made to force their way through the Chinese lines. In this they were unsuccessful, and while the lives of the women and children were spared by the special orders of Kinshun, no restraining hand was put on the soldiers to prevent the slaughter of the garrison. From this point onwards the Chinese triumphed all along the line, and though Yakoob Khan intervened on behalf of the rebels, he failed utterly to turn back the tide of war. After several defeats this celebrated leader returned to Korla, where he died from disease, or, as was broadly stated at the time, by a dose of poison. Aksu, Yarkand,

Kashgar, and Khoten fell before the victorious Chinese generals, who thus in the year 1878 were able to report to the Throne that the Emperor was again master of his own. Honours were showered on the successful commanders, and Tso was admitted to the Grand Secretariat, was made a member of the Tsungli Yamên, and was promoted to be Viceroy of the two Kiang provinces.

It is necessary now to revert to the period at the close of the war of 1860. In order to make the sequence of events intelligible it was considered advisable to trace " from the egg to his apples " the history of the T'aip'ing movement and the rebellions which may be said directly or indirectly to have sprung from it. The system of administration in China is a very disjointed one, and events of high moment and concern may, and often do, occur in one part of that unwieldy Empire, and yet leave no trace on the rest of the country. The rebellions which have been dealt with in this chapter may be considered in this sense to be little more than local outbreaks, and can scarcely be said to have affected the affairs at Peking. So soon as the Allies left for the south in 1860 the Grand Council of State took into consideration the question of the future management of foreign affairs. Up to this time the Government, with that contemptuous disregard of everything relating to the Outer Barbarians which belongs to them, had relegated the management of foreign affairs to the *Lifan Yuan*, or "Colonial Office." That is to say, European affairs were classed with the trivial concerns of Mongolian and Central Asian

24

nomads. The continuation of this system was plainly impossible now that relations with foreign governments had become closer, and it was determined therefore to establish a Bureau, called the Tsungli Yamèn, or "Yamèn of General Superintendence," which should serve the purposes of a

COURTYARD OF TSUNGLI YAMÈN AT PEKIN.

Foreign Office. Prince Kung was nominated the first President, with Wènhsiang and Kweiliang as his colleagues. As the business increased additions were made to this board, and at the present time it numbers eleven magnates, who daily discuss foreign affairs, and do very little else. Sir Harry Parkes likened a visit to the Tsungli Yamèn to lowering buckets into a bottomless well. The first few years of T'ungchih's reign passed quietly enough, and the Government discussed with the Foreign Ministers, who were now established in Legations at Peking, the means by which they might so strengthen the Empire as to make it a really independent State. Much good advice was lavished on these occasions, and some faint efforts were made to carry out the recommendations given. The main desire of the Regency was to strengthen the army, and with this object drill books were translated from English into Chinese, and arsenals were established at Foochow, Nanking, and Shanghai. At the first-named port a French naval officer, M. Giguel, was appointed Superintendent, and at Nanking Dr. Macartney, now Sir Haliday, presided over the management. These three establishments did good work within certain limits. But the Chinese military service suffers under the extreme disability of being a despised profession, and so long as this is the case arsenals may continue to turn out guns, and dockyards may produce ships, but the officers will be always inefficient and the men untrustworthy. But the Chinese have from all time depended more on negotiation and diplomacy to keep their enemies from the gate than on weapons of defence. Already they had repented themselves that they had granted many of the concessions which were embodied in the treaties, and they at once began to whittle down the more generous clauses of those agreements. The admission of Foreign Ministers into Peking was regarded as such an enormous privilege, and the Chinese took every means in their

power to magnify the boon, that the first representatives of the European Courts in the capital were
overawed by the position which they were called
upon to occupy, and in response to civil words and
pleasant phrases from members of the Tsungli
Yamên, showed a disposition to barter away the
rights acquired by their countrymen. Among these
officials was Mr. Burlingham, the representative of
the United States of America. He was a man of
considerable eloquence, of an enthusiastic tempera-
ment, and of a nature malleable by skilful treatment.
In the hands of Prince Kung and Wênhsiang he
was as clay in the hands of the potters, and while
readily accepting their views of the situation, believed
implicitly in their loudly expressed desires for reform
in the administration of the Empire. Having
thoroughly indoctrinated him with their pretended
opinions on these subjects, they invited him to lay
aside his official position as regarded his own country
and to accept the rôle of Chinese Minister to the
Courts of Europe and America. In this character
he visited the capitals of the Western world, and
gained some share of success for the objects of his
mission, which mainly consisted of the plea that
China should be allowed to manage her own affairs
irrespective of treaty obligations and foreign rights.
While this enthusiastic envoy was describing to
European listeners the wisdom, tolerance and
liberality of the Chinese officials and people, an
event occurred at Yangchow, in the province of
Kiangsu, which shook the confidence of his hearers
in the accuracy of his generous professions. Mr.

Hudson Taylor the leading spirit in the China Inland Mission, taking advantage of the clause in the treaty which provided that " since the Christian religion, as professed by Protestants and Roman Catholics, inculcates the practice of virtue, and teaches man to do as he would be done by, persons teaching it or professing it shall alike be entitled to the protection of the Chinese authorities, nor shall any such, peaceably pursuing their calling, and not offending against the law, be persecuted or interfered with," established himself at Yangchow. It was never denied that he and his people had lived quietly with the people, and the only charges which were brought against him were the usual groundless accusations that he and his followers were in the habit of killing children and of using their eyes and hearts for medicinal purposes. Ridiculous as these charges were, they found ready acceptance with the mob, who, far from being held in check by the mandarins, were openly encouraged by them in their demonstrations against the foreigners. A Chinese mob is easily roused, and when once aroused is capable of great fury. In this case they assaulted the missionaries, burnt down their houses, and drove them from the city. An immediate demand for reparation was made by Mr. Medhurst, H.B.M. Consul at Shanghai, who required that the local mandarins should be degraded ; that certain *Literati* who had instituted the riots should be punished ; that two thousand taels should be paid as compensation for the wounded and ejected missionaries ; that these ministers of the gospel should be officially received back; and that a tablet should be erected on which should be inscribed the history of the riot, with a declaration that foreigners have a treaty right to visit the interior of the Empire. At this time Tsêng Kwofan, who it will be remembered won his laurels in engagements against the T'aip'ings, was Viceroy of the two Kiang provinces, and so soon as Mr. Medhurst's terms were referred to him he at once vetoed the demands for the punishment of the *Literati* and for the erection of the tablet. Both Mr. Medhurst and Sir Rutherford Alcock, who was the British Minister at Peking, had been trained in the pre-Legation-at-Peking system of dealing with the local authorities, and with the full permission of his chief, the Consul, quite in the old and most efficacious manner, steamed up the Yangtsze with a small naval squadron, and anchored his ships opposite the walls of Nanking. The effect was instantaneous, as similar demonstrations have always proved with the Chinese, and every condition was promptly complied with, the only modification being that the tablet which Mr. Medhurst had declared should be of stone was, in consideration for Tsêng Kwofan's feelings, set up in wood. At the same time a proclamation was issued in which the local authorities were held up to reprobation, the condign punishment of the ringleaders was announced, and the Viceroyal consent was given to the other terms of reparation proposed. The effect of Mr. Medhurst's judicious treatment of the emergency has since shown itself to be lasting and salutary. Since the memorable day in which he entered Yangchow, accompanied by an escort of four hundred marines and sailors, the city from having been one of the most anti-foreign centres in the Empire, has become eminently peaceable and law-abiding.

It is noticeable that the anti-foreign outbursts which have so frequently occurred have been generally, though not always, accompanied by similar riots in other parts of the country. Just about this time anti-missionary rebellions took place in Formosa, at Swatow, Foochow, and in the province of Szech'uan, where Père Rigaud was unfortunately murdered. Following the example set by Mr. Medhurst, M. de Rochechouart went personally to the scene of the last outbreak, and was able successfully to arrange terms which were satisfactory both to the Minister and to the Government which he represented. These matters were scarcely settled when an outbreak of more than usual violence occurred in Tientsin (June, 1870).

XIII

THE CLOSE OF T'UNGCHIH'S REIGN AND THE FIRST YEARS OF THAT OF KWANGHSÜ.

FOR some time ill-will had been manifested towards the Roman Catholic establishments at Tientsin, and more especially against the orphanage which had been established by Sisters of Mercy ; and at the end of May an epidemic, which occurred in that establishment, and which proved especially fatal, aroused the popular feeling to frenzy. There has always been a superstitious belief amongst Chinamen that Europeans are in the habit of using the eyes and hearts of deceased infants for medicinal purposes, and the numerous deaths which occurred at this time led the ignorant townspeople to give credence to the folly. So threatening did the mob become that the Sisters thought it wise to offer to allow a committee of five from among the rioters to examine the premises. How far this concession may have met the necessities of the case it is difficult to say. But the French Consul, deeming it an unworthy surrender to menace, repaired to the orphanage and drove the committee of five into the street. Against this summary proceeding the Chinese District Magistrate strongly protested, and expressed fear that unless some such arrangement were made with the people the consequences might be serious. This threat was speedily fulfilled, and on the 21st of June a surging crowd assembled around the Orphanage. The French Consul, recognising the stormy outlook, hurried off to Chung How, the Superintendent of Foreign Trade, who was the senior native authority on the spot, and urged him to take steps to quell the mob. It is said that the Consul was in a "state of excitement bordering on insanity." But however that may be, Chung How was either unwilling or unable to act as demanded, and the Consul made his way out into the mob, pistol in hand. Accounts vary as to what subsequently happened. It is said that he fired into the crowd, but, whether this be so or not, it is certain that he was speedily knocked down and beaten to death.

The mob, having once tasted blood, rushed to the Sisters' Orphanage, where they murdered the unfortunate ladies, after inflicting on them all kinds of nameless barbarities. They then set fire to the buildings, having, however, had the humanity to allow the children to escape. In their mad fury they murdered a Russian and his young bride, whom they took to be French, and who were trying to make their escape to the foreign settlement. In all twenty foreigners were killed, and as many more Chinese attendants. This fiendish massacre was doubtless due partly to ignorance, but principally to the appearance at this time of a work entitled " Death

Blow to Corrupt Doctrines," which describes the
worship of the Christians in terms so nearly identical
with those used by Gibbon in his history of the early
persecutions at Rome, that we are tempted to quote
the words of the author of the " Decline and Fall of
the Roman Empire." In the passage referred to
Gibbon states that the Christians " were regarded
as the most wicked of human kind, who practised in
their dark recesses every abomination that a depraved
fancy could suggest, and who solicited the favour of
their unknown God by the sacrifice of every moral
virtue. There were many who pretended to confess
or to relate the ceremonies of the abhorred society.
It was asserted that a new-born infant, entirely
covered over with flour, was presented, like some
mystic symbol of initiation, to the knife of the
proselyte, who unknowingly inflicted many a
secret and mortal wound on the innocent victim
of his error ; and as soon as the cruel deed was
perpetrated the sectaries drank up the blood,
greedily tore asunder the quivering members, and
pledged themselves to eternal secrecy by a mutual
consciousness of guilt. It was as confidently affirmed
that this inhuman sacrifice was succeeded by a
suitable entertainment, in which intemperance
served as a provocation to brutal lust ; till at the
appointed moment, the lights were suddenly ex-
tinguished, shame was banished, nature was forgotten ; and, as accident might direct, the darkness
of the night was polluted by the commerce of sisters
and brothers, of sons and of mothers." Vigorous
protests were made to the Chinese Government

against the continued distribution of this infamous
work, and at the same time the Foreign Ministers
presented a united demand for the punishment of
the ringleaders of the riot, both official and non-
official, and for compensation for the murders committed.

At this time Tsêng Kwofan, who had been promoted from the Viceroyalty of the two Kiang, to the
same position in the metropolitan province, was
residing at Paoting Fu, the provincial capital. By
Imperial decree he was appointed, together with
Chung How, to inquire into the circumstances of the
massacre. But Tsêng was getting old, and the strong
prejudice which he had always exhibited against
foreigners disinclined him to take any active steps to
punish the perpetrators of the atrocities. Sir Thomas
Wade, who at this time represented England at
Peking, was not a man, however, tamely to submit to
be put off by unsympathetic officials, and on Tsêng
showing signs of dilatoriness, he addressed a remon-
strance direct to Prince Kung in these terms. " As
to the atrocities committed, although there is no
doubt about the popular exasperation, there is the
strongest reason to doubt that the destruction of the
religious establishments, and the murder of their
occupants, were exclusively the work of the ignorant
multitude. The chief actors in the affair are stated to
have been the fire brigades, and the banded villains
known as the Hunsing Tzŭ. These were ready for
the attack, and as soon as the gong sounded, fell in,
provided with deadly weapons. They were reinforced
by soldiers and Yamên followers, and conspicuously

directed by a man with the title of Titu (Major-
General), the ex-rebel Chên Kwojui. . . . Yet after
more than seventy days' delay what has been done
towards the satisfaction of justice? Some few of the
lower class of criminals have been arrested, the more
important of these not having been discoverable until
their names and their whereabouts were supplied by
the French Legation. The guilty magistrates were
left for twenty days after the massacre at their posts,
their energies being devoted throughout that period,
not to the detection of persons guilty of a share in
the crime, but to the examination under torture of
unfortunate Christians, from whom it was hoped that
confessions might be extorted in such a form as
to tell favourably for their persecutors. . . . The
common people, seeing no punishment inflicted on
any one, persuaded themselves that the massacre was
a meritorious act. Songs are sung in honour of it, and
paintings of it are circulated representing officials as
approving spectators of the crime. . . . I must add, in
conclusion, what it will give your Imperial Highness
little pleasure to read, as little certainly as to myself
to write; but the occasion requires that I should
speak out. It is very generally believed that, although
your Imperial Highness and the wiser of your colleagues are opposed to any policy that would involve
a rupture with foreign Powers, there are other leading
men in China whose dream is the expulsion of the
Barbarian, and who, if they were not the immediate
instigators of the movement of the 21st of June, have
heartily approved its atrocities ; have exerted themselves to prevent the punishment of the guilty parties,

official and non-official ; and are even now urging on the Central Government the expediency of directing a like murderous enterprise against all foreigners that may be found on Chinese ground."

This, and other remonstrances from Sir Thomas Wade's colleagues at Peking, at length compelled the Government to take action, but at the same time it was generally acknowledged that the continuance of Tsêng Kwofan in his existing post stood as a bar to the satisfaction of the foreign demands. It so happened that at this juncture the Viceroy of the two Kiang provinces was murdered by a fanatic in the streets of Nanking, and the opportunity was seized upon, therefore, of transferring Tsêng to this thus vacated office, and of bringing Li Hungchang from Hukwang to the metropolitan province. "We command Li Hungchang," so ran the Imperial Edict, "who has been translated to the Viceroyalty of Chihli, to proceed post to Tientsin, there, in concert with Tsêng Kwofan, Ting Jihch'ang, and Chêng Lin, to conduct the inquiry still open, and take the necessary action. . . . Respect this." Though thus commanded to act in concert with his colleagues, a free hand was practically given to Li, who at once, taking a firm grip of the situation, gave the people of Tientsin plainly to understand that any recrudescence of the anti-foreign agitation would be sternly repressed. Under this new *régime* the investigations proceeded apace, with the result that the Prefect and District Magistrate were sentenced to banishment to Manchuria ; that twenty of the rioters were condemned to death ; and that twenty-one were consigned to banishment. It is always difficult to estimate the real value of such a sentence as that passed on the culpable officials.   It not unfrequently happens that in response to foreign pressure a mandarin is removed from a post, and ostensibly degraded, while in fact he may only be moved to an office of greater honour and emolument, and a certain amount of doubt must always rest on the just identification of rioters, who are offered up on

THE COURTYARD OF AN INN IN MANCHURIA.

the execution ground to propitiate outraged foreign feeling.   Cases have happened of prisoners, who have been condemned for other crimes, being executed to satisfy the numerical balance of victims to be punished for murders committed.   In this instance, however, no doubt seems to have arisen about the guilt of sixteen of the malefactors, and these were therefore executed on the 18th of October, 1870.   The circum-

stances, however, which attended their decapitation
were such as to show that they were rather regarded as martyrs in a holy cause than as criminals
guilty of heinous crimes. In a report to Sir Thomas
Wade the Consul on the spot thus describes the
scene : "About two hundred police and soldiers
escorted them (the criminals) from the jail to the
magistrate's court room, where they were marshalled,
sixteen in all. None of them would kneel to be bound
when ordered to do so. They were all dressed in what
is everywhere stated to be a Government present,
viz., new silk clothes, and wore on their feet shoes
of elegant manufacture. Their hair was dressed after
the female fashion, in various modes ; and ornaments
such as those seen on the heads of Chinese ladies were
stuck in their head-dresses." The Russian Ambassador not being satisfied that the four men charged with
the murder of his compatriots were really guilty of
the crime laid to their charge, secured them a reprieve,
which resulted in two being sent into banishment, and
the remaining two following their associates to the
execution ground. Subsequent inquiry proved that
the sentence on the prefect and magistrate was of
the illusory nature common to such cases. Instead
of going on a weary journey to Manchuria they were
allowed to return to the bosom of their families,
where no doubt they received the ovations which are
commonly lavished on patriots.

The Titu, Chên Kwojui, of whom Sir Thomas
Wade spoke, was a veritable stormy petrel. His
career had been chequered by many vicissitudes. He
had begun life as a T'aip'ing rebel, and had deserted

the banners which had sheltered him for the Imperial
ranks in return for promotion and increased pay. His
hatred of foreigners amounted almost to a mania, and
his presence in the same town with Europeans was
invariably the precursor of riots and disturbances. It
is said that an accident led him to visit Tientsin at
the moment of the outbreak and certain it is that he
led on the mob to the attack. Being a *persona grata*
with the Powers at Peking he was carefully shielded
from all harm, and the utmost step that Sir Thomas
Wade could persuade the Tsungli Yamên to take,
was to send him back to Nanking and there to place
him under surveillance. They agreed, however, to
pay the sum of 400,000 taels to France as compensation for the murder of the Sisters of Mercy, and
consented to despatch Chung How on a special
embassy to Paris to express the regret of the Government for the murderous outbreak. It will be remembered that Chung How was the presiding mandarin
at the time of the massacre, and it was therefore
peculiarly fitting and proper that his should be the
lips to utter the apologies and regrets.

The excitement which had been stirred up in connection with the missionary question by these events
was by no means confined to Tientsin and the neighbourhood, but was widely spread over many parts of
the country. Distinct evidence had been furnished
that this unrest was fomented, as Sir Thomas Wade
had pointed out, by some of the highest officers of
state, and the occasion was characteristically seized
upon by the Tsungli Yamên to attempt to minimise
the Treaty rights as regarded the teaching of Christ-

ianity. With this view the Yamên drew up eight articles for the regulation of missionary undertakings, and enclosed them in a letter addressed to the various foreign Legations, which in each case ran as follows :

" SIR,—In relation to the missionary question, the members of the Foreign Office are apprehensive lest in their efforts to manage the various points connected with it, they should interrupt the good relations existing between this and other Governments, and have therefore drawn up several rules upon the subject. These are now enclosed, with an explanatory minute,. for your examination, and we hope that you will take them into careful consideration."

Sufficient comprehensiveness cannot be denied to these eight articles, which, briefly stated, were " that foreign orphanages should be abolished ; that women should not be allowed to enter the churches, nor Sisters of Charity to live in China ; that missionaries must conform to the laws and customs of China, and must submit themselves to the authority of the Chinese magistrates ; that since the individuals who commit disorders ordinarily belong to the lowest class of the people, accusations, in case of riots, must not be brought against the *Literati ;* and that before a man be permitted to become a Christian, he must be examined as to whether he had undergone any sentence or committed any crime." These articles were so palpably contrary to the spirit of the treaty, that the ministers one and all declined to entertain the consideration of them for a moment, and matters were allowed to

revert to the *status quo ante.* The Chinese have
always shown themselves singularly tolerant of faiths
other than their own, more especially when the new
religions are professed only by strangers and are not
of a proselytising nature. They have allowed Mohammedans to live in their midst and to hold offices of
all ranks, without imposing on them the slightest
disability, and it is only when native converts decline
to fall in to the popular customs, and to take part in
the national festivals which mark the seasons of the
years, that they come into collision with their fellow-
countrymen.   In China, as in other polytheistic
countries, innumerable deities are closely interwoven
with all business and pleasure, and with every act of
public and private life.   To renounce these gods and
goddesses is therefore to interfere with every custom
and practice of society.   It is held impossible for
Christians to take part or lot in any matters polluted
by the stain of idolatry, and with holy horror they
decline to subscribe to the celebration of the high
days and festivals which are kept at the solstices, the
opening of spring, and other public holidays in the
year.   All this places them in antagonism with their
fellow-citizens.   But the mandarins have a still more
definite cause of complaint when native Christians,
who are accused of crimes, enlist the advocacy of the
missionaries in the native courts.   The existence in
their midst of congregations which observe rights and
ceremonies apart from those practised by the people
at large, gives rise to much ill-feeling, and one can
only admire the courage and self-sacrifice of those men
and women who, knowing the dangers to which they

are exposed, devote their lives to the dissemination
of the doctrines of Christ in the midst of a hostile
population.   From the nature of the case it is inevitable that offences will come, and so long as Christianity is represented by a small struggling minority,
we must expect persecutions and troubles to arise.

While all these matters were disturbing the counsels
of the Government, the Emperor was growing in
years, and in 1872 he had reached the time of life
(sixteen) when, according to Chinese ideas, he should
take to himself an Empress.   The event was one of
momentous national importance, and vast preparations were made to secure the selection of a fitting
consort for so lofty a monarch.   By the dynastic
rules it is laid down that the Empress shall always be
a Manchu by race and the daughter of a member of
one of the eight military banners.   Apart from these
conditions there is nothing to prevent the daughter
of a Manchu private from being raised to the
" Dragon Throne."   Custom forbids that an Imperial
bridegroom, any more than bridegrooms of lower
degree, should even see his bride before the wedding
night, and it was plainly impossible, therefore, that
His Majesty T'ungchih should take any personal
part in the selection.   This duty devolved by necessity on the Dowager Empresses, and in their zeal for
the Emperor's happiness they threw a wide net over
all the eligible young ladies in the country.   The
position of the Empress has so many disabilities that
it is not sought after with the eagerness that might
be expected, and it is said that a number of young
ladies affect a limp, or a hunch back, or some other

deformity, in order to escape from the Imperial honour. In this case, however, between six and

A MANCHU SWEETMEAT-SELLER.

seven hundred Manchu maidens were brought to the palace for the Empresses' inspection. By a process of elimination these great ladies, in some weeks, reduced the number to two, and finally their choice fell on a young lady named Ahluta. The father of this damsel was a man of distinction, having taken the highest literary honours obtainable at the competitive examinations, and had imparted, so it was said, some of his learning to the future Empress.

So soon as the choice was made preparations were begun for the ceremony, and as a preliminary step the Astronomical Board was called upon to determine by the stars the day and hour which would present the most felicitous moment for the august union. Meanwhile, in preparation for the duties of his new state, four young ladies, known as Professors of Matrimony, were introduced into the Emperor's Palace, who, as was generally reported, satisfactorily performed their vicarious *rôles* until the arrival of Ahluta. The midnight of October 16, 1872, was the time chosen for the ceremony, and for days beforehand countless processions passed from the bride's home to the palace bearing her *trousseau* and belongings. The road leading to the palace was made smooth, and, to mark the occasion, was thickly covered with sand of the Imperial yellow colour. On the day preceding the wedding high officials bore in solemn state a tablet of gold constituting Ahluta Empress, together with a sceptre and a seal, which they presented to the lady ; and at the hour appointed the bridal procession left for the palace attended by a large sprinkling of State officials with escorts and aides-de-camp. As it was essential that Ahluta should reach the palace at the exact

moment prescribed by the Astronomical Board, a
member of that learned body walked by the side
of the bridal chair with a burning joss-stick in his
hand, which was so arranged as to mark the progress
of time. The result was satisfactory, and the Emperor
had the pleasure of receiving his consort neither
before nor after the felicitous instant which had been
proclaimed. Following this great lady came four
other young maidens who were destined to play the
part in the Imperial harem of secondary wives of
the first rank. By the laws of the Empire the
Emperor is entitled to fill his cup of felicity with
four ladies of the first grade, twenty-seven of the
second, and eighty-one of the third. T'ungchih,
however, contented himself with the first arrivals,
and probably it was well for him that he did so.

The marriage of an Emperor of China is always
held to announce his arrival at years of discretion,
and is therefore equivalent to coming of age amongst
ourselves. With the advent of an Empress to share
his throne the Regency disappears, and the Emperor
is acknowledged to be, theoretically, a fit and proper
person to govern his immense Empire, and to exercise rule over the four hundred million subjects who
obey his will. Among the duties which T'ungchih's
new position imposed upon him was that of holding
communication with the ministers of the Treaty
Powers. This obligation his father had accepted by
the terms of the treaty of 1858, but by his judiciously
timed retreat to Jehol he had successfully avoided
carrying it out. The long minority of T'ungchih
had further placed in abeyance the question of

Imperial audiences—a delay for which the Tsungli Yamên was profoundly grateful. The question had always been a thorny one. The idea of any representative of a foreign State entering the Imperial presence without striking his forehead on the floor was so preposterous in the eyes of the mandarins that they resisted the introduction of all discussion on the subject so long as they were able. But the time had now come when it had again to be faced. They were perfectly aware that the k'ot'ow would have to be given up. But though thus driven from their first entrenchment they were prepared strenuously to defend every succeeding line. Lord Macartney had bent the knee on entering the presence of Ch'ienlung. They pleaded, therefore, that foreign ministers should follow this notable example. The foreign ministers, however, pointed to the treaty, in which it was laid down that no minister "should be called upon to perform any ceremony derogatory to him as representing the Sovereign of an independent nation on a footing of equality with that of China," and explained that to bend the knee would obviously be to perform a derogatory ceremony. This answer was conclusive, and it was finally agreed that whenever it should please the Emperor to grant an audience to the foreign ministers they should be expected only to bow thrice on entering the Imperial presence.

In June, 1873, the Emperor was moved to receive the ministers in solemn audience. It was reported at the time that this determination was mainly due to curiosity on the part of T'ungchih, who was desirous of seeing what sort of men the Envoys were who had come from so great a distance to his Court. But however that may be, on the 15th of the month an edict appeared, couched in the following terms: " The Tsungli Yamén having presented a Memorial to the effect that the foreign ministers residing in Peking have implored us to grant an audience that they may deliver letters from their Governments, We command that the foreign ministers residing in Peking, who have brought letters from their Governments, be accorded audience. Respect this." The tone of this decree was not of hopeful augury. There was a dictatorial and discourteous air about it which, whether due to ignorance or impertinence, was, to say the least, unfortunate. Its appearance, however, put the Tsungli Yamén in a flutter, and for ten days a brisk discussion was carried on with the Legations as to the etiquette which was to be observed on the occasion.

In a land such as China, where etiquette is the very breath of the nostrils of the officials, any modification in ceremonial practice, however trifling it may appear to Europeans, is regarded as being of vital importance. The mandarins had been obliged to yield the points of the k'ot'ow and the genuflexion, but there still remained to them the possibility of humiliating the ministers by inducing them to make their bows in a hall where it is customary for the Emperor to receive the envoys of tributary states. This hall, the Tzŭkwang Ko, or " Pavilion of Purple Light," is situated outside the palace, and is, as the native guide-books tell us, the place where New-Year

receptions are granted to the outer tribes, and where
wrestling and military exercises are performed for
the amusement of the Emperor. All this must have
been perfectly well known to the foreign ministers,
who were, however, so elated at the idea of entering
the presence of the "Son of Heaven" that they
agreed to accept the slur implied by the choice of
the building. The 29th of June was the day fixed
for the ceremony, and the time determined by the
Emperor was the very inconvenient hour of six
o'clock in the morning. Etiquette entailed upon
the ministers the necessity of being in readiness
even still earlier. On arriving at the palace grounds
the six ministers, representing England, France,
America, Russia, the Netherlands, and Japan, were
escorted to the "Palace of Seasonableness," a temple
in which the Emperor is accustomed to pray for rain.
Here light refreshments were offered to their expect-
ing Excellencies, and after half an hour had been
wasted in the consumption of confectionery and tea
the envoys were conducted to a large tent pitched
near the "Pavilion of Purple Light." A delay of an
hour and a half was here endured, and at last the
Japanese Ambassador, in virtue of his ambassadorial
rank, was summoned to the presence. So soon as
this official was dismissed the Western ministers were
admitted into the hall, at the end of which T'ungchih
was discovered, seated cross-legged, after the Manchu
fashion, on a raised daïs surrounded by princes and
ministers of State. In accordance with the pre-
arranged programme, the ministers advanced bow-
ing, and an address in Chinese having been read,

Prince Kung fell on his knees and went through the
form of receiving the return message vouchsafed by
the Emperor. Charged with the weighty words of
the "Son of Heaven," he rose and descended the
steps from the daïs with his arms extended in imitation of the way in which Confucius, that great
master of make-believe, used to practise leaving
the presence of his Sovereign as though in a state
of agitation and alarm. The ministers then, having
placed their letters of credence on the table which
stood before His Imperial Majesty, made their bows
and retired à reculons.

The whole history of this ceremony, like that of
most of our dealings with the Chinese, is a signal
example of the glamour which the Celestials have
ever succeeded in throwing over their pretensions in
the eyes of Europeans. The chief blot in our policy
with China up till the Japanese War has been the
half-concealed admission that we were in China
purely on benevolent sufferance. In the relations
between ourselves and the mandarins we have in all
cases been the suppliants, and they the dispensers
of privileges. Their haughty attitude of stand-off-
wardness has in these circumstances had its effect,
and our communications with them have been too
often marked by undue deference. The attitude of
our Government towards Li Hungchang during his
recent visit to this country was an instance in point.
Neither his official position nor his private character
entitled him in any way to the adulation which was
shown him, and which he, after the manner of
Orientals, repaid by acts of grave discourtesy.

Nevertheless, these last were entirely overlooked by a mistaken consideration, and he doubtless left our shores satisfied that his countrymen are correct when they hold that we are but hangers-on to the Imperial bounty of the "Son of Heaven" and his ministers. That the reception of the foreign ministers by T'ungchih was a step in the right direction there can be no doubt, but it is also plain that a mistake was made in consenting to accept the "Pavilion of Purple Light" as the scene of the ceremony. The remark made by a member of the Tsungli Yamên to one of the foreign ministers, that "The princes who waited on the Emperor had been surprised and pleased at the demeanour of himself and his colleagues," effectively displayed the patronising attitude which the mandarins chose to adopt on the occasion, and to which we unfortunately submitted.

Though for the nonce the foreign relations of the Empire were at this time peaceful, the internal affairs of the country were far from being undisturbed. The rebellion which had decimated the province of Yunnan for so many years had been, it is true, brought to a conclusion by the surrender of Tali Fu. But the country was left desolate. The ravages of both the insurgents and the Imperial forces had robbed the surviving wretched inhabitants of everything that makes life worth having, while disease and famine carried off thousands of those who, as by a miracle, had survived the sword. In response to an appeal from the distressful country the Emperor remitted all the taxes due up to date, and by gifts of land and other inducements attempted to entice yeomen from the neighbouring provinces to take up the deserted farms. The success of these efforts was only partial, and to this day the province bears traces of the iron heel of the Mohammedans. In the north-western provinces of Kansu and Shensi legislative endeavours were made to restore to those districts some glimpse of their former prosperity, and it is amusing to find, in the light of recent experience, that the military authorities could suggest nothing better for the preservation of the peace of the provinces than that the army, which had apparently been allowed to revert to civil life, should be mustered again and armed with bows and arrows. Not only, however, had the troops become disorganised, but according to the Literary Chancellor of the Viceroyalty, the civil population was suffering demoralisation from the suspension of the competitive examinations, and with all the weight of his authority he went on to recommend, in the pages of the *Peking Gazette*, that these should be resumed, and, if this should be done, he did "not despair of the Book of Poetry having its duly mollifying effect on the manners of the people." The same implicit faith in the humanising tendency of this ancient work was, according to the same periodical, held at this time by the Governor of Canton, who suggested that a dissemination of its classic verses would be a fit and proper remedy for the clan fights which were then (1873) disturbing the peace of his province.

While these matters were claiming the attention of the Imperial Government a despatch from Li Hanchang, a brother of our late visitor, announced the outbreak of a rebellion in Hunan, and at the same time the Yellow River, "China's Sorrow," burst its banks and flooded thousands of square miles of territory.

Before the year closed a cloud arose on the Eastern sea which seriously threatened a foreign war. Japan had long had grievances against her huge neighbour, and like other foreign Powers had found unassisted diplomacy inadequate to extract the reparation which was due. On repeated occasions shipwrecked Japanese sailors had been cruelly put to death by the inhabitants of the Island of Formosa. For these outrages the Chinese declared themselves unable to make any compensation, or to apply any remedy. In these circumstances the Japanese landed a force on the island, and despatched a special envoy to Peking to make a final attempt at arriving at a peaceful solution of the difficulty. In presence of these energetic measures the Chinese were disposed to yield, but they did so with an ill grace. They admitted their liability but declined to name any fixed sum which should be paid, or any date as to when it should become due. This attitude was so eminently unsatisfactory that the Japanese envoy had no other course to pursue than to prepare to leave Peking, and was on the point of taking his departure when Sir Thomas Wade intervened as a mediator between the disputants, and prevented a breach of the peace by making himself personally responsible for the payment of the 500,000 taels demanded by the Japanese.

It is always difficult to determine whose is the

power behind the Throne which directs political
events in China. In the early days of T'ungchih's
accession to power it was commonly reported that
he was inclined to resent the imposition of the
leading strings by which the Dowager Empresses,
and his ministers, attempted to direct his course.
Rumours were even afloat that, like another Haroun-
al-Raschid, it was his wont to escape from the palace
at night time and wander through the city that he
might become acquainted *in propriâ personâ* with
the actual condition of his subjects. It was said
that Prince Kung's influence was particularly distasteful to him, and the people of the capital were,
therefore, not much surprised when an edict appeared degrading that prince for the use of
"language in very many respects unbecoming" to
his Imperial kinsman. That this degradation was
fiercely resented by the Empresses is proved by the
fact that on the very next day a decree appeared
under their signatures manual, reinstating the Prince
in his hereditary rank and honours. It would appear
from this that the Emperor had resisted the pressure
brought to bear upon him by the Dowager ladies,
and that when they insisted, had saved "his face"
by throwing the responsibility of the measure upon
them. In fact at this period there was as little peace
inside the palace walls, as there was in the outlying
provinces of the Empire. No secrets are allowed to
escape beyond the pink walls of the palace, and it is
only possible to guess at much that goes on within
those sacred precincts by the announcements which
are officially promulgated. Towards the end of the

year 1874 an edict appeared in the *Peking Gazette* stating that the Emperor was "happily" ill with an attack of small-pox, and an effusively dutiful decree was thereupon published in his name, in which he besought the Dowager Empresses to undertake in their "overflowing benevolence" the administration of the Empire during his illness. For some days the Imperial patient was said to be progressing favourably, and honours were heaped on the physicians who had charge of his case. But the good effected by these learned men was only temporary. A turn for the worse set in, and on the 12th of January, 1875, he became "a guest on high."

This event gave rise to one of those palace intrigues which are common in Eastern countries. As has been indicated the Dowager Empresses had on many occasions found the young Emperor a refractory pupil, and they were naturally desirous of taking advantage of the opportunity thus afforded them of regaining the control of affairs, which custom had compelled them to give up when T'ungchih took to himself an Empress and proclaimed his majority. The one obstacle in their way was the now widowed Empress who, as was well known, might possibly have given birth to an heir to the throne. In such a case she naturally would have become the Regent during her son's minority, and this the elder ladies determined to put beyond the range of possibility. With a total disregard of the regulations ordering the Imperial succession, they, without any delay, set about making a choice of an heir to T'ungchih. There were two candidates for this distinguished

honour. One was the son of Prince Kung, who had
arrived at years of discretion, and the other was
Tsait'ien, the infant son of Prince Ch'un. Prince
Kung's son was naturally the one which should have
been chosen as being the eldest son of the eldest
uncle of the late Emperor. But in the eyes of the
Dowager Empresses there were two fatal objections
to his candidature. He was of age, and therefore
would have supreme control of affairs, and, besides,
his accession would have necessitated the retirement
of Prince Kung, who could not, in accordance with
the Chinese ideas of filial piety, have served under
his son. Neither of these objections were prominent
in the case of Tsait'ien, who was barely four years
old, and whose succession to the throne would give a
new lease of power to the intriguing ladies. His
father also, not having taken any public part in
political life, would have no office to vacate.
Tsait'ien, therefore, was chosen, and by a pious
fiction, common to Chinese practice, he was adopted
as the son, not of T'ungchih, but of the preceding
Emperor, Hsienfèng. But Ahluta still remained,
and it did not surprise those who had watched the
course of events to hear that the poor lady had been
seized with illness which in a few days proved fatal
(29th of March, 1875). It suited nobody's purpose
to inquire too closely into the nature of the malady
which had so conveniently removed a political difficulty, and certain it is that whatever may have been
the Dowager Empresses' attitude towards her when
alive, she had no sooner passed into the shades than
they lavished encomiums upon her. The pages of the

Peking Gazette were filled with her good deeds, and by common consent the posthumous title was conferred upon her of "The filial, wise, excellent, yielding, chaste, careful, virtuous, and intelligent Queen I, who governed her actions by the laws of Heaven, and whose life added lustre to the teachings of the Sages."

Meanwhile strangely demonstrative decrees were issued under the signature of the infant Emperor proclaiming, in all the fanciful verbiage of the East, his imaginary grief at the death of his predecessor, and belauding the virtues which he chose to attribute to him. "Prostrate upon the earth," he wrote, "We bewail Our grief to Heaven, vainly stretching out Our hands in lamentation." It now only remained to choose an Imperial epithet for the infant "Son of Heaven," and in accordance with the prescribed forms a number of complimentary titles were submitted for selection to Tsait'ien, who is supposed to have chosen the designation of Kwanghsü or "The Succession of Glory."

One of the grievances which the Dowager Empresses had against T'ungchih was, that by a laxity of administration he had allowed the palace eunuchs to assume functions and exercise powers to which they were in no wise entitled. One of the first acts of the Regents, therefore, was to put these assuming courtiers in their proper places. Seven of the principal offenders were consequently put on their trial, with the result that three were transported to the Amur, there to act as slaves, and four others were severely bastinadoed. These salutary lessons brought these pests of the palace to their bearings.

To those on the spot who had followed the course
of current events in China it was obvious that, since
the conclusion of the treaty, there had been rather
a decrease than an increase in the friendly feeling
towards foreigners on the part of the officials.   In
fact, since the establishment of the legations at
Peking there had been a marked change in a hostile
direction, and though the Chinese Government professed friendly feelings towards the Treaty Powers,
there were not lacking signs that there was a desire
on the part of even the most highly placed officials to
restrict the provisions of the treaty so far as possible.
Before the death of T'ungchih, it had been arranged
that the Viceroy of India should send an expedition
viâ Bhamo, in Burma, into Yunnan, for the purpose
of opening commercial relations with that district.
In December, 1874, the members of the mission
arrived at Mandalay, and as soon as their arrangements were complete, started for Bhamo.   To further
the success of the undertaking it was determined to
send Mr. Margary, of the Chinese Consular Service,
who besides being a good Chinese scholar was a
thoroughly capable man, to meet the expedition at
Bhamo.   On his way from Shanghai to the western
frontier he met with every civility from the local
mandarins, and eventually joined hands with Colonel
Browne at Bhamo, on January 26, 1875.   After
some delay, during which reports had reached Bhamo
that a Chinese force was collecting in the mountain
passes to bar the passage of the expedition, Colonel
Browne's party started eastward.   By the light of his
experience *en route* from Shanghai, Mr. Margary con-

sidered the rumour of opposition to be unworthy of credit, and with the consent of Colonel Browne, went ahead of the expedition to inquire exactly into the condition of affairs. On the 19th of February he arrived without difficulty at Manwyne, a town within the Chinese frontier, where he was hospitably received by the officials. On the following day he was invited to visit a mineral spring in the neighbourhood, and while on this excursion he was savagely assaulted and murdered. At the same time a Chinese force attacked Colonel Browne's party. These assailants were beaten off without much difficulty, but the murder of Margary, and the hostile attitude of the people, determined Colonel Browne to give up any thought of proceeding further, and he returned to Bhamo.

So soon as the news of this outrage reached Peking, Sir Thomas Wade made strong remonstrances at the Tsungli Yamên, and insisted that a joint Commission of English and Chinese officials should proceed to the spot to investigate the circumstances of the murder. But the Tsungli Yamên was in a more than usually obstructive mood, and for months Sir Thomas Wade's demands were met with consistent prevarications and delay. When no unemployed subterfuge for shelving the question at issue remained to them, they, in quite their approved manner, named a Taot'ai of inferior position as the colleague of Mr. Grosvenor, a secretary of Legation, in the commission of inquiry. Sir Thomas Wade refused to accept this appointment on the ground of the comparatively mean rank of the officer nominated, and finally induced Prince

Kung and his colleagues to appoint in his stead Li Hanchang, the Viceroy of the two Hu Provinces. This was only the preliminary difficulty to be overcome, for Li, imitating the conduct of his superiors, required two months to make his preparation for the journey. But everything must come to an end, even a Chinaman's delays, and eventually the Commission arrived at Manwyne and opened proceedings.

Meanwhile Sir Thomas Wade put forward seven demands to the Chinese Government, which he considered should be satisfied before there could be any reasonable possibility of bringing the matter to a satisfactory conclusion. The first of these had reference to improving the condition of diplomatic intercourse at Peking ; the second to the enlargement of trading facilities ; the third to the provision of a sufficient escort to Mr. Grosvenor ; the fourth to the promise of an escort for another mission from India ; the fifth to requiring the Viceroy Ts'ên to state how it happened that nearly six months after the murder of Margary no definite information concerning it had reached the Yamên ; the sixth to insisting that a minister should be sent to England to express the regret of the Chinese Government at the outrage ; and the seventh to demanding that the decree, directing the appointment of this minister to England, should be published in the *Peking Gazette*. To the first of these the Tsungli Yamên returned a characteristic answer. The ministers stated it was not customary for Chinese officials who were not charged with the management of foreign affairs to hold intercourse with foreigners, "and it consequently behoves them," they added, "not to be in relations with the foreign representatives at Peking." They declined also to send a mission of apology, and added, "that it was not open to the servants of His Majesty the Emperor to make suggestions regarding his decrees." At this time Sir Thomas Wade was at Tientsin and had used Li Hungchang as an intermediary with the Government. The course which the proceedings now took, however, was so eminently unsatisfactory that he had made up his mind to return to Peking, and was on the point of departure, when the following laconic Imperial Decree was brought to his notice. "Let Li Hungchang and Ting Jihch'ang negotiate respecting the Margary affair with the British Minister, Mr. Wade at Tientsin." This edict appeared to constitute Li a plenipotentiary, and Sir Thomas Wade was, therefore, not unnaturally surprised when the Tsungli Yamèn subsequently declined to endorse certain concessions made by their representative, and further announced at the same time "that it did not follow that what his Excellency Li might guarantee at Tientsin should be given effect to at Peking."

The position of affairs in Yunnan was in every way as unsatisfactory as the course of the negotiations at Peking. Every obstacle was put in the way of the English Commissioner, and it was rendered quite impossible for him to arrive at the true conclusion of the matter by the withholding of much important evidence, and by the obtrusion of other so-called testimony which was absolutely valueless. It was plainly the intention of the supreme authorities to shelter the Viceroy Ts'ên from all blame in the matter. This man's record was bad, and was blood-stained with every species of cruelty. During the suppression of the Mohammedan rebellion in the province he had sent to the execution ground hecatombs of victims, and in the opinion of all unprejudiced observers, it was plain that in this case he was primarily responsible for the murder. But it was impossible to get any witnesses to give evidence against him. Men who were in close relations with him professed to know nothing of his attitude in the matter, while at the same time they gave voluble testimony against a number of men of a border tribe, who were as far from their cognisance as Ts'ên was near. Of only one official had they a word of disparagement to say. This was Colonel Li (Li Sieht'ai) who had begun life as a brigand, who had then turned rebel, and who had eventually transferred his valuable services to the provincial authorities. By all accounts this was the man who led the troops which opposed Colonel Browne's party.

So thoroughly unsatisfactory were the results thus obtained, that Sir Thomas Wade refrained to press for the punishment of the accused, and finally despair-ing of arriving at a satisfactory arrangement with so tortuously minded a Government as that at Peking, hauled down his flag, and took ship for Shanghai. This step seriously alarmed the Tsungli Yamên, and after some negotiations Sir Thomas Wade agreed to meet Li Hungchang at Chifu (Chefoo) to discuss the terms

of a settlement. The result of the discussions which
ensued was the Chifu Convention, which after having
been unconfirmed for twelve years was at last
ratified.

One result of these long-drawn-out negotiations
was that a permanent Chinese Minister was sent to
the Court of St. James's. The choice of the first
Envoy Plenipotentiary was an eminently fortunate
one. Kwo Sungtao had had relations with foreigners
in China, and was possessed of a conciliatory and
courteous demeanour. As Mr. Gladstone once said
of him, "he was the most genial Oriental whom he
had ever met," and during his tenure of the Legation in Portland Place, international matters went
smoothly and well. While the foreign relations of
the Empire had thus been disturbed, the attention of
both officials and people at Peking had been absorbed
by the details of the funerals of the late Emperor
and Empress. Vast preparations were made for the
august ceremony, and it was determined that both
the young Emperor and the Dowager Empresses
should follow the *cortège* to the Imperial mausolea in
the eastern mountains. The sudden and unaccounted
for death of Ahluta had agitated the Pekingese not a
little, and one censor, more bold than the rest, took
upon himself to suggest that an extra title of honour
should be conferred upon her late Majesty in commemoration of her many virtues. This was regarded
as an implied censure by the Dowager Empresses, who
issued an angry decree in response declaring the
suggestion to be absurd, and ordering the unfortunate
censor to be severely punished. On the 16th of

October, 1875, the funeral *cortège* left Peking, and on
the 25th the Emperor returned to his capital.   More
than usual magnificence was lavished on the procession and accompanying ceremonies.   The coffins
were each carried by a hundred and twenty-eight
bearers, who were relieved sixty times during the
day; and the cost incurred amounted to 189,000
taels.

These Imperial dead were scarcely laid to rest in
the costly tombs raised to their memory, when their
unhappy country, which was just recovering from the
effects of wars and disturbances, was afflicted with
one of the most severe famines which have been
known in the recent history of the world.   Over a
large portion of the north of China, consisting of an
area as large as France, there lies a deep deposit of
the geological formation known as Loess.   This
formation consists of a light friable soil, and covers
the country to the depth of a hundred feet or more,
levelling up the valleys and bringing low the hills.
In favourable seasons when rains are frequent and
temperate, the crops grown on the loess are full and
generous.   It is only necessary for the farmer to
scratch the surface and sow his seed.   Manure is
unnecessary, and the usual succession of rich crops
which are commonly yielded has earned for the
district the name of the " Garden of China."   But all
this fertility depends on the fall of sufficient rain and
snow.   In seasons when the clouds refuse their
moisture, the winds which prevail blow away the
surface soil, and leave the seed grain exposed to the
desiccating influences of the sun and wind.   It is

these conditions which afford a substantial reason for the prayers which are offered up by the Emperor in person, for rain and snow in seasons of summer drought and when the winter coating of snow is persistently withheld.

During the years 1874–75 there had been a marked deficiency of moisture, a want which was

A HOUSE IN SHANSI.

further intensified in the following year, and which ultimately ended in rendering absolutely sterile the seed sown by the farmers. The results were disastrous in the extreme. With such imperfect means of communication as the Chinese possess, it is impossible to supply the deficiencies of one district by the superfluities of others with sufficient speed to prevent the occurrence of famine. Over the four provinces of Chihli, Shansi, Honan, and Kansu a dire scarcity prevailed, and though every effort was made, both by foreigners and natives, to bring aid to the starving people, upwards of nine million perished before succeeding crops supplied food for the survivors. In this emergency Li Hungchang succeeded in collecting as much as 289,394 taels, and a foreign relief committee at Shanghai was able to hand over 204,560 taels to provide grain for the unfortunate sufferers. It is illustrative of the deeply grained dishonesty which pervades China that, even in the presence of such a fearful calamity, the peculating tendencies of native officials remained too strong to be overcome. In these circumstances Li Hungchang set a worthy example, and reported a number of his subordinates who had been taken red-handed in intercepting the monies subscribed for the purchase of grain. These men were severely punished, and it is a pleasure to know that one agent, who had mixed alum with the flour which he distributed in such proportions as to make it uneatable, met with exemplary punishment.

Li, who has always had an eye for business profits, made large use of the vessels of the China Merchant Steam Navigation Company, of which he was the promoter, for the conveyance of the grain to the famine districts, and the result was undoubtedly satisfactory. But the bad roads and imperfect conveyances made the transport of the grain from the ports to the inland localities a matter of serious difficulty. The prominence which was thus given to the faulty native means of intercommunication, brought once more to the front the question of introducing railways into the country. Already a small company of foreign merchants had, with the permission of the Viceroy of the two Kiang provinces, constructed a line from Shanghai to Wusung, at the mouth of the river, a distance of about twelve miles. For a time all things went smoothly with the new venture. The line was popular with the people, who crowded the carriages to such an extent that some would-be passengers were left behind on almost every railway platform. But though it quickly secured the favour of the people, its success was gall and wormwood to the *Literati*, to whom any new foreign innovation is anathema. Confucius laid it down that his countrymen should not accept any new devices from abroad, and with curious pertinacity the students of what is known as the Confucian literature have steadily adhered to his advice. Life is not counted as being of much value in China, and when it became known that it would be a convenience to the official classes if a man were run over and killed, the event at once took place. This supplied the well-known Chinese device in such cases of a demand of a life for a life. A reference to the Consular Court naturally disposed of this preposterous proposition. Another means had therefore to be employed to arrive at the same end. Nothing is easier than to get up a riot in China, and it soon became evident that the appeal of the *Literati* to the people would meet with its usual success. So serious did affairs become under the influence of these mischief-makers, that the Viceroy was obliged to intervene, and the matter was referred for decision to Sir Thomas Wade and Li Hungchang, who at the time were negotiating the Chifu Convention.

Li disclaimed all administrative power in the matter, and, in face of the opposition which had been roused, Sir Thomas Wade recommended that the trains should cease to run until a decision should be arrived at. Events in which foreigners were implicated had in those days a tendency to develop in one direction. This was no exception to the rule, and after much discussion, it was agreed that the Chinese should become owners of the railway by purchase. This sealed its fate, the rails were at once ruthlessly torn up, and were exported to the Island of Formosa, where they were allowed to rot on the sea shore. The practical utility of railways is so palpable that Li, in common with all men of intelligence, has always fully recognised their advantage, and being at the time interested in the development of some coal mines within his jurisdiction, he proposed to make a line to connect these pits with Tientsin and Taku. The district through which this line was to run was sparsely inhabited, and was entirely free from the presence of obstructive scholars. Li's influence, however, was sufficient to have overcome any opposition which might have existed, but as none appeared, no difficulty arose in the construction of the line which still carries coal between K'aip'ing and the sea, to the infinite advantage of the province. The object lesson taught by this railroad has not been lost on the natives of the locality, and at the present

moment the only lines which exist in the Empire—
one from Taku to Peking, and the other a continuation
of K'aip'ing line to Shanhaikwan—are in this immediate neighbourhood.

In so vast an Empire as China, with so many feudatory states owing allegiance to her, it can seldom
be that complete peace reigns within her territories.

A ROADWAY SCENE IN KOREA.

A rebellion which broke out in Annan at this time
was put down after some difficulty with the assistance
of Chinese troops, and later the Court of Peking was
disturbed by the news of a serious outbreak in Korea.
Japan had already opened diplomatic intercourse
with that country, and had claimed, as she always
had done, suzerainty over it. At this time, as has

not uncommonly happened in the annals of that unhappy country, Korea was a house divided against
itself. The King who still reigns is a well-meaning
man, but without sufficient character to give effect to
his good intentions in the face of opposition. He
also suffered under the disadvantage of having
witnessed during a long minority his father rule, or
rather misrule, in the country. This man's external
policy had been consistently anti-foreign. He had
successfully opposed attempts made by French and
American expeditions to enter the country, and when
at length he handed over the reins of power to his
son, he attempted to direct his successor's policy on
the lines which he himself had followed. Finding,
however, that his son was unwilling to accept his
guidance in these matters, he used all his arts of
intrigue to carry his points. He had bitterly opposed
the Japanese Treaty, and finding the King obdurate
on the question, he determined to effect by violence
that which he could not gain by argument. At his
instigation an attack was made on the Japanese
Legation at Seoul, and so fierce was the assault that
the Japanese after defending the building so long as
it was tenable, sallied out against the mob, and fought
their way to the sea coast, where they found shelter
and protection on board a British gunboat. The ex-
Regent T'aiwён Kun was now supreme. The young
King was made a prisoner, and the Queen was only
saved from assassination by the devotion of one of
her ladies who met death in her stead. On receipt
of the news of this outrage Li Hungchang, who was
ordered by an Imperial edict to take the matter in

hand, despatched an official named Ma with a fleet
of ironclads to suppress the riots, while at the same
time the Japanese Government re-established their
Legation with the support of a strong escort.

It was plain to Li, and to his lieutenant Ma, that
so long as the ex-Regent was at liberty to plot and
intrigue, peace was impossible. They determined

A KOREAN SEDAN-CHAIR.

therefore, that it was for the good of the country that
he should be deported for a while. The kidnapping
of officials in such circumstances is not an unusual
practice in the East, and Ma was only acting after
the manner of his countrymen when, having invited
the T'aiwèn Kun to an entertainment on board his
ship, he steamed off to China with his unsuspecting

visitor. On the arrival of this Korean plotter on Chinese soil an Imperial edict was issued ordering that he should, for the remainder of his life, " live at peace at Paoting Fu in Chihli. . . . Let the Governor-General of Chihli," so ran on the document, " continue bountifully to afford him such support as his rank demands, and strictly keep watch over him, that thus a cause of trouble and calamity to Korea may be removed, and the breach of the laws of kindred towards the prince of that kingdom be healed."

Meanwhile Japan had made demands for compensation for the insult offered to her flag in the attack on the Legation at Seoul. Five hundred thousand dollars were claimed as an indemnity for the cost of the expedition ; a new treaty port was insisted on ; and it was required that a mission of apology be sent to Japan to satisfy the *amour propre* of the Mikado's Government. Being absolutely powerless to refuse consent to these, or any other conditions, the Korean Government readily yielded all that was asked.

For some time Li Hungchang and those who acted with him had observed with growing anxiety the advances which Japan had been making in the equipment of her army and navy, and in 1882 a secret memorial was presented to the Throne by Chang Peilun, a man who has since become notorious in many ways, and who further rejoices in the position of son-in-law to Li Hungchang, detailing the reforms which were being introduced into the Japanese army, and urging that it was the duty of " our Empire to check in time threatening evil from Japan, and to establish definitely the supremacy of China over its neighbour." Chang was careful, however, to explain that an invasion of Japan would, in existing circumstances, be a hazardous undertaking, and he very reasonably advocated the necessity of adding strength to the forces and fortifications of the Empire. Li, to whom this and other memorials of a similar kind were referred, advised caution, as was his wont, and summed up his recommendations in these words : " It is above all things necessary to strengthen our country's defences, to organise a powerful navy, and not to undertake aggressive steps against Japan in too great a hurry."

We have seen the miserable figure which the Chinese forces cut in their late encounter with Japan, and if it is possible to imagine a greater disproportion of strength than was then displayed, it would have been found at the time of which we speak. For years the Japanese had been organising their army on the European model, and had armed their troops with the newest weapons invented at Elswick and by Krupp ; while the Chinese soldiers, with the exception of a small body enlisted by Li, were still trusting in their bows and arrows and in the scarcely more effective gingalls. In accordance with Li's advice the trial of strength was postponed, and if his subsequent counsel had been followed the battles of 1894 and 1895 would never have been fought.

But though the Chinese Government were successful in avoiding a war with Japan, they were unable to escape complications which ended in the outbreak

of hostilities with France in connection with affairs
in Tongking. For many years the French Government had had relations with Annam, which, however,
had never been carried on in any other than an
intermittent fashion in accordance with the changes
and chances of home politics. French missionaries
had with indefatigable zeal attempted to introduce
the knowledge of Christianity among the Annamese,
and consequent persecutions had from time to time
broken out which had not unfrequently ended in the
massacre of the foreign priests. In this desultory
and unsatisfactory manner relations were maintained
until 1858, when, in consequence of the refusal of the
King to carry out the terms of a treaty negotiated so
far back as 1787, the French fleet destroyed the forts
of Tourane and captured the town of Saigon. At
this last-named city they established themselves, and
when, after the war of 1870, the enthusiasm for a
Colonial Empire became so pronounced in France,
they used it as a base from which to attempt to
extend their influence over the neighbouring province of Tongking. One or two expeditions, which
were rather of the nature of fillibustering adventures,
were sent against Hanoi, the capital of the province,
and gained temporary success. Annam, including
Tongking, had for centuries been a feudatory state
of China, and had acknowledged fealty by despatch-
ing at regular intervals tributary missions to Peking.
As in duty bound, the King on this occasion reported
to his liege lord the efforts which the French were
making to gain possession of his northern province,
and rather than risk a rupture Li Hungchang, as the

Chinese representative, agreed in response to hand over to France that portion of the country which was south of the Songkoi River. We have already seen that Li's recommendations were not always accepted at Peking, and on this occasion, both in that capital and in Paris, the conditions proposed were peremptorily rejected. For ten years matters remained in this unsatisfactory condition; the French being ever aggressive and the Annamese doing their utmost by force and by intrigue to oppose the advance of the invaders. At length, in 1884, the important towns of Sontay and Bacninh were threatened by French armies. The garrisons of these cities were mainly composed of Chinese troops, and the Marquis Tsêng, who represented China at Paris at the time, was instructed to inform the French Government that China would regard an attack on those positions as an act of war.

This threat, however, proved to be utterly unavailing, and, in defiance of the Marquis's warning, the two cities were attacked and occupied by the French. It has never been the practice of the Chinese Government, until the outbreak of the recent war with Japan, to make a formal declaration of war, and as the French saw no necessity for going through that formality, the two countries, while contending in the field, remained diplomatically at peace. In Peking a strong party, headed by Li Hungchang, were desirous of coming to terms with the enemy while they were in the way with him, and the Dowager Empresses took occasion to emphasise their sympathy with the peace party by issuing a decree depriving " Prince Kung and several other ministers of all their offices, and imposing condign punishment upon all who were responsible for the failure in Tongking." In these circumstances Mr. Detring, of the China Customs Service, was encouraged to suggest the opening of negotiations between Captain Fournier, of the French Navy, and Li Hungchang. Both parties being favourably disposed towards the conclusion of peace, terms were readily arrived at, and a convention was eventually signed between the two plenipotentiaries. By this instrument it was agreed that France should respect and, in case of need, protect the southern frontier of China, which separates that country from Tongking, and at the same time China undertook to withdraw at once all her troops from Tongking.

Unfortunately for the permanence of the peace proposed by this treaty, the plenipotentiaries had omitted to name the date at which the Chinese troops were to be withdrawn, and, as it afterwards turned out, the two contracting parties held different views on this very important subject. Li was under the impression that it had been arranged that the movement should take place at the end of three months; Fournier, on the other hand, believed that three weeks was the limit allowed. Neither date, however, seems to have been mentioned to Colonel Dugenne, the commander of the troops in the neighbourhood of Langson, when notice was sent him of the conclusion of peace. With the impatience of a new possessor, therefore, he marched towards the town, and on arriving at a defile some distance from

the city he was met by a considerable Chinese force
drawn up to oppose his advance. When he demanded a passage through the lines of this hostile
array, three mandarins came forward, and, explaining that they had had no intimation of the suspension
of hostilities, demanded time that they might communicate with the commanding officer at Langson.
Dugenne interned these men as hostages, and then
professed his willingness to wait for the required
reference. By some misadventure the Zephyrs, or
criminal corps of the army, opened fire upon the
Chinese, and brought about an engagement. Two
of the hostages, perceiving the mistake, attempted
to ride back to their army to stop the fighting.
Their intention, however, being misunderstood, they
were both shot, while the third met the same fate
by the discharge of a pistol. The action now
became general, and the French were completely
defeated. Their losses were heavy both in men and
in baggage, and the troops would have been entirely
overwhelmed had it not been for the gallant action
of a body of *Chasseurs d'Afrique*, who checked the
pursuing Chinamen.

This misadventure gave rise to mutual recrimina-
tions between the two negotiators of the Convention.
Captain Fournier averred that he had agreed with
Li as to the dates on which the fortresses were to
be given up, while Li asserted that when he protested against the impossibly short time named,
Captain Fournier had run his pen through the
clauses in dispute. In defence of his conduct
Captain Fournier wrote to Monsieur Ferry affirm-

ing upon his honour that he had neither cancelled nor evaded any of the dates and stipulations of the note handed to Li Hungchang. In opposition to this very categorical statement, Ma, the captor of the Taiwên Kun of Korea, and Lo Fênglu, the present Minister at our Court, signed a letter addressed to the *North China Herald*, in which they stated that they "saw with their own eyes Captain Fournier with his own hand make the said erasures and put his initials thereto."

After these events peace became impossible, and both in Tongking and Formosa the French again began operations. In the former province General Négrier took the field, and with some difficulty captured the stronghold of Langson (February 13, 1885), while Admiral Courbet attacked, though unsuccessfully, Kelung, on the northern coast of Formosa. Finding his efforts there to be unavailing the admiral steamed across to Foochow. Of this intended movement the Chinese had notice, but Chang Peilun, of whom mention has already been made, and who was commanding at Foochow at the time, entirely disregarded the intimation. With a certain disingenuousness Admiral Courbet, on the plea that war had not been declared, steamed by the forts at the mouth of the Min river, and anchored among the Chinese fleet in rear of the defences. Secure in his position, Courbet demanded the immediate surrender of the fleet and forts, and on this being refused, opened fire on the Chinese ships as they lay at anchor. In seven minutes the destruction of the enemy's vessels was complete, and the harbour was full of wreckage and drowning sailors. Between the natives of the provinces of Kwangtung and Fuhkien there has always been a standing feud, and the horrors of the situation were increased on this occasion by the fact that as the Kwangtung sailors scrambled up to the shore they were murdered by their Fuhkien countrymen. So complete was the disaster that it might fairly be considered impossible that even a Chinaman could have described it otherwise than as a defeat. But Chang P'eilun was equal to the occasion, and with splendid mendacity reported to the throne that he had gained a complete victory over the French, and had sunk several of their ships. The facts, however, which immediately transpired were too plain to make any such statement credible, and Chang P'eilun escaped execution by accepting transportation to the frontier. Being a protégé of Li Hungchang, his exile was only temporary, and before long he returned to marry Li's daughter, and to take an active part in the management of his patron's concerns.

After his exploit in the Foochow harbour Admiral Courbet, after having made five unsuccessful attacks on the forts near Kelung, at length succeeded in taking them (March, 1885), and further occupied the Pescadores. In Tongking, however, the French cause was not so successful. A system of guerilla warfare, while it failed to bring glory to the Tricolour, had an exhausting effect on the troops, and it was found necessary in April to evacuate Langson. Both sides were now heartily tired of the war, and the Tsungli Yamên was relieved to hear from Sir Robert Hart

that the negotiations which they had authorised him
to carry on with M. Billot in Paris had been brought
to a successful issue. The announcement of this
welcome conclusion of peace was made by Sir Robert
Hart in an enigmatic fashion which is so much
affected by the Chinese. Sir Robert called one day
at the Tsungli Yamên, and, addressing the ministers,
said : "Nine months ago you authorised me to open

INTERIOR OF THE TSUNGLI YAMÊN, PEKING.

negotiations for peace, and now——" "The baby is
born," said the ministers before he could proceed
further. "Yes," said Sir Robert, "the preliminaries
of peace are arranged." Congratulations followed,
and it was agreed that the details of the treaty
should be left to the consideration of Li Hungchang
and M. Patenôtre, the French Minister at Peking.
On the 9th of June, 1885, the treaty was signed by

these plenipotentiaries, and it is eminently confirma-
tory of Li's prescience that after a year's conflict,
which had cost his country 60,000,000 taels and the
loss of the Foochow fleet, the Chinese Government
had been willing to accept terms almost identical
with those which he had arranged with Fournier in
the preceding year.

Meanwhile disturbances had again broken out in
Korea. Notwithstanding the Imperial assertion that
the transportation of the Taiwên Kun was to be for
life, he was, in a moment of weakness, allowed to
return to his native country. The result of this
manumission was disastrous. He found on his
return to his familiar haunts that the King had
in his absence introduced extensive reforms, and
amongst others a postal system modelled on European lines. To this and all other innovations he
was, as ever, determined to offer strenuous opposition, and, by skilful intrigue, he so contrived that on
the occasion of a dinner given to celebrate the
inauguration of the new post office, a band of
rebels was introduced into the banqueting-hall, who
attempted to lay violent hands on the King. For
some days fighting in the capital continued between
the two contending parties, the reformers and the
reactionists, and in the course of the hostilities a
determined attack was made on the Japanese Legation, when for the second time the minister and his
staff had to fight their way to the coast. In response
to this outrage, and in defence of their national
honour, the Japanese landed a force at Chemulpo,
the port of Seoul; while at the same time a Chinese

army entered the Korean capital. The situation of
1882 was thus repeated, and, as on that occasion, it
seemed only too probable that the two protecting
powers would be drawn into a war. Happily the
danger was averted, and negotiations between the
two states were entered upon at Tientsin, Count Ito
representing Japan and Li Hungchang China.

After considerable discussion a convention was
signed by which it was agreed that both China and
Japan should withdraw their troops from Korea
within four months of the date of the signature of
the treaty; that the King of Korea should be
invited to instruct and drill a sufficient armed force
to assure the public security of the kingdom; and
that "in case of any disturbance of a grave nature
occurring in Korea, which may oblige the respective
countries or either of them to send troops to Korea,
it is hereby understood that they shall give, each to
the other, previous notice in writing of their intention
so to do, and that after the matter is settled they
shall withdraw their troops and not further station
them in the country." This last clause is worthy of
attention, as it was the infringement of it, or alleged
infringement of it, on the part of China, which led
to the outbreak of the recent war with Japan.

The war with France which had lately been brought
to a close, and the threatened hostilities with Japan,
awoke, for a moment, at Peking a desire to strengthen
the forces of the country. Ships were added to the
navy, and advice poured in from Censors and others
as to the best means of protecting the Empire against
foreign foes. A Board of Admiralty was instituted

of which Prince Ch'un, the father of the Emperor, was made first lord, and so seriously did he regard his position that in the summer of 1886 he took the unprecedented step of leaving the capital to inspect the fleet and arsenals at Tientsin and Port Arthur. Under this new naval administration Captain Lang, of the British navy, was appointed admiral of the northern fleet, which by that curious system of decentralisation which prevails in China was alone placed under the control of Prince Ch'un and his colleagues, the southern fleet, with its headquarters at Foochow, being administered by the local provincial magnates. This curious arrangement led to some strange results in the recent war with Japan. At Wei-hai-wei, when the Chinese fleet surrendered, a ship of the southern squadron happened by chance to be amongst them. The captain of this vessel, not in the least understanding why he should be held a prisoner when his presence with the northern fleet had been the result of an accident, represented his case to the Japanese admiral, and requested that he and his ship should be released as otherwise he might fall under the censure of his superiors !

The year 1886 was a busy year in foreign politics, more especially so far as relations with Great Britain were concerned. At this time King Thebaw's misdoings had led to our occupation of Upper Burma, a territory over which China claimed suzerain rights. With that tender regard for the feelings of the Emperor and his ministers which has always distinguished our Foreign Office, it was agreed that if China would consent no longer to interfere in

Burmese politics, the decennial tribute mission should continue to be despatched to Peking. The folly of this arrangement soon became apparent. Since 1842 our main endeavour in dealing with the Chinese had been to bring home to their consciousness the fact that as a nation we were to be treated on terms of perfect equality with themselves. At this eleventh hour, therefore, to proclaim ourselves tributary to Peking was one of those acts of folly which are to be accounted for only by presupposing on the part of the Foreign Office a complete ignorance of Asiatics and their modes of thought. With a return to a more reasonable mind the arrangement was discontinued.

The latest outbreak in Korea, described above, had disquieted other countries besides China and Japan. The Russians protested that such disturbances, recurring at such short intervals, presented a danger to the peace of their provinces across the frontier which was not to be endured, and there were not wanting the usual signs of a threatened move southwards on the part of the Colossus of the North. In these circumstances our Admiralty determined, as a protective measure, to occupy Port Hamilton, an island off the southern coast of Korea. In obedience to the following laconic telegram "Occupy Port Hamilton, and report proceedings," Admiral Sir William Dowell hoisted the British flag on the island. This move aroused, as might have been expected, considerable Russian opposition, and the Czar's minister at Peking was instructed to warn the Chinese that if the occupation was persisted in, Russia would be compelled to take possession of a similar foothold in self-defence.   Happily under the influence of the Ito and Li Convention a more peaceful state of affairs had supervened in Korea, and the British Government felt justified, under the favourably altered circumstances, in yielding the point.   It was, however, laid down as a condition of the restoration of the island, that under no circumstances whatever should it at any time be handed over to any other foreign Power, and simultaneously the Chinese Government extracted from the Russian minister a categorical undertaking that his country would not, under any circumstances, interfere with Korean territory. On February 27, 1887, the British flag ceased to fly over Port Hamilton.

The year which followed was an uneventful one as far as foreign politics are concerned, but the internal affairs of the Empire gave plenty of occupation to the Emperor's ministers.   The reforms in the army were still being carried on, although in the usual ineffective Oriental way.   How deplorable was the condition of this branch of the service may be inferred from memorials presented to the Throne at this time.   The Governor of Shensi proposed to inspect the troops of the province, who for thirty years had never presented themselves on the parade ground.   The troops in the province of Yunnan were perhaps not quite in so parlous a condition.   They were, however, mainly armed with bows and arrows, and the Governor with some show of reason reminded his Imperial master that though archery is a good gymnastic exercise, the weapons with which battles are won are rifles and cannon, and he therefore proposed to arm his men, so far as possible, with these weapons. Doubtless the miserable condition of the army is attributable to the fact that at earlier periods the enemies whom the Chinese have been accustomed to meet have been even worse armed and worse drilled than themselves.

At the time of which we speak a war was being waged in Hainan against the aboriginal tribes who inhabit and disturb that island. After many engagements and a lengthened campaign, the Chinese general announced the suppression of the revolt and received from the Emperor characteristic rewards for his martial valour. His Majesty presented him with a jade thumb-ring, a dagger with a jade handle, a pair of large pouches and a pair of small ones. An incidental reference in the general's despatch to the unhealthiness of the climate and the malarious evils arising from it awakened the sympathy of the Dowager Empress, who was good enough to present the army with ten boxes of *P'ingan Tan*, or "pills of peace and tranquillity."

In the beginning of 1887 an announcement was made that that the young Emperor having now reached years of discretion, that is to say the ripe age of sixteen, he would accept the reins of power. But this apparently did not harmonise with the wishes of the "Son of Heaven." "When I heard of the decree," he wrote in his Edict in response, "I trembled as if I were in mid-ocean, not knowing where the land is. Her Majesty will, however, continue to advise me for a few years longer in important affairs of State. I shall not dare to be indolent, and, in obedience to the Empress's command, I have petitioned heaven, earth, and my ancestors, that I may assume the adminstration of the Government in person on the 15th day of the first moon in the thirteenth year of my reign. Guided by the counsel of her Majesty, everything will be done with care." As a matter of fact the Dowager Empress did not retire from the control of affairs until 1889, and even since then she has exercised considerable influence in the administration of the Empire. It is not to be wondered at that the Emperor desired to put off as long as possible the weight of government. The life of a " Son of Heaven " is certainly not to be envied. With rare exceptions he remains a State prisoner within the palace walls, and even on the Progresses which he is occasionally called upon to make, the heavy duties of his position are still constantly with him. Even at the time when the Dowager Empress shared his responsibilities, his duties were onerous, and from notices which appeared in the *Peking Gazette* some idea of his official thraldom can be gained. In March, 1887, he visited the tombs of his ancestors in the Western Hills, and each day at fixed hours batches of memorials were sent after him to occupy his leisure moments at the halting-places. On arriving at the mausolea he performed at the tombs the sacrifices which were necessary for the repose of the dead, who, if his object were gained, would appear to have been the only ones benefited by the process.

For weeks beforehand the people living on the highway were charged with the duty of repairing the
road and mending the bridges. This duty they, on
this occasion, failed to perform to the complete satisfaction of the traveller, who made a formal complaint
that he had observed wheel tracks on the roadway
over which his chariot should have been the first to
travel.

It must always be a matter of wonder how the
national accounts, being of an extremely fluctuating
nature, can ever be made to balance. In the year of
which we are speaking the Yellow River was more
than usually capricious in its ebb and flow. On
several occasions it burst its banks and flooded the
country far and wide. As a natural consequence
farms were desolated and whole villages were swept
away. From people in such straits it was plainly
impossible to expect payment of taxes, and neither
from the provinces of Honan nor Shantung was a
tithe of the usual revenue received. The currency
also is of so variable a value that large losses are
constantly incurred by the mints, and Kwanghsü's
ministers had not only to bear the brunt of a monetary crisis in Peking, but had to meet the consequences of several financial panics in different parts
of the Empire. At Foochow, as elsewhere, the local
banks had issued paper currency far beyond the due
proportion of reserve coin in their chests. The
natural results followed, and as the banks closed
their doors they were attacked by angry mobs who
wrecked them utterly, and attempted, vainly, to
recompense themselves by plunder for the losses

they had sustained. In the midst of these money
difficulties the Emperor, in a lofty manner, issued an
edict calling upon his officials to exercise the
strictest economy in the administration of the
Empire, and warning the Court mandarins to avoid
all unnecessary expenditure in the palace ceremonies,
for, as he said, "the Court should stand forth as an
example of frugality to the whole nation."

At this time the war with France had given a great
impetus to the extension of telegraphs throughout
the Empire, and in 1887 the line was completed
which connected Peking with the capital of Yunnan,
the extreme south-westerly province in the Empire.
The old-fashioned notion that the *fêngshui* of the
districts through which the wires passed would be
affected by their presence had ceased to exist, and
there were not wanting signs that the days of that
venerable superstition were numbered. At Jehol in
Mongolia large quarries were opened for Imperial
purposes, and, to prevent all misunderstandings, an
order was issued by Li Hungchang that no one should
dare to suggest that the disturbance of the earth's
surface would in any way affect the *fêngshui* of the
neighbourhood. In this he was implicitly obeyed, as
he had also been in the case of the K'aip'ing railway,
and the Emperor got his stone without arousing any
of that opposition which twenty years ago would,
under similar circumstances, have been rampant.

Notwithstanding the Emperor's protest in favour
of economy, the year 1887 was marked by the preparation of several magnificent Court ceremonies.
Since the Emperor had been declared to be of age,

it was necessary that he should think of taking to
himself a consort, and under the direction of the
Dowager Empress he arranged to espouse a young
lady named Yehonala, the daughter of the Empress's
brother, General Kweihsiang ; and after the manner
of the country it was determined that he should also
take to himself two concubines, who owned to the
youthful ages of thirteen and fifteen. For rather
more than a year the Emperor was left to enjoy
the pleasures of anticipation, and it was not till
March, 1889, that the Imperial wedding took place.
The officials of the Astronomical Board chose, as was
their duty, a day which was believed to augur well
for the happiness of the young couple, but in a
moment of carelessness announced that the usual
preparatory worship would be offered two days
before, instead of one day before, the ceremony.
For this error they were roundly taken to task
by the Dowager Empress, who, being a staunch
ceremonialist, decreed that they should suffer severe
penalities for their mistake. By an Imperial Edict
the rites and ceremonies which were to be carefully
observed consisted of seven parts. First came the
sending of presents ; then the actual marriage ;
next the joint worship of their ancestors by the
Imperial pair ; the conferring a patent as Empress
on the bride ; her presentation to the Dowager
Empress ; the reception of felicitations ; and an
Imperial banquet.

Honours in commemoration of the event were
bestowed on Sir Robert Hart and numberless other
officials, while the carriers of the bride's sedan-chair

and even the torchbearers who attended upon her received royal largess. With this final assumption of manhood the Emperor passed out of the leading strings by which the Empress Tzŭhsi had so long directed his course, and one of the first of his new duties was to prepare a palace for the reception of the ex-Regent. The choice of his residence had, as we are told in the *Peking Gazette*, been a subject of long and anxious consideration to the Emperor, who, in well-rounded sentences, declared in a decree his anxiety to procure for her Majesty a place of rest and peace after the eighteen wearisome years of administration which had fallen to her lot. In an appreciative edict the Empress returned the compliments paid her by the Sovereign, and took the opportunity of giving utterance to the following excellent advice : " The Emperor is now advancing to manhood, and the greatest respect which he can pay to us will be to discipline his own body, to develop his mind, to pay unremitting attention to the administration of the Government, and to love his people." From all accounts the young Emperor has endeavoured to obey these wholesome admonitions, and from the records of his daily life there seems to be very little time left for the enjoyment of the pleasures of existence after he has shown his love for his people by attending to the administration of the Empire. The following programme of a by no means uncommon morning's work is enough to justify this assertion. At 2 a.m. he leaves the palace for the Temple of Earth, where he sacrifices to the gods of the five grains,

At 4 a.m. he returns to the palace, where he betakes
of an early breakfast; and then proceeds to the
Temple of the God of Fire, where he burns incense,

and, after having offered up the usual prayers,
returns to the palace to receive the reports of his
ministers and to discuss the affairs of the Empire.

The years during which the Dowager Empress had held the reins of power had been full of difficulties and anxieties, and it says much for her ability that she was able to steer the ship of State in safety through the ruffled waters of the time. The assumption of power by Kwanghsü brought no relief to this strain. Local rebellions immediately broke out in the provinces of Yunnan and Hunan and among the bordering tribes of Lolos ; and though these were successfully suppressed, the peace of the country was for a time seriously disturbed.

During the long minority of the Emperor the foreign ministers at Peking had been obliged to forego the right of audience. But, as in the case of T'ungchih, the time had now arrived when they might fairly ask to be received by the " Son of Heaven." Having, however, intimated their desire to appear in the Imperial presence they took no other step to accomplish their desire, and without further negotiations the following edict appeared in the *Peking Gazette* of the 12th of December, 1890: " Since the treaties have been made with the various nations letters and despatches under the seals of the Governments have passed to and fro, making complimentary inquiries year by year without intermission. The harmony which has existed has become thus from time to time more and more secure. The ministers of the various Powers residing at Peking have abundantly shown their loyal desire to maintain peaceful relations and international friendship. This I cordially recognise, and I rejoice in it. In the first and second months of last year, when there were special reasons

for expressing national joy, I received a gracious
decree (from the Empress Dowager) ordering the
ministers of the Yamên for Foreign Affairs to entertain the ministers of foreign nations at a banquet.
That occasion was a memorable and happy one. I
have now been in charge of the Government for two
years. The ministers of foreign Powers ought to be
received by me at an audience, and I hereby decree
that the audience to be held be in accordance with
that of the twelfth year of the reign of T'ungchih
(1873). It is also hereby decreed that a day will be
fixed every year for an audience, in order to show my
desire to treat with honour all the ministers of foreign
Powers resident in Peking. . . . The ministers of the
Yamên for Foreign Affairs are hereby ordered to
prepare in the first month of the ensuing new year a
memorial asking that the time for the audience may
be fixed. On the next day the foreign ministers are
to be received at a banquet at the Foreign Office.
The same is to be done every year in the first month,
and the rules will be the same on each occasion.
New ministers coming will be received at this annual
audience. At all times of national congratulation,
when China and the foreign countries give suitable
expression to their joy, the ministers of the Foreign
Office are to present a memorial asking for the
bestowal of a banquet to show the sincere and increasing desire of the Imperial Government for the
maintenance of peace and the best possible relations
between China and the foreign States."

The fact that this decree was published spontane-
ously, and that the terms in which it was dictated

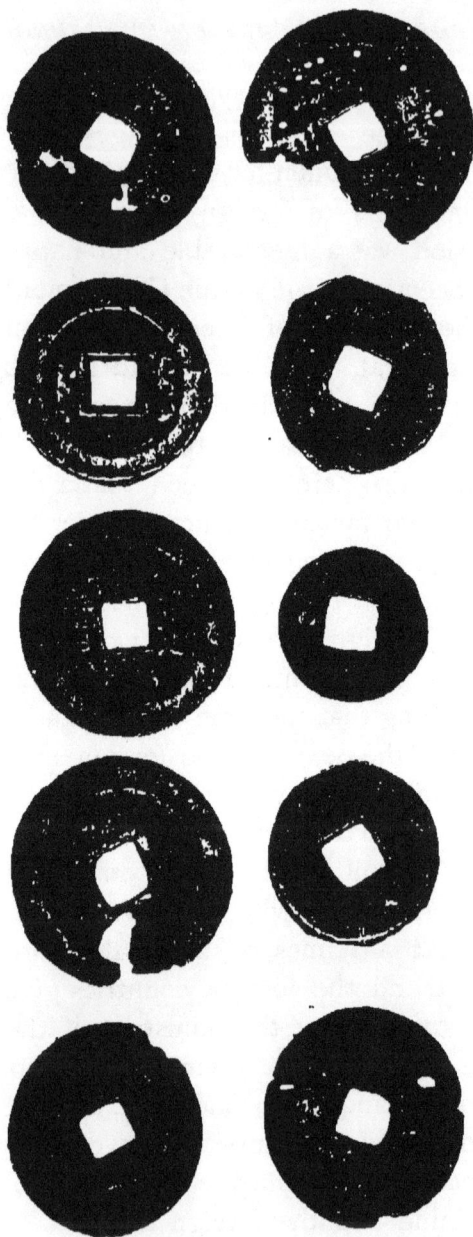

CURRENT COIN.

evinced a desire for friendly relations, encouraged the foreign ministers to hope that a brighter day was dawning on their relations with the Imperial Government. These anticipations, however, were not destined to find fulfilment at once. The building named for the ceremony was the same hall dedicated to inferior uses as that in which T'ungchih received the diplomatic body in 1873, and in one respect an act was at this time imposed which formed a distinct relapse from the level reached in 1873. In that year the ministers placed their letters of credence with their own hands on the table in front of the Emperor's throne. Now they were expected to hand them to an attendant prince, who, in this respect, acted in their stead. Though this change may appear insignificant to Western minds, it meant much, and it was intended to mean much, to the native onlookers who crowded the outskirts of the hall in an inconvenient and especially indecorous manner. The Emperor's reply to the congratulations of his visitors was most cordial, and his manner was then, as it always has been since, as courteous as circumstances permitted. On the whole, however, the audience cannot be said to have come up to what might reasonably have been expected, and the ministers on reviewing their position came to the determination that in future they would rather forego the right of audience than present themselves again in the Tzŭ-kwang Ko. The result of this decision might have taught them the very useful lesson that if they had previously shown an equally firm front, they need never have submitted to the degradations to which they had been subjected. In the following year both the Austrian Minister and, a little later, Mr. O'Connor, the British Representative, were received by the Emperor in the Chêng-Kwang Tien, a building which, though outside the palace, had never been used as a reception-hall for envoys from tributary States.

But what diplomacy had failed to accomplish in this matter, political complications brought about without discussion. The war with Japan inclined the Chinese Government to seek for the countenance, if not the support, of the European Powers by granting timely concessions, and in November, 1894, the following edict appeared in the *Peking Gazette* : " On Monday last the Emperor gave audience in the Wênhwa Tien to the following ministers : American, Russian, English, French, Belgian, Swedish, and the Acting Minister for Spain." The hall here mentioned stands within the walls of the Imperial Palace, and thus for the first time an audience was granted in a manner which demonstrated the equality with China of the nations represented. Since then, however, events have marched apace, and foreigners, taking advantage of the weakness of the Empire, have occupied strategic positions which until now have been beyond the dreams of their ambition. The attitude of the Emperor towards foreign Sovereigns reflects this changed position of affairs, and we are now told (May, 1898) that Prince Henry of Germany was received by the Emperor standing, and was honoured by a return visit from the " Son of Heaven " !

It is necessary now, in order to preserve the general

chronology and sequence of events, to revert to the year 1887. For some time it had been felt by the less bigoted members of the Imperial Government that use should be made of European science to enable the authorities to place their country in a position of safety. As long ago as 1866 Prince Kung and others had presented a memorial to the Throne recommending the study of mathematics for Chinese students, and advising the Emperor to found a college at Peking where that and cognate sciences might be taught. The college was established and European professors were appointed. But this reform was in advance of the age, and failed of the success which it had been hoped it might achieve. Twenty-one years later a more practical step was taken in the same direction, and the Tsungli Yamên in 1887 presented a united request to the Throne that mathematics should be included in the list of subjects required from students at the competitive examinations. The Imperial assent was given to this proposal, and with more or less cordiality, in accordance with the proclivities of the officials of each province, the new subject has been placed side by side with the " Book of Changes " and the " Sayings of Confucius."

No doubt this innovation was eminently distasteful to the general body of *Literati*, whose instincts and interests are bound up in the continuance of the existing condition of things. To these men any concession to foreigners, or any adoption of Western appliances, is hateful, and with one consent large bodies of them banded themselves together to oppose the foreign taint by every means in their power.

A CHINESE PROFESSOR.

Of all the provinces in the Empire Hunan has, until within the last few months, shown the most determined and implacable distaste for everything European, and in 1891 there proceeded from this hotbed of reactionism a series of vile anti-foreign placards accusing the European missionaries of every crime which disgraces humanity. The prime mover in the publication of these gross libels was a certain Chow Han, who was of official rank and was possessed of considerable scholarship. With the fiercest invective he described how missionaries gouged out the eyes of their converts, and cut out parts of their intestines for medicinal purposes, and how they led astray the unsuspecting natives by their vile arts and evil designs. These placards were profusely illustrated, and every device was employed to cast obloquy both on the missionaries and on the Supreme Being whom they worshipped. It happens that the term which the Roman Catholics use for God, *T'ienchu*, or " Lord of Heaven," is almost identical in sound with words meaning the " Heavenly Pig," and it suited the fancy of these impious caricaturists to represent the Deity under this infamous disguise. An expression for " Foreigners," *Yangjin*, might, in the same way, be understood to mean " Goat Men," and this play on words was in the same way abundantly made use of by Chow Han and his confederates. On the basis of these slanders, rumours were circulated that children were being kidnapped and vivisected by the missionaries, and, in consequence, as has always happened in China in similar circumstances, the people in their ignorance broke out into riot and disorder. In rapid succession the mob rose at Wuhu, Wuhsueh, Tanyang, Wusieh, Chingkwan, Yangwu, and Kiangyen. Christian churches were demolished, the houses of the missionaries were wrecked and looted, and at Wuhsueh two British subjects, one a missionary and one an officer of the Maritime Customs, were murdered. In accordance with the invariable precedent in such matters, the representations on the subject made by the British Minister to the Tsungli Yamên were met with evasive replies ; and the Chinese Minister at St. James's was even instructed to suggest to Lord Salisbury that he should check the zeal of Sir John Walsham in pursuing his inquiry into the *fons et origo* of the riots. So eminently unsatisfactory was the attitude of the Chinese Government throughout the investigation that the foreign ministers at Peking found themselves compelled to place on record " that no faith could be put in the assurances of the Chinese Government." To this grave assertion Sir John Walsham added, " The charges (against the mandarins) remain unaltered, and the repeated assertions of Chinese agents in foreign countries that the Chinese Government has acted with good faith and energy can be disproved by facts, and are as plausible as the assurances that native officials might now be safely entrusted with the protection of foreigners."

This being the attitude of the Tsungli Yamên, not much could be expected in the way of compensation for the outrages. After long and dreary negotiations certain monetary recompense was granted, but the only official who suffered punishment was the man who at the risk of his life saved English women and

children from the fury of the mob! Meanwhile the
prime mover in the whole matter, Chow Han, was
allowed to remain at large, although the Yamên went
through the form of holding an inquiry into his
conduct. A commission was appointed to adjudicate
upon the charges brought against him, and the result
of the investigation amounted to the assertion that
he was a wild, erratic creature whose actions were not
to be regarded seriously. Without hesitation the
Yamên accepted this view, and left the malefactor at
liberty to work any further mischief which might be
in his power. The one favourable feature in the
episode was the edict issued by the Emperor in
response to a memorial presented by the Yamên on
the circumstances connected with the riots. This
document ran as follows :—

"The propagation of Christianity by foreigners is
provided for by treaty, and Imperial decrees have
been issued to the provincial authorities to protect
the missionaries from time to time. . . . The doctrine
of Christianity has for its purpose the teaching of
men to be good. . . . Peace and quiet should reign
among the Chinese and missionaries. There are,
however, reckless fellows who fabricate stories which
have no foundation in fact for the purpose of creating
trouble. Villains of this class are not few in number,
and are to be found everywhere. The local authorities must protect the lives and property of foreign
merchants and missionaries and prevent bad
characters from doing them injury. . . . Let this
decree be universally promulgated for the information of the people."

After the appearance of this edict matters quieted down for a time in the disturbed district, but a strong anti-foreign feeling still existed, and two years later two Swedish missionaries were murdered at Sungpu, in circumstances which were especially brutal. But the same course of political events which opened the Imperial Palace to the foreign ministers produced a calm so far as Europeans were concerned in the provinces, and, though outwardly satisfactory, this peaceful situation was in one sense evidence of one of the worst features of the attitude of the Chinese towards foreigners. It has always been contended by those who understand the situation best, that as a rule the anti-foreign riots are made to order, and it is at least eminently noticeable that they never occur when it is to the interest of the Government that peace should reign. With the outbreak of the Japanese war it became the interest of the Chinese to seek in every possible way to conciliate the foreign Powers, and a *mot d'ordre*, therefore, went forth that the elements of disorder were to remain quiescent. So long as the war lasted, outrages in China Proper ceased completely, and it was not until peace had been signed that mob law again prevailed in parts of the central provinces, more especially in Szech'uan. In the capital of this province every missionary establishment was razed to the ground, and nearly a hundred foreigners were compelled to take refuge in places of safety. A little later in the same year (1895) a peculiarly savage onslaught was made on the missionary settlement of Hwashan, in the province of Fuhkien. With the ordinary natives in the neighbourhood the missionaries were on excellent terms, but it so happened that a local society of vegetarians, for some quite unknown reason, professed deadly enmity to the foreigners. This state of things was perfectly well known to the local authorities, who, however, took no steps to check the evil which they saw to be gathering about them. At early dawn one morning, without any immediate warning, a band of two or three hundred of these miscreants attacked the station, and succeeded in murdering ten foreigners and wounding others, besides destroying the mission premises. This outrage was a shock to the sensibilities of Europe, and so strong were the diplomatic expressions used with regard to it, that the Chinese Government showed a somewhat more complacent demeanour than usual in the conduct of the subsequent inquiries. The recent murder of a German missionary in Shantung has been productive of a useful lesson. It has brought a comparatively new Power into the field, and has called forth action on the part of the German Government which is likely to bear good fruit in the future. As has so often been said, the Chinese will yield only to force, and it is by such measures alone as those now adopted in Shantung, that the lives and goods of Christian missionaries will continue to be preserved from harm.

XIV

THE WAR WITH JAPAN, AND RECENT EVENTS

KOREAN politics have, as we have seen, constantly formed bones of contention between the Chinese and Japanese Governments. The country has been overrun at different periods by the troops of both nations, and with that curious elasticity of obligations common to the extreme East the Korean Government has owned itself a feudatory at one and the same time of both China and Japan. It will be remembered that by the convention signed by Count Ito and Li Hungchang it was agreed that, in case circumstances arose which demanded the presence of the troops of either country in Korea, each should send notice to the other of her intention to land soldiers. In 1894 such a contingency arose. The *Tong Hak*, or followers of the Eastern Doctrine, rose in revolt primarily against the Roman Catholic converts, but also against the government of the country. A force sent against them from Seoul met with a serious reverse, and in his difficulty the King, in accordance with precedent, appealed to Peking for help.

With the contemptuous disregard for international obligations which distinguishes the Chinese, they in response to the King's appeal landed troops in Korea without, as the Japanese aver, giving any notice of their intention so to do. As a protest against this step the Mikado's Government despatched a *corps d'armée* in all haste to Korea, and thus once again the troops of the two states were brought face to face in a semi-hostile attitude. Neither, however, was inclined to fight, and the Japanese contented themselves with advocating the introduction of reforms into the administration of the country. To this eminently sensible course the Chinese took exception, and warned the Japanese that all questions relating to the reformation of the country should be left in their hands. To this political snub the Japanese submitted, and even made no protest against a further preposterous demand that all men-of-war flying the Mikado's flag should leave the Chinese ports by the 20th of the July following. Though so far compliant, the Japanese warned their opponents that they should consider any further importation of troops into the country as an act of war. They were, however, too well versed in Chinese methods to accept blindly the assurances that were made them on this point, and took the reasonable precaution of sending three cruisers to the gulf of Pechihli to ensure the fulfilment of the understanding. The event proved that this measure was justified, for on the morning of the 25th of July the Japanese squadron encountered a Chinese transport loaded with troops, and accompanied by two men-of-war, making for the coast of Korea. There could only be one outcome of this breach of faith, and the cruisers on both sides cleared for action. In less than an hour one of the Chinese warships was disabled and beached, and the other steamed off, leaving the transport to be dealt with by the Japanese commander, who signalled to the captain to make for a Japanese port. To this summons the captain explained that he was unable to comply, owing to the attitude of the Chinese soldiers on board, who further prevented him from leaving the ship when he was subsequently warned to do so. In this deadlock the Japanese, after a brief interval, hoisted a red flag and poured a broadside into the transport. The scene which followed was one of helpless terror and alarm, and before any steps could be taken to save the life of a single person on board, the ship went down, carrying with it most of its passengers and crew.

This act led to a declaration of war on both sides, and both Powers poured troops into Korea. The first battle was fought in the neighbourhood of Asan, a port in the south-west of the peninsula. A Chinese force occupied the town commanded by General Yeh, who no sooner learnt of the approach of the Japanese than he marched off with the bulk of his forces to Pingyang, a strongly fortified position to the north of the capital, leaving his rearguard to defend the city. The natural result followed. At the end of a brief skirmish the Japanese took possession of the place, and after having captured the Chinese stores and munitions of war, left a

garrison in the forts and marched northwards in
the pursuit of the fugitive Yeh. At Pingyang Yeh
had joined hands with two *corps d'armée* and a force
of cavalry which had marched south from Manchuria.
The position was naturally a strong one, and if the
fortifications had been effectively defended, it might
well have withstood any attack that the Japanese
could have brought against it. But Yeh was ignorant
as well as being a coward, and when General Tso,
who was the only brave and capable officer in Korea,
urged him to make preparations for the defence of
the town he laughed the necessity to scorn. This
folly was fatal to the Chinese cause in Korea. From
the east, south, and west three Japanese divisions
converged on the doomed city. Early on the
morning of the 15th of September the attacking
force arrived in position. This was enough for the
redoubtable Yeh, who straightway performed another
strategic movement by marching his troops out of
the north gate of the city, and onwards with all haste
to the Yalu river, which forms the northern boundary
of the kingdom. This evil example was followed by
General Wei, and Tso was thus left alone to face the
enemy as best he could. He fought well and bravely,
dying at the head of his men, over whose bodies the
Japanese streamed into the city. It is some satisfaction to know that for this gross act of cowardice
General Wei was beheaded, and that Yeh, though he
has by a liberal expenditure of money kept his head
on his shoulders, is still confined in the Board of
Punishments at Peking.

Before the fate of Pingyang was decided, the

Chinese had despatched a strong force of troops under the convoy of the northern fleet to the Yalu river. There they arrived in safety, and were in the act of landing when, on the morning of the 17th of September, the Japanese fleet hove in sight. The position was one in which Admiral Ting, who commanded the Chinese fleet, could not resist

A HOUSE IN MANCHURIA.

fighting, and he steamed out to meet the enemy, having marshalled his fleet in a V-shaped formation, with two of his most powerful ironclads in the centre. In point of numbers the two fleets were equal, twelve ships carrying the nation's flag in each case. Both sides fought with determination, but, as in every engagement during the war, the Chinese were from the first out-manœuvred. The Japanese ships, being faster than those of their opponents, were able to take up the positions which suited them best, and to avoid as far as possible the Chinese guns. In these circumstances the result was a foregone conclusion, and by the end of the day five Chinese ships were sunk and the rest were in full flight. So severe had been the battle that the Japanese ships were unable to follow in pursuit, and seven of the retreating fleet reached Port Arthur in safety.

Meanwhile Marshal Yamagata marched northwards from Pingyang, and on the 8th of October occupied the town of Wiju on the south bank of the Yalu. Korea was now swept clear of Chinese troops, and the Japanese were at liberty to carry the war into Manchuria. Without meeting with any serious opposition Yamagata crossed the Yalu river and joined forces with General Nodzu, who on the 25th of October gained a signal victory over the Chinese at Hushan. From this point the invaders had almost a march over, and some of the strongest places in Southern Manchuria surrendered without striking a blow.

While Nodzu and Yamagata were thus making their triumphal march northwards, General Oyama landed in the neighbourhood of Kinchow, a city which stands on the narrow neck of land to the northward of Port Arthur. On the 5th and 6th of November Talienwan and Kinchow opened their gates to the invaders, and Oyama was consequently set free to attack Port Arthur from the land side. The intervening country being very rough and hilly, and the roads bad, the difficulties were of no mean order, but by the 21st of the month the troops were in position to deliver their assault. Here, as elsewhere, the Chinese failed to distinguish themselves for courage, and after some show of resistance, deserted the batteries and escaped along the shore flanking the Japanese troops. The fall of this place

A MANCHURIAN CART.

was a crushing blow to the Chinese cause. It was the position on which Li Hungchang had expended vast sums of money, and which had always been regarded as impregnable. To the Japanese, however, the achievement represented only an incident in the war, and with unabated energy Oyama waited only to garrison the captured stronghold, and then

marched northwards into Manchuria, capturing by
the way the cities of Fuchow and K'aipingchow.
This series of disasters induced the Emperor to
listen to the advice tendered by Li Hungchang that
overtures of peace should be made to the enemy, and
two futile missions, the first headed by Mr. Detring,
of the Customs Service, and the second by a mandarin
named Chang, were consequently despatched to
deprecate the further advance of the Japanese troops.
As neither of these envoys had either plenipotentiary
powers or appropriate rank they were promptly sent
back to those who had commissioned them. While
time was thus wasted the Japanese were repeating
at Wei-hai-wei, the one fortress remaining to China,
the tactics which had secured the capture of Port
Arthur ; but here the task was a more difficult one.
The Chinese fleet in the harbour was commanded by
Admiral Ting, who had fought a good fight in the
battle off Yalu river. His back was now against the
wall, and he was determined to defend the position
to the last. Unhappily his command did not extend
to the soldiers, and when he wished to dismantle the
outlying forts to prevent the Japanese from taking
them, and turning their guns on the fortress as they
had done at Port Arthur, the soldiers refused to
carry out his instructions. The result was exactly
as he had foreseen. Without much difficulty the
Japanese made themselves masters of the outer lines,
and brought the captured artillery to bear on the
town ; but Ting still held the citadel and the fleet,
and, from these standpoints, offered a determined
resistance to the enemy. It was obvious, however,

that in the end the Japanese must secure the prize, and when this became apparent beyond question Ting made final arrangements with Admiral Ito for the surrender of the town and fleet (February 7th). Having agreed to the necessary conditions, and having secured the lives and freedom of his men, Ting committed suicide, an example which was

A JINRIKSHA.

followed by his second and third in command. It is gratifying to know that Admiral Ito did honour to his late gallant opponent by detaching a captured Chinese man-of-war to carry the Admiral's remains to Chifu. This final disaster brought home to the Emperor and his advisers the inevitable conclusion that if any remnant of sovereignty was to be left to them, they must at once make peace with the enemy. It also emphasised the lesson which they were beginning to learn, that it was useless to try to impose any more *pseudo* plenipotentiaries on Japan, and in this dilemma the Emperor turned to the one man who, from his rank and abilities, was clearly marked out as a fit and proper person to represent the Empire in its present straits. With the patriotism of the kind which has always distinguished him, Li Hungchang at once undertook the mission at the bidding of his sovereign ; and after some delay, due to his efforts to gain European support against any demand on the part of Japan for territorial acquisitions on the mainland, he for the first time in his life landed on a foreign shore.

In the negotiations which followed, Li first attempted to secure an armistice during the discussion of the terms of peace. To this the Japanese made no objection on the conditions that the Taku forts, Shanhaikwan, and the railway to Tientsin should be handed over to the Japanese generals. As the fulfilment of these terms would entail the virtual command of Peking from the coast, Li declined to accept them, and the plenipotentiaries therefore proceeded at once to arrange the terms of a permanent treaty. With the exception of the regrettable incident of the wound inflicted on Li by a crazy would-be assassin, the discussion proceeded favourably, and on the 17th of April the treaty of peace was solemnly signed. By the terms of this document the Liaotung peninsula (including Port Arthur), Formosa, and the Pescadores were ceded to the conquerors, and an indemnity of 200,000,000 taels was exacted for the expenses of the war.

Although a strong party in Peking were opposed to the ratification of this humiliating treaty, the Emperor gave his approval to it, and on the 8th of May the ratifications were exchanged at Chifu. But though China had thus pledged her honour to the terms demanded, a strong appeal was made to the European Powers to intervene on her behalf. This entreaty was partially successful, and the combined Governments of Russia, Germany and France were induced to remonstrate so strongly and persistently against the cession of Liaotung that the Japanese thought it wise to restore the peninsula to their conquered foe.

The disorder and uncertainty which had overclouded the Empire during the continuance of the war seriously interfered with one of those national rejoicings which appeal with especial force to the Chinese mind. In 1895 the Dowager Empress completed her sixtieth year, and as such an event is of rare occurrence among members of the Imperial family, it was early marked out to be the subject of a grand national rejoicing. With that respect for precedent which so distinguishes the backward-looking intellect of the Celestials, the officials of the Board of Ceremonies searched in the records for the occurrence of a similar event in the annals of the dynasty. Their researches were rewarded by finding that during the reign of the Emperor Ch'ienlung the Dowager Empress had reached the venerable age of eighty, and that on that occasion, in addition to numberless ceremonies, the Emperor on horseback had escorted her sedan-chair from her residence to the palace, where, dressed in a fantastic garb, he had danced and gesticulated before his aged parent. It is needless to say that this device was not original, but was carried out in imitation of one of the twenty-four national models of Filial Piety, who at the age of seventy dressed himself up as a child and frolicked before his parents in order to cheat them into the belief that they were still untouched by age. The more sedate part of the ceremonial was loyally adopted by the Emperor, who, however, with some show of wisdom, declined to disport himself in the motley proposed.

But though the Government was able occasionally to divert its attention from the necessities of the hour by this and other pageants, it was soon called upon again to consider the difficulties which had arisen from the war. The three European Powers which had posed as friends in need soon made it plain that they required a *quid pro quo* for their intervention in the matter of the Liaotung peninsula. In this regard Russia was first in the field and demanded the right of carrying the Siberian railway through Manchuria to Vladivostok with a branch line to Kirin Mukden and Port Arthur. France followed next and claimed that the Chinese should meet the Tonking railway at the frontier and continue it as far as Nanning Fu, in the province of Kwangsi. Germany was for the moment less ambitious and was satisfied with asking for certain mining and financial privileges. To these

several exactions China was in no position to return
a negative answer, and indeed her position since the

A DAGOBA AT MOUKDEN.

war has been one of limp impotence without any
guiding principle to direct her policy, or the slightest

vestige of power to uphold her rights. One of her chief needs throughout has been that of money with which to pay off the indemnity due to Japan, and being completely helpless so far as her own resources were concerned, she appealed to England for assisttance. Lord Salisbury, acting on the traditional policy of his country towards China, was willing to arrange a loan to the amount of twelve millions, and the negotiations had advanced several stages when Russia intervened, and protested so vehemently against the proceedings that the terrorised Chinese begged to be allowed to withdraw from their bargain. They had, however, sufficient sense to decline a loan proffered from St. Petersburg, and eventually the money was borrowed, with £4,000,000 in addition, from the Hongkong and Shanghai Banking Corporation, with the assistance of a German bank. But worse difficulties were still in store for the distracted country. In an ill moment a native mob rose against a German missionary establishment in Shantung and murdered two of the priests. This incident supplied the excuse wanted by Germany for obtaining a substantial hold on the country, and, without notice, the Admiral on the station steamed into Kiaochow Bay in the incriminated province, and took forcible possession of the harbour and its surroundings. It was only necessary for the Germans to say that they were there, and intended staying, to make the Chinese acquiesce, however unwillingly, in the arrangement. The example thus set was speedily followed. Russia demanded a lease of Port Arthur and Talienwan on the same terms as that granted to the Germans at Kiaochow, and as a counterblast to this last move Sir Claud Macdonald was instructed to ask for a lease of Wei-hai-wei so soon as the Japanese, who had been holding it as security for the payment of the indemnity, should have rendered it again to China. Later still France, not to be behindhand, has taken possession of Kwangchow Bay on the Lienchow peninsula in Kwangtung. The danger of this system of seizing at will ports along the coast soon became sufficiently obvious even to the Chinese, and in their own defence they readily listened to the proposals of Sir Claud Macdonald to open three more ports, Yochow on the Tungt'ing Lake, Funing Fu on the coast of Fuhkien, and Chinwang in the Gulf of Liaotung, to which, on their own motion, they added Wusung, near Shanghai. In addition to these new trade centres, three ports on the west river of Canton had already been declared open in compensation for the British Shan territory of Kiang Hung, which by a breach of treaty had been alienated to France.

The policy of throwing open the whole coast line to trade is the only one which will secure the Empire against the attack of grasping Powers. By the favoured nation clause no power can acquire any rights at the treaty ports which are not shared by all the signatories. Any attempt therefore to grasp at exclusive privileges on the part of any one nation would be met by the united opposition of the rest of their number, and in the present helpless condition of the State, and the known greed of various governments, this is the only sure and certain means of defence that the Empire possesses.

It is, as it always has been, the true policy of England to look to China for commercial privileges rather than for territorial aggrandizement, and, with the exception of the lease of Wei-hai-wei, every move on her part has been in the direction of opening the country to the traffic of the world. It was in this spirit that in recognition of her share in the new loan she urged the Chinese Government to open the inland waters to steam navigation ; and to undertake that on no conditions should the valley of the Yangtsze-kiang be alienated to any foreign Power. These terms have been agreed to, and additional conditions have been framed, by which it is arranged that so long as British trade is predominant in China Sir Robert Hart's successors shall be British subjects, and that the collection of the Likin tax at the ports of Soochow and Kiukiang, with the districts of Sunghu and Eastern Chehkiang, as well as the salt Likin of Ichang, and of the districts of Hupeh and Anhui, shall be placed forthwith under the control of the Inspector-General of the Imperial Chinese Maritime Customs. It is difficult to over-estimate the importance of this last condition. It is a blow at that corruption which has hitherto made progress in China next to impossible, which has prevented the construction of railways, which has hide-bound the trade of the country, and which has made the army and navy of the Empire the laughing-stocks of the world. If once the political administration of the provinces could be placed on a sound and honest basis, the progressive leaven which, though small, does exist in the country, could gain life and energy, and China might yet succeed in occupying the position in the world to which her teeming population, her immense wealth, and the industry of her people justly entitle her.

FINIS.

INDEX

Ningpo, occupation of, 227
Ningyuan, defence of, 74
Nurhachu, 65 ; his seven grievances against the Mings, 68 ; his victory over the Chinese, 70 ; his death, 74.

O.

Opium, trade in, 210, 213
Osborn, Captain Sherard, 336

P.

Pa Chung, General, 168 ; commits suicide, 169
Pan Ch'ao, march to Khoten, 18
Panshen Lama, death at Peking, 166
Parkes, Sir Harry, 238; appointed consul at Canton, 259 ; taken prisoner, 294
Pereira, 112
Philippines, the, arrival of Spaniards, 56 ; massacre of Christians at, 57
Pingyang, capture of, 436
Portuguese, mission to Peking, 48 ; massacre of, 50 ; aid sent to Peking, 71
Pottinger, Sir H., minister, 226 ; concludes treaty of Nanking, 232 ; sails for England, 234

Q.

Queue, institution of, 72

R.

Railways, Wusung line, 395 ; its destruction, 396
Regency, the, 383
Remusat, 20
Ricci, 51 ; death of, 52
Rome, See of, 21 ; embassy to the Chinese Court, 21
Rubruquis, Friar, 27 ; his description of the Chinese, 28
Russia, embassy (1664), 100 ; defeat of at Albazin, 113 ; college at Peking, 203 ; concessions to, 444

S.

Sankolinsin, 279, 293
Schaal, J. A., his arrival in China, 60 ; his death in prison, 61
Senhouse, Sir F., 225
Seymour, Sir M., takes Canton, 262
Shang dynasty, the, 7
Shennung, Emperor, 4
Shih Hwangti, 14
Shih K'ofa, champions the Ming cause, 91 ; his attempted defence of Yangchow, 93
Shun, Emperor, 5
Shunchih, Emperor, 95 ; death of, 101
Siamese tribute, 192
Soochow, Negotiations for surrender of, 329 ; capture of, 330
Sung, Minister, 199
Sung dynasty, the, 22

T.

Taku forts, capture of, 271 ; defeat before, 277 ; recapture, 284
Taki, concubine of Chow Sin, 7
T'aip'ing, establishment of dynasty of, 248 ; unsuccessful advance on Peking, 250 ; later successes, 315
T'ang dynasty, the, literature of, 21 ; conquests, 21 ; persecution of Christians, 22
T'ang, the "complete," 7
Taokwang, Emperor, his accession, 201 ; his martial habits, 202 ; his death, 255
Tashilumbo, taken by the Gurkhas, 169
Terrien de Lacouperie, Professor, 2
Texeira, Gonsalvo de, 70
Three kingdoms, the, 19
Tientsin, massacre at, 361 ; rioters executed, 365
Tinghai, recapture of, 227
Ting, Admiral, 437 ; commits suicide, 441

www.ingramcontent.com/pod-product-compliance
Lightning Source LLC
Chambersburg PA
CBHW031820270326
41932CB00008B/485